Mind Fields

AC / SS — Adolescent Cultures, School & Society

Joseph L. DeVitis & Linda Irwin-DeVitis
General Editors

Vol. 16

PETER LANG
New York • Washington, D.C./Baltimore • Bern
Frankfurt am Main • Berlin • Brussels • Vienna • Oxford

Thomas J. Cottle

Mind Fields

Adolescent Consciousness
in a Culture of Distraction

PETER LANG
New York • Washington, D.C./Baltimore • Bern
Frankfurt am Main • Berlin • Brussels • Vienna • Oxford

Library of Congress Cataloging-in-Publication Data

Cottle, Thomas J.
Mind fields: adolescent consciousness
in a culture of distraction / Thomas J. Cottle.
p. cm. — (Adolescent cultures, school & society; vol. 16)
Includes bibliographical references.
1. Adolescent psychology. I. Title. II. Series.
BF724 .C635   155.5—dc21   00-062953
ISBN 0-8204-4922-9
ISSN 1091-1464

Die Deutsche Bibliothek-CIP-Einheitsaufnahme

Cottle, Thomas J.:
Mind fields: adolescent consciousness
in a culture of distraction / Thomas J. Cottle.
–New York; Washington, D.C./Baltimore; Bern;
Frankfurt am Main; Berlin; Brussels; Vienna; Oxford: Lang.
(Adolescent cultures, school, and society; Vol. 16)
ISBN 0-8204-4922-9

Cover design by Dutton & Sherman Design

The paper in this book meets the guidelines for permanence and durability
of the Committee on Production Guidelines for Book Longevity
of the Council of Library Resources.

© 2001, 2003, 2005 Peter Lang Publishing, Inc., New York

Printed in the United States of America

For Kay Mikkelsen Cottle

Grant me intention, purpose, and design—That's near
enough for me to the Divine.
Robert Frost, "Accidentally on Purpose"

Rest not till you rivet and publish yourself of your own Personality.
Walt Whitman, "To a Pupil"

We are far more out of touch with even the nearest approaches of the
infinite reaches of inner space than we now are with the reaches of outer
space. We respect the voyager, the explorer, the climber, the space man.
It makes far more sense to me as a valid project—indeed, as a desperately
and urgently required project for our time—to explore the inner space and
time of consciousness.
R. D. Laing, *The Politics of Experience*

Contents

Acknowledgments

As everyone knows, writing is a solitary activity, but no book gets published without the help and encouragement of many people. This project began with letters and conversations with a wonderful new friend, Professor Joseph DeVitis, who has been a perfectly exemplary editor. Then there is the faculty in the School of Education at Boston University, notably my colleagues in the Special Education Department, Arthur Beane, who has been particularly helpful, Leroy Clinton, Donna Lehr, Rose Ray, Kathleen Vaughan, Sandra DiIeso, and above all Gerald Fain. In addition, Edwin J. Delattre, Stephen Tigner, Allan Gaynor, Roselmina Indrisano, Victor Kestenbaum, Mary Shann, and David Steiner have all been exemplary colleagues and teachers. Special thanks must go as well to Jim Stone, Man Leung, Donald Palladino, Jr., and Lisa L. Paine, Chairman of the Department of Maternal and Child Health at the Boston University School of Public Health. A special thank you too, to the librarians at the Brookline Library, Brookline, Massachusetts. Above all, I wish to thank the students at Boston University whose writings and classroom discussions have greatly informed this volume. It should not go unnoticed that many of these people will be devoting their lives to the well being of children and adolescents.

I am blessed with many friends who not only are willing to listen to my book ideas, but on occasion read early drafts of manuscripts and offer invaluable commentary and support. In this regard I wish to thank Sara Lawrence Lightfoot, Robert Melson, Robert Coles, Gerald Platt, Barry O'Connell, Jan Dizard, Joan and Robert Weiss, Judy and David Lahm, Naomi Zigmond, Oliver Holmes, Brigitte Cazalis and Joseph Collins, Lane Conn, Scott Horton, Dianna Townsend, Daniel Frank, Richard and Anne Rosenfeld, Paul Strudler, Anne and Martin Peretz, and Patricia and Salvador Minuchin.

At the press, Chris Myers has shown extraordinary forbearance guiding me through the various steps of publication, and Phyllis Korper has done a masterful editing job.

No one supports and encourages me as much as the members of our family, Claudia and Tony, Jason and Sonya. I suspect too, that our grandchildren, Luke Thomas, Nicole Kate and Anna Carey, have also played a part in the production of this book.

Finally, I have chosen to dedicate the book to my wife, Kay Mikkelsen Cottle, extraordinary teacher, mother, partner and friend.

PART I

THE FIELDS OF DISTRACTION

Chapter 1

The Language of Distraction

Introduction

This book begins with the notion that we are, perhaps, only the stories we tell. Even small children's lives are predicated on stories, but adolescents bring these stories to new and complex levels. I suggest that people of every age are constantly conversing not only with the outside world but with their inner world as well. In addition, each of these conversations affects the others, because each is not only a momentary reading of the exterior or interior worlds, it represents the way we construct these worlds. Reasoning in this manner, we are nothing more, nothing less than the stories we tell to ourselves and to others. The story I tell about you is not only my representation of you, it signifies the construction I have made of you in my mind.[1] Elie Wiesel said it this way: "Memories, even painful memories, are all we have. In fact, they are the only thing we are. So we must take very good care of them."[2]

Never is this more true than during that period labeled by psychologists as adolescence. Truth be told, and this is one of the stories we will be examining throughout the book, the very notion of adolescence is itself a construction, just another story we tell about ourselves or about people of a certain age.[3] Everyone knows the inconsistencies of the adolescent story: Too young to drink but not to go to war. The inconsistencies are part of the ongoing story each of us constructs about adolescence and the young people constituting this arbitrary age group.[4] Hold in mind, however, that adolescents themselves perpetuate these stories as well, believing, apparently, that they are no longer children, though not quite adults, and that their identities, as Bradford Brown[5] suggested, are provisional, not quite fully formed.

Making these stories possible are the neurological development of young people and, more explicitly, as David Elkind[6] has noted, adolescents' capacity to engage in formal operational reasoning. Simply put, adolescents discover they are able to reflect on the stories they tell about others and themselves just as they are able to reflect on their own reflections. Their work, as it were, is to construct identities and develop a consolidated sense of self[7] which they do in part from private reflection and in part from trying out bits of themselves, the products of these self-reflections, on the world. In sharing their reflections, adolescents open themselves to the possibility that their developing selves will be confirmed by others, although there is always the possibility of disconfirmation as well. Moreover, adolescents discover that many others are undergoing the same process of self-development and the consequent experiments with self-confirmation. Erik Erikson expressed the notion this way: "The sense of ego identity, then, is the accrued confidence that the inner sameness and continuity prepared in the past are matched by the sameness and continuity of one's meaning for others. . . . "[8] Believing this to be true, peer groups and gangs assume new significance, because peers contribute to the development of an individual's most private readings of his or her self.[9]

Conjoining these notions, we see that the work of adolescents is to construct a consolidated sense of self that integrates the most private explorations of that inner world we will call the mind fields. The explorations, however, are themselves affected by social values, norms, expectations, morality, conventions, rules, procedures, rituals, all stories of the culture, all stories of those who populate the culture of the adolescent. This becomes another major theme in our discussion. For we will argue that although the world of self-exploration, what many adults perceive as the selfishness or self-indulgence of adolescence, is precisely what is meant to characterize this stage of development, the culture often works to mislead adolescents by pushing them off the intended paths of self-exploration and self-reflection. It does this inadvertently at times by distracting adolescents as they undertake their narrative work. It also does this knowingly, with clear-cut intent and purpose.[10] It would be lovely to think that the well being of children and adolescents is first and foremost within the culture, but this is not always the case.

The story of adolescents growing up in a culture of distraction is a story of thinking and, more precisely, the sort of thinking about self that adolescents necessarily undertake as a function of their newly found capacity to reason at post-conventional levels, often with great sophistication.[11] Although many theories of adolescence rest on a physical or biological foundation,[12] that it is the emergence of secondary sex characteristics that symbolize this particular stage of life, I will argue that adolescence is inevitably about consciousness, thinking, personal reflection of a profound order, the development of the self, story telling in which the audience is sometimes the culture, sometimes the individual adolescent and where the story's source is sometimes the individual adolescent, and sometimes the culture, replete with distractions. *def'n adolescence*

Let me say a brief word about distraction, which I will be defining throughout this chapter.

Possessing several distinct meanings, the word "distraction" is intended to denote any cultural stimulus, fashion, fad, style, norm, that leads the *def'n distraction* adolescent away from the sort of reasoning and reflection required to produce an authentic, not to mention healthy, moral sense of self and identity. In its most fundamental form, distraction disrupts reflection, thinking, reasoning, thereby causing adolescents to perceive of themselves more in the forms, beneficial or not, the culture desires, than in the forms they themselves construct. In other words, distracting cultural stories lead to perverse personal stories and more fragile and incomplete identities.

Adolescence may be a period of consternation, confusion, conflict, anxiety, as popular conceptions have it, but it is also a period in which personal freedom and magnificent opportunities for creativity are possible. As has been said, adolescence is the storm before the lull; the adolescent requires the storm, creating it even, while the culture seeks to end it as soon as possible so that adulthood—yet another story—may commence.

Although this hardly represents the common conception of adolescence, I will argue that the whole point of this stage of development is to accomplish nothing less than the construction of a personal story, itself representing the construction of the self, one that genuinely works for the individual young person. Inevitably, while the mind fields and personal caves of the inner world are filled with stories, one question remains: Are adolescents themselves the true authors of their stories, or, by dint of the power of a distracting culture, are their stories little more than the internalization of others' stories? Has individual consciousness, in other words, been plagiarized?[13]

To make these notions more concrete and understand how personal stories and narratives come to be constructed, let us consider anorexia nervosa, an eating disorder found mainly in girls and women.[14]

Seemingly in competition with herself, the often-perfectionist anorectic girl has determined that nothing about her is good enough. One observes her fighting to win the power struggles with other people, notably her parents, and, especially, her mother. At the same time, however, she seeks to control her inner and outer worlds, all the while believing that she possesses no power whatsoever, hence she lives perpetually defeated, at a loss, isolated, and, probably, resentful. This is the opening chapter of her personal story.

The struggle she experiences—still more of her story—reveals her difficulty in developing an identity, an image really, of which she herself can approve. In seeking approbation of others and thereby taking her private story to the public, she fears the criticism she has heard again and again, much of it generated in her own head. Eventually she finds it impossible to express anger at anyone except, of course, herself. Her mother typically is viewed as a saint, a self-sacrificing woman who, after all, does provide the girl with support and sustenance. Eventually the resentment, anger and disapproval are turned toward the self—the process is called "acting in"—and more precisely toward the body. It is easier to work out one's struggles on the body than in their true habitat: the mind fields.

The rest of the story is familiar to students of adolescents. There are essentially only two transformations open to the young woman: She can become clinically obese or abnormally thin, stuff or starve, as it is said, acts often leading to bingeing and purging, the trademark behaviors of yet another eating disorder, bulimia. The decision is simple, the message from the exterior world unequivocal: Everything in the public media screams thinness. Become thin and the world ("of the look") embraces and approves of you. America, ironically, has an insatiable appetite for not eating; every adolescent girl knows this to be true.

A glance at the characteristic family structure of the anorexic young woman, another part of her developing story and personal identity, is especially revealing.[15] Some children feel smothered by their families or, to use the language of family systems theorist Salvador Minuchin and his colleagues,[16] they feel enmeshed in relationships. It is an apt word, enmeshment, particularly for girls with anorexia, for it bespeaks the boundaryless nature of human connections of the sort that in physical reality cannot exist. There are, after all, boundaries separating embryo from mother without which the embryo's and mother's health is imperiled. In the anorexic family, one observes this boundaryless behavior to the extent that one can barely discern where one person's interior or emotional life begins and the other person's interior and emotional life ends. Enmeshed people are more than joined at the hip; they are joined in the gut; their interior worlds are more than overlapping, thereby preventing each from becoming differentiated from one another though never truly independent. Enmeshment suggests not knowing where one person's story ends and another person's story begins. According to Minuchin: "The anorectic family is a system whose adaptive and coping mechanisms have become unavailable."[17]

Enmeshment characteristically commences early in the daughter's development, her happiness becoming the happiness of her parents, and, later and more significantly, her successes and failures becoming the parents' successes and failures. Enmeshment carries the concept of vicarious experience to unbearable extremes, with vicariousness itself emerging as an ability to live, as it were, within the stories and boundaries of another person. The characteristic response to adolescent enmeshment is total separation, an utterly implausible degree of manifest independence. Some psychologists label it "pseudo independence" although this too may be distractive thinking. How can anyone be totally independent or totally self sufficient despite the culture's insistence on just such (implausible) ideals?[18]

The healthy goal is for people to become differentiated from one another according to the language and grammar of their personally authored stories. This means that lives overlap and touch, connect and unite, but no person's life or self ever wholly encompasses or obliterates another's. There can be no such thing as a human eclipse wherein one life conceals the existence of the another, although in many families one observes attempts at just such a constellation.

Properly differentiated from others although still attached to them, adolescents are free to focus on their interior world primarily because they are able to bring the same loving attitude to themselves that others continue to bring to them. Needless to say, enmeshment never substitutes for love, even though in distractive thinking, some may confuse it as a form of love. Borrowing from the writings of John Dewey[19] to whom we will turn in later chapters, it might be alleged that enmeshment is to love as distraction is to enslavement.

In the case of anorexia, much of enmeshment activity takes place around food. Consider one subtle but significant daily ritual, still another part of the young girl's story. Mother prepares food and daughter eats it, or more likely, eats a bit of it. "But why not all of it?" inquires the mother. "Is something wrong with it? Is something wrong with me? Is something wrong with you? Is something wrong with us?" Enmeshment now is speaking, for the mother has not yet confronted the question of whether the child is eating for herself or for her, the mother. Just whose needs are being gratified by the child's eating? Just whose story is taking precedence? Is the mother feeding to nurture the child or merely to quiet her?

Although not focusing on anorexia, Erikson expressed his concern for these sorts of parents this way: "But they love intrusively and desperately. They themselves are so hungry for approval and recognition that they burden their children with complicated complaints."[20]

For boys, and once again we observe the power of the mass media and contemporary ideology, discussions of food assume wholly different forms. Boys elicit dinner table commentary such as, "Look what that child devours! I'd rather clothe him than feed him." Or conversely, "Don't worry, when he's hungry, he'll eat." All the while the boy's sister is feeling smothered, even abandoned, because of her "bad" behavior: refusing to eat. Perhaps she has heard too many words about looks, appearance, weight, thinness, public presentation, body. Everything in the family, everything about life suddenly revolves around food. Every emotion, every interpersonal crisis or problem-solving dilemma joins with fundamental definitions of independence and personal identity to focus on the consumption of food. "If you're hungry, you'll eat" turns into "If you loved me, respected me, truly wanted to please me, cared enough about this family, you'd eat!"

Not eating represents a flagrant defiance of everything for which the parents stand. It is pseudo-self-sufficiency, pseudo-independence, and good-old-fashioned adolescent rebellion writ large. Yet notice that amid the conflicts caused by the anorexia, for which the young woman does receive some attention, she deliberates the question of what literally and symbolically she wishes to incorporate, internalize, digest. Although the outside world declares her actions to be unequivocal rebellion or clinical disorder, her own narrative depicts her behavior in the form of a deliberation about what to accept and what to reject. In her mind she isn't at all ill. Obviously recognizing that she is in some distress, she perceives her story neither as rebellion nor disorder but rather one of refusing to take orders and battling against the suffocating power of enmeshment. Ironically moving closer to death with her precariously low weight, her story has her believing that she is at long last nearing a life-saving plateau.

The distraction part of this scenario should be evident; it certainly is in the minds of seriously aggressive boys: Erect armor; let no one get to you; let no one inside; avoid intimacy; tell no one anything of what lives within you, and practice these policies often enough that you yourself begin to lose touch with your interior world or, conversely, discover that these are the requisite conditions for exploring your own interior world. In these instances, it is almost as if adolescents strive to be independent not only from the society but from themselves as well. Acting and feeling in this alienated manner, the young anorectic woman needn't reflect on any matter that might trouble her. She can avoid every square inch of her mind fields and focus solely on controlling the one thing in her life that appears controllable—her weight. In her mind she is now totally independent and self-sufficient, exactly as the culture claims it wishes her to be. She needs no one, especially not her parents, nothing, not even food. Or so she imagines.

The onset of anorexia is frequently ignited by personal loss, a good friend moving away or the breaking up of a significant relationship. It is ignited as well by a transition, one often involving the pressure to mature, like graduation or the commencement of a new life status. Igniting transitions of this sort also include the death of a loved one or one's parents getting a divorce, suggesting that *interpersonal* decoupling begins a process in some adolescents of an *intrapersonal* decoupling, a sense of the inner world falling away as if one has lost an understanding or control of it. This matter, too, we will examine in a later chapter.

Equally intriguing, many girls who respond to common competitive situations by becoming anorexic, are the very ones who once excelled in these same competitions, such as academics, dancing, gymnastics, running, swimming, diving. In the end, these girls appear to be acting out exactly what Erich Fromm described in *Escape from Freedom*.[21] They wish to excel, stand out as exceptional persons, as we all do, shouting their independence to the rooftops. Yet underneath, feeling unlovable and defective, as Heinz Kohut[22] warned, they are desperate for security, affection, comfort, and healthy attachments, especially with adults.[23] No one knows better than they that independence is completely unattainable despite the unrealistic urgings of a distracted culture and the perverse sense of an accomplishment consisting of having lost a dangerous amount of weight.

Anorexia is distraction gone mad. It is a buying-in to public icons and images as a way of handling mistrust of others and alienation from one's own mind fields. The young woman has suddenly lost the ability to value or approve of herself, love or care for herself. The nurturance, security and capacity for intimacy that Felton Earls and Mary Carlson[24] advanced as requirements for a healthy family have all but vanished. In their place stands a frightfully thin, angry, resentful, self-hating, and, let us not forget, hungry child at war not with the world at large but with the world of her own impulses, dreams, desires, needs, which are fueled by that same world. Valiantly she attempts to recast her story, make things right, unconsciously wishing perhaps, to turn herself into a little boy, all the while projecting these distressing reflections on to the external world that she views as untrustworthy and perilous. With anorexia, everything gets played out in the public arena, for in a sense, the private arena has been shut down, as it often is when one seeks unalloyed independence and the repudiation of the self. One's very symptoms keep one, and perhaps entire families as well, distracted.

Anorexia, the disorder of self-sacrifice, purity, holiness, humility, has one final component that plays into the themes of our discussion of adolescence and distraction.

Quite regularly, anorexic girls describe uncomfortable, brittle, or even openly hostile relationships between their parents. Granted, their passive-aggressive type disorder demands that their family attend to them. Yet might it be that these girls wish to take the spotlight off their parents? Might they even feel enobled by this action? Perhaps they are the rodeo clowns distracting the bull so that he doesn't mangle the cowboy. Whatever the causes, the result is a daughter painfully dependent on a family that at the same time is dependent on her although few wish to read the story this way. The interdependence of the family stories is witnessed in the oscillating actions of anger and forgiveness, nurturance and neglect. For these families, and in the mind fields of these daughters, it is always feast or famine.[25]

As for the child herself, how possibly can she explain her actions? How does she explain herself to herself? Is she not doing exactly what society requires? Thinness and beauty, after all, are evidence of will and power, discipline and success. Everything in the culture pushes her to become independent, self-sufficient, autonomous, self-directed, able to withstand any form of competition; she is a woman under her own control. And as she strives, nay, works like a dog to reach that ideal weight and attain that ideal look, she succeeds in getting everyone to look at her and possibly feel the same disgust for her she holds for herself. Still, they are looking, and so is she.

Distraction as Diversion or Being Drawn Away

We turn now to four fundamental definitions of distraction, each one having significant implications for developing adolescents and the selves they are constructing. Each definition, in part, is born in cultural forms and dynamics, just as each eventually finds its way in to the adolescent's mind fields. To appreciate the felt sense of distraction, imagine stepping outside your home on an especially dark evening. With no lights around, you find that in the first few moments you cannot see anything. Gradually your eyes become accustomed to the darkness, and you discern the outlines of shapes and figures. Perhaps you recognize certain objects, although many of them are already familiar to you.

Now you discover that by looking not directly at an object but a few feet to the left or right of it, you can discern it more clearly. Aware of it or not, you have switched on your night-vision lenses, a physiological process causing the objects you perceive to fall on a spot of your retina meant primarily for night vision (different spots of the retina are employed for day vision). The process is a familiar one, although it's a bit awkward holding your head in just that perfect position that allows you to see an object that in the daylight would require no effort.

Most of us are familiar with these experiences of day vision and night vision, which now serve as a metaphor for experiencing the ways in which adolescents pursue reality and distraction. In pursuing reality, a person looks dead on at an object in the brilliance of the light of day. We even use the expression, "This will look differently to you in the daylight." Conversely, in pursuing distraction, adolescents urge their minds, consciously or not, to look away from what is there before them in order to come up with or render a perception that satisfies them, even though at some level they know they are not looking directly at that which they claim to identify or encounter. It's close enough, they think; it will suffice. This becomes the image of the adolescent pursuit of distraction, something we all do.

To illustrate the phenomenon, consider an example of looking not at the (real) object before us, the truth of the matter or the day version, but at something close by, the object of distraction or the night version. Suppose that a man enters a doctor's office complaining of severe chest pains. Solicitous and sensitive, the doctor orders a series of tests. The patient feels relieved that he is at last being cared for, but the chest pains persist. Finally, on the basis of the test results, the doctor pronounces the man to be perfectly healthy and sends him on his way. So far so good. But let us now consider two scenarios to this story.

Delighted to learn that his chest pains are "nothing," the man's health quickly improves; all he needed was a physician to proclaim there were no physical reasons for his pains. Doctors, we all know, possess some magic in their little black bags. In another scenario, the man goes out into the hall and drops dead while waiting for an elevator. His friends are incredulous: "It's impossible to believe; there was nothing wrong with him!" they say. "The doctor even said so."

Here then the first definition of distraction: the inability or reluctance to look at the truths of a particular event or experience. By not looking directly at the heart of the matter but away from it, we are, in effect, having our attention drawn away or diverted from essential truths. Literally speaking, to distract means to *divert* or *draw the mind away* from something, just as we do when something tends to trouble or bore us. We even employ the word when we say: "I need some distraction."

When my mind is drawn away from something, be it a noxious, boring, or anxiety-provoking stimulus, I may be wholly unaware that distraction is taking place. Conversely, aware that I require distraction, I may be totally unaware of what lives within me from which I now want to be drawn away. Convicted of so-called "technical crimes," Michael Milken may have spoken for generations of distracted souls when he stated: "I allowed myself to get too caught up in what I was doing to consider the consequences or to stop myself from doing what I knew was wrong."[26]

The essential or nondistracted truth is the complaint of chest pains or the knowledge that I am acting immorally. The drawing away from the truth is captured in the diagnosis of perfect health in a man who will suffer a fatal heart attack within an hour. If we weren't drawn away from the truth of the matter, we wouldn't say things like "It's impossible to believe; there was nothing wrong with him!" Instead, we must aver that there *was* something wrong with him, but the doctor couldn't find the problem. We could even refine this statement by saying that it was the tests that failed to detect the man's problem in the first place.

Throughout this book, we are going to see that much of the business of our culture is meant to draw us away or divert us from something, a phenomenon that assumes inordinate significance for adolescents in the throes of seeking to determine the truths of their own being. We are going to learn, moreover, that it is not always in the best interest of some businesses and social institutions to have adolescents perceive the world or the world's products in that dead-on manner we adopt when examining objects in the daylight. We are going to discover that it may be better for the culture, although not necessarily for its young people, to lower the lights and have them grope about in darkness. That way they need not see the truths of their own ways, their own experiences, their own lives, not to mention the ways of the culture in which they are being raised.

Notice, however, that even in this introductory explanation, we have already encountered a form of distraction. For the idea of businesses distracting adolescents is itself a distraction, because adolescents possess the ultimate power to combat distraction. So part of the adolescent-distraction story is an exploration of why in their personal and public endeavors, adolescents may desire to look away from the realities of their lives and, hence, the realities of the culture. Why do they wish to keep turning down the lights in their lives (as, for understandable reasons, they do at their high school dances) in order to avoid looking at what is really going on within their personal mind fields? Why are they willing to be so easily drawn away or diverted from something? Why are they willing to be so distracted?

Distraction as Confusion and Conflict

Consider now the second definition of distraction, the felt sense of *confusion* or *conflict*, the existence of two competing elements in our mind, which, when examined closely, may not be competing at all. Let us now look at several examples of this second definition of distraction, each of them related to the world of adolescents.

When disappointed with certain political actions, even young students are heard to grumble, "That's the way it's always been. Nothing's ever going to change." Most of us recognize that this attitude actually consti-tutes the mechanism perpetuating the political structure and decision mak-ing apparatus that appalls us in the first place. We label the attitude cyni-cism or apathy, but the result of the attitude is the perpetuation of much of what we presently observe in America—a political system that works well for some citizens, adequately for others, and not at all for still others.

The conflict aspect of distraction in this illustration, leading as it often does to unproductive thinking, represents a rather extraordinary political experiment. The positive aspects of democracy we know well. Conversely, conflicts arise when democracy is seen as unworkable. The very rituals of nominating and electing candidates, political polling, campaign financ-ing, and television reporting of elections, though not intended to be de-structive or nefarious, in fact tend to perpetuate the "unworkability" of the system. Moviegoers recognize this as the point of the movie *Bullworth*. An editorial in *The New York Times* makes the point of distraction even more succinctly:

> What 200 years of democracy have come to is a tawdry system where poll takers wield more influence than economists and scientists, where negative advertising makes legislators afraid to debate (much less act on) controversial issues, where the costs of running for office render the effective exercise of office impossible.[27]

In 1848, the problems of American politics already had taken form. We know this from reading Alexis de Tocqueville's two-volume portrait, *Democracy in America*.[28] (Americans, incidentally, learned early in their history to trust foreigners' perceptions of the country.) Among Tocqueville's more trenchant observations was that the "best people" in America do not enter politics, choosing instead to work in voluntary associations.

Some people still hold this observation to be true, but others would call it the epitome of cynicism. Some believe "the system" to be immutable, etched in stone, something to which, alas, one must adjust. To depict the flaws of the political system too vociferously makes one a radical, a whistle-blower, un-American, worse of all perhaps, an adolescent! Psychoanalyst Bruno Bettelheim once described the young protesters of the Vietnam War as acting out Oedipal anger toward their fathers. Notice the Bettelheim version of distraction as confusion or conflict. Not only did he see the world in psychoanalytic terms—his personal realm of thinking—he overlooked any possible political legitimacy of the protesters' ideology. Some people tend to do this with most ideologies to which adolescents subscribe.

One extension of the Bettelheim position is to suggest that political protest is a sign of ill health, requiring either psychotherapy or hospitalization as was advocated in the former Soviet Union. So now the conflict or confusion is revealed: We are angered by and distrustful of the system we believe to be immutable, but then find that we are angered as well by the people seeking to change it, people we best not trust because they are transforming their rage against their fathers into a protest against the (mother) country. Besides, how can we ever trust adolescents exhibiting the audacity to change what we claim to be unchangeable?

To elaborate this example of (distractive) confusion and conflict in the political realm, we reflect on what has been written about the politics of America's high school and college students during the 1980s and 1990s. For decades, scores of articles were written on why America's students have grown politically quiet, apathetic, and why they embraced the status quo of the American system, precisely as their elders wished them to do.

Once again we have encountered the conflict aspect of distraction. In one moment, experts diagnose political protest among adolescents, in the next they diagnose the *absence* of protest. It's not a matter of whether or not the young *should* protest, but how in our own conflicted and confused attitudes, we the observers assess the political process and those who would have either a strong reaction to it or no reaction whatsoever.

Another example of the confusion aspect of distraction, one that regularly filters into the mind fields of adolescents, presented itself several years ago when the cover of *Us Magazine* revealed the face of actor Kevin Costner.[29] In 1991, Costner was as hot as they come in Hollywood, having hit the critical and financial jackpots with his movie *Dances with Wolves*. Clearly a public relations piece, the article announced that Costner was as honorable and decent a man as he was handsome. What better publicity could a man want! Yet the cover carried the headline of Costner as "Rebel." That's a rather strong word for a man making that much money from a film, accepting Oscar nominations, and undertaking the publicity activities intended to increase box office receipts. Rebel? Really?

Costner was gutsy to undertake a film like *Dances with Wolves,* but describing him as a rebel seems appropriate only in the context of distraction. To the untrained viewer such as myself, *Dances with Wolves* appeared to be a relatively enlightened cinematic rendering of the world of Native Americans. However, unlike most American Westerns, for once the "Indians" weren't the bad guys; they were real people, touching, intelligent, sensate. Taking the path toward depicting truth made this multi-millionaire filmmaker/actor a rebel. Here's the distraction: Because American film makers have consistently portrayed Native Americans as warlike and immoral, the handsome and honorable Costner emerged as a rebel. In the world of (public relations) distractions, everyone, apparently, accepts life as ugly, dishonorable, and indecent.

For adolescents the message is straightforward. Does the culture maintain conflict with those people wishing to tell genuine stories? Is it the point of the culture, moreover, to get adolescents out of their characteristically rebellious posture and become conforming "proper" citizens? We certainly would not want to conclude that everyone seeking to portray reality is a rebel. Or would we?

Come to think of it, the two populations ostensibly devoting their lives to articulating "truth," artists and academics, regularly are portrayed in the media as being illegitimate or unusual. Conjure up the image of artists and academics; think about their hair and clothes. Even well-intentioned children's television programs frequently portray artists and scientists with stereotypic characteristics like long, messy hair and outrageously sloppy clothing. The point is to make certain that young people recognize that artists and intellectuals are "different" and perhaps in some ways dangerous as well, essentially because they speak of freedom and constraint, liberty and oppression. Put these same people in three-piece suits and they will be perceived as far less threatening.

It's interesting that those people associated with white-collar crime—be they lawyers, bankers, CEOs, politicians, brokers—rarely if ever are viewed as rebellious. Indeed, they are the ones who speak to us of law and order.

Interesting, too, that public images rarely depict women as artists, scientists, and intellectuals. This matter, too, is also relevant to the lives of adolescents, and falls into the category of distraction as conflict and confusion.

Distraction as Boredom

We arrive at the third definition of distraction, one which some readers may find perplexing. For many of us, boredom hardly seems an appropriate facet of distraction. Granted, some young people are forced to engage in activities they find uninteresting, unstimulating or outright boring. Simply put, they are not engaged in activities that excite or energize them. They may fake interest or, more likely, go through the paces from the time they arrive at school to the time they leave, disliking most everything they do and barely able to keep their minds on school work they describe as boring. For these young people, school serves to distract them from their genuine sense of their own beings while demanding the attention of the consciousness they wish they could dismiss. Their sense of a good solution to their boredom, ironically, is to seek forms of distraction that they hope will take their minds off their boredom rather than focus on precisely what it is they genuinely are thinking and wish to do and become.

The familiar advertising slogan, directed at the young, "Weekends Were Made for Michelob" appeals to the bored because it exploits this tendency to seek a distraction intended to mute the fundamental concerns of consciousness, in this case the felt sense of boredom. Alcohol, adolescents learn early on, normally dulls their boredom but does nothing to help them focus on what they must do, think, and feel in order not to be bored. Nonetheless, boredom momentarily is counteracted with alcohol, and everyone seems happy, particularly those corporations making money on antidotes to boredom.

In the meantime, bored adolescents have been distracted from the real effort required to re-think the nature of their school or family situations, as well as those aspects of modern life evidently causing them unhappiness, depression and boredom. Even young adolescents recognize that for slogans like "T.G.I.F." and "Happy Hour" to capture one's imagination, Monday, Tuesday, Wednesday, Thursday, and Friday, up until the later afternoon anyway, must be awfully dull.

Teachers are quick to acknowledge that many of their students define the academic experience as an oscillation between boredom and anxiety. It is hoped that the resulting agitation will be relieved by daily gym classes and recess. Yet, again, what traditionally has been the solution to this common school problem of boredom and agitation? Too regularly we discover that well-meaning people turn to distractive techniques, more competition for the child's consciousness, and probably, too, more inauthentic emotional and cognitive exercises and curricula meant to distract the child from the anxiety, boredom, conflict, and agitation he or she already experiences by dint of living a distracted life, one which schools unwittingly perpetuate. In this context, I recall a high school junior saying, "I really like school; it's the classes I can't stand!"

Even small children use the word "bored" to describe their distracted states. Observing certain children, we discern an agitation or discomfort in the way they move about or play with toys and friends. Something appears to be stirring them up. We know the internal worlds of the young often reach a fever pitch of activity as if their conscious and unconscious states conspire to heat up the molecules of their mind fields. Did we not just last night go into their rooms and comfort them as they expressed dread of the monsters under their bed, terror of the thunder outside, or their most recent nightmare? Did we not just now kneel down beside them and help them select a toy since they seemed unable to decide which one would satisfy their present need? And if we are being completely truthful, don't we offer children and adolescents distractions when it is the distracted consciousness that has caused this expressed boredom, anxiety, and agitation in the first place?

Distraction as Madness

The fourth and final definition of distraction, derived in great measure from the earlier definitions, probably captures the felt sense of distraction better than any other description. If we combine diversion with conflict, confusion, and boredom, we wind up with an almost crazed consciousness or sense of madness. At bottom, this is precisely what adolescents experience in distracted states. It is the felt sense not only of enormous numbers of stimuli simultaneously hitting their consciousness, but their inability to process or handle all of these stimuli. More than a few adolescents have experienced the sensation of something about their lives they can barely describe, literally making them go mad. In these moments, they appear to have lost all control of their mind fields.

To understand this final definition of distraction, it seems worthwhile to point out that everything has the power to affect the consciousness of adolescents. Every stimulus with which they come into contact, every word or sign, every image on a television or computer screen, every sight on the street, every sound of every song fills their consciousness or at least looks to find a little room for itself. "Our minds are like crows," Thomas Merton wrote. "They pick up everything that glitters, no matter how uncomfortable our nests get with all the metal in them."[30]

Memories, too, compete to find a little space in the minds of adolescents.[31] Just because something no longer exists hardly means it doesn't live within one's consciousness. For that matter, things that are yet to arrive fill up the space of consciousness in the form of expectations, anticipations, wishes, apprehensions, as do messages and impulses of which adolescents aren't even aware, although they could be if pointed in that direction. This is what Freud[32] meant by the pre-conscious: the contents of the mind one can reach with the barest suggestion. The adolescent picks a fight with his mother because she irritated him when she reminded him to clean his room. Eventually the young man discovers that his real anger is with a friend who betrayed him earlier that day. For the moment, he is not yet aware of what precisely fuels his irritation with his mother, yet all of this stuff fills his consciousness, along with a reminder that he must study for an exam, write a term paper, take out the garbage, walk the dog, and try to accomplish everything before the Knicks and Lakers tip off.

In more general terms, American society reveals a host of forces seeking to capture the attention, the fancy, the consciousness of adolescents. One focuses on the advertising industry and the media, particularly television, because they are the most obvious examples of industries intent on planting their messages into the mind fields of adolescents; they make no bones about it. They want the young to buy their products, watch their programs, have their logos indelibly lodged in adolescents' minds. Whether they wish to teach adolescents something or merely entertain them, these industries demand the adolescent's complete (conscious and unconscious) attention.[33] Periodically, one may focus on the subliminal messages of advertisers, but the conscious, purely liminal messages are all one need consider in this discussion. Whether the beer bottle is a phallic symbol remains a question for psychoanalysts. The point is that the beer industries want to push the idea of drinking into the adolescent's consciousness and the beer into the adolescent's mouth.

Political elections are conducted in much the same manner. At any given moment, even during sleep, there's not a lot of wiggle room left in one's consciousness, so political candidates had better do something extra special, or look extra special, or sound extra special if they're going to get a front row seat in anyone's consciousness. None of these people are all that different, actually, from the teacher standing before a class that will not quiet down. "May I *please* have your attention *now!* " she shouts at them, for a moment, anyway, becoming the center of her students' consciousness, trying to quell the madness of a classroom.

Along with advertisements, public relations campaigns, television programs, political candidates undertake the same endeavor, hawking their messages at the young like merchants at a street bazaar hoping to rein in customers. The only problem is that their messages are hardly trinkets; they are substances shaping the nature of adolescent consciousness and, ultimately, the entire culture as well. They shape the words the young employ to describe, examine, and interpret the world and their existence in it.[34] They shape the way adolescents assess and feel about themselves just as they shape the nature of an adolescent's capacity to think critically and his or her sense of morality and responsibility.

Recognizing now how encompassing and complex is this matter of distraction, let us consider an all-too-appropriate illustration of what we are calling distraction as madness.

One wonders how many perfectly healthy young people are practically driven mad trying to keep up with the latest fashions, styles, trends, fads, looks. The messages of the culture battling for adolescents' attention, while causing distraction in their wake, may appear to some observers as superficial and transitory as the clothes adolescents (are meant to) purchase. As the seasons change, fashions change. One minute a young woman would die to own a particular sweater; the next moment she can't find a place for it in her wardrobe. She comes to believe that the entirety of her being is symbolized by the way she looks,[35] the makeup she applies, the clothes she wears. Boys are not immune from this form of distraction either; we still say, "Clothes make the man." The products and messages of the culture, therefore, are hardly baseball caps holding the attention of adolescents for a few moments; they turn out to be the very ingredients of adolescent consciousness. For adolescents seem vulnerable to these handsomely packaged directives.

Young people may grin upon hearing the slogan, "When the going gets tough the tough go shopping." They know how often they themselves have hit the malls, having decided to reward themselves with a small treat, a little nothing, perhaps, in cashmere. Some of them know as well, the feeling of peering into a closet so filled with clothes they cannot shut the door and with despair crying out, "I have nothing to wear!" In these instants of what only can be described as confusion and madness, their entire consciousness seems to be filled with and defined by the closet. It would take something stupendous to distract them from their agitation and unhappiness. They think of calling a friend in order to borrow something or dashing out to a store to buy something but are halted in their tracks by a dilemma: What can they put on that's appropriate for going shopping?

Does this not sound like madness? In these moments, the messages of the culture own the adolescent. Fashion, beauty, style, appearance, image, latest trend or fad have grabbed all the front row seats of the adolescent's consciousness. A parent enters their room and tells them they are beautiful no matter what they wear, but their consciousness repels this: "Get out of here; there's no room (in my consciousness closet) for that rubbish!" Suddenly they have forfeited anything resembling human freedom, will, or sanity. For the moment, this story seems to have ended.

In their states of distraction, it often appears that adolescents are driven not by sexual or aggressive drives, as Freud alleged, but by malls, images, ideal visions, advertisements, television programs, movies, role models, and worst of all, a self-concept constructed in their own mind fields and generated by materialism. In these instants, adolescents have become a living compilation of things, clothes, fads, fashions, all contrived to get them thinking and feeling exactly as they now are thinking and feeling. Suddenly, young people have become nothing but the fashion statement they hope to make through their appearance or behavior, or the void left by the statement they are unable to create precisely because they have nothing to wear. Their consciousness now imprisoned, they only naturally feel madness all around them. For the moment, they have lost sight of the mind fields; everything has become public distraction.

At this point, you may be feeling that, although our theory of distraction is reasonably provocative, when it is you standing before that totally filled and yet utterly empty closet, life itself seemingly hangs in the balance (as well as in the closet). Still, if this seems exaggerated, then think of the numerous idioms employed to express feelings about fashion and appearance and ask yourself whether these idioms do not seem somewhat mad: "Now *there's* a sweater you could *die* for." "She looked so awesome I could have *killed* her." "I'd rather *die* than be seen in public wearing *that!*" "Wow, what a *drop-dead* gorgeous gown!" And finally: "I'd *kill* for that jacket."

To repeat, as all of this is going on, adolescents are not merely reacting to the culture,[36] they are directly influencing its shape with their desperate feelings and worship of fashion. They are in a state of distraction, for the moment alienated from the genuine activities "intended" for the human mind, which include a search for and examination of human realities, which, in great measure, means the ongoing construction of the self. They are neither challenged by the activity of finding the perfect garment to wear nor critical, this one day, of the value of their hunt for perfection. They accept the despair or desperation as being natural, given the state of their closet and bank account, and remain unaware of what it is their consciousness is doing or of what it is in this moment comprised.

In the end, the energy spent in this desperate search will prove wasteful, for in a few hours, days, or weeks, irrespective of how successful their intermittent shopping sprees or other voyages to distraction may be, they once again will experience these same feelings and thoughts of madness. And don't think that the malls of America won't be delighted with this latest bout of fashion madness. Let us, however, hold that other notion in mind as well, the one having to do with individual consciousness helping to shape culture just as culture shapes individual consciousness. Remember that when one laments his or her difficulty in keeping up with fashions when "they" keep changing them, it is the state of one's own consciousness that legitimates and encourages people called fashion designers to play with one's consciousness in the first place. Inevitably "we" create "they," or more precisely, our story writes their existence into our mind fields.

Let's review the definitions of "distract" or "to be distracted": To draw the mind away from something or divert its attention, to cause conflict or confusion, to experience boredom, and, lastly, to feel crazed or mad. All these definitions play into the state of adolescent consciousness as well as the individual's felt sense of consciousness. All these definitions should appear relevant to adolescents' descriptions of themselves standing in front of a surfeit of clothes desperate because they have nothing to wear, a surfeit of stimuli to which they cannot properly respond.

In that instant, adolescents have forfeited authentic conscious activities and (literally) bought into what the culture wishes them to do with their sometimes noisy desperation. In that instant, moreover, adolescents have totally forgotten (or forfeited the notion) that they themselves have the power to construct reality and fill the emptiness or, better yet, leave it empty; they forever remain the authors of their own stories. By forfeiting this birthright, they have imprisoned themselves or at least feel as if their mind fields had been confiscated, which, as we will note in later chapters, is precisely what has taken place when they live in distracted states.

Finally, in pursuing distraction, adolescents are not only going about their everyday lives, they are constructing the lives that constitute their culture and, thereby, shaping the entire culture through their conscious activities. A perfect example of this is heard in this announcement of a television newsperson: "Here are the stories making news at this hour." Read his words closely: We have said that we are, perhaps, nothing more than the stories we tell, but stories don't make news; people select events and transform them into stories, and, by dint of being reported, the stories come to be defined as news. In this way, the culture is being constructed or, more precisely, reconstructed. This is not to say that culture is nothing more than a collection of individual lives; it is far more complicated. As Christopher Lasch wrote: "Communities shape us in ways that we are not free to reject, and they are held together not by love and friendship, but by descent, early training, and the enforcement of collective norms."[37]

Adolescents are not only reflecting on the ways they think about things, they are creating, reinforcing, and constructing the ways they think about things.[38] In fact, they do this with such intensity, they actually feel their thought processes to be perfectly normal and natural and that others had best conform to them. How often do adolescents recognize they are pursuing distraction? My own sense is that although they may not pick up the inherent fallacy in a statement like, "Here are the stories making news at this hour," they do, in fact, recognize the faces and sounds of distraction even when they opt to ignore them. There isn't an adolescent alive who hasn't wondered about that peculiarly illogical expression that precedes a spanking: "This is going to hurt me more than it will you!"

This volume is divided into four parts. In this first chapter, I have defined the concept of distraction and examined how it plays out in the minds of adolescents as they attempt to construct a healthy sense of themselves and build a functioning identity. In the next chapter, I continue this discussion on distraction, taking a closer look at what goes on in the social and public worlds of young people, and how they tend to respond to these allegedly distracting stimuli.

In Part II I focus more specifically on adolescence and what young people and, of course, the culture in which they are developing construct as normal or typical behavior and activity. In Part III, I turn to a discussion of modes of thinking, which is the central concern in this study of adolescents. If what the adolescent thinks in great measure determines the self under construction, then how the adolescent thinks would seem to be of equally vital importance.

Part IV is devoted to the mind fields themselves, the modes of being, and, most especially, the supreme antidote to distraction available to every adolescent by dint of normal neurological and cognitive maturation. If one form of thinking gets young persons into some difficulty, as we say, distracts them, then might there be another form of thinking that pulls those people to safety while offering security and a healthy sense of self that will support and define them throughout life?

The clue to this form of thinking is captured in the title of the last chapter, "The Prize of Self-Reflection." For what we are doing in this entire work is precisely what adolescents do as they invent and construct themselves or, more precisely, their selves. We are engaging in a reflection of self and culture, constantly seeking to discern what it is that makes us think about the world and ourselves as we do. We thereby open the possibility that because we are little more than our stories, we may create for ourselves and our culture whatever it is we choose to create. This book, in other words, is but another story.

Although these last notions may sound somewhat, well, adolescent, to believe that the world order and, most especially, our culture and ourselves are set in stone, determined by forces either long dead or over which we have no control, is to live without will, purpose, or anything resembling freedom—the very freedom many of us imagine we see, and perhaps envy, as we watch children emerge into adolescence.

Notes

1   D. Udall, "The Power of Stories: Learning from the Lives of Young People." *The Journal of Experiential Education. 14*, 34, 1991: 35–38; Israel Rosenfield, "Memory and Identity." *New Literary History.* Winter, 1995: 197–204; S. Engel, *The Stories Children Tell.* New York: Freeman, 1995.

2   Cited in "Claims of Memory." *Bostonia,* Spring, 1999: 67.

3   See G. H. Elder, "Adolescence in Historical Perspective." In J. Adelson (Editor). *Handbook of Adolescent Psychology.* New York: Wiley, 1980; R. Takanishi. "Changing Views of Adolescence in Contemporary Society." In R. Takanishi (Editor), *Adolescence in the 1990s.* New York: Teachers College, 1993; R. D. Enright, V. M. Levy, D. Harris and D. K. Lapsley, "Do Economic Conditions Influence How Theorists View Adolescents?" *Journal of Youth and Adolescence, 16,* 1987: 541–559; and A. Garrod, A. Smulyan, L. Powers, S. and Kilkenny, R., *Adolescent Portraits* (3rd Edition). Boston: Allyn and Bacon, 1999.

4   See A. C. Petersen, "Creating Adolescents: The Role of Context and Process in Developmental Trajectories." *Journal of Research on Adolescence, 3,* 1993: 1–18.

5   Bradford Brown, "Peer Groups and Peer Cultures." In S. S. Feldman and G. R. Elliot (Editors), *At the Threshold: The Developing Adolescent.* Cambridge, MA: Harvard University Press, 1990.

6   David Elkind, *All Grown Up and No Place to Go.* Reading, MA: Addison-Wesley, 1984; B. J. Wadsworth, *Piaget's Theory of Cognitive and Affective Development.* New York: Longman, 1996. I. Sigel, *Cognitive Development from Childhood to Adolescence.* New York: Holt, Rinehart and Winston, 1977; and R. S. Siegler, *Children's Thinking.* Englewood Cliffs, NJ: Prentice-Hall, 1991.

7   Heinz Kohut, *The Chicago Institute Lectures,* Paul and Marian Tolpin (Editors). Hillsdale, Illinois: Analytic Press, 1996.

8   Erik H. Erikson, *Childhood and Society.* New York: Norton, 1950, page 261.

9   B. Brown, M. Lohr, and E. McClenahan, "Early Adolescents' Perceptions of Peer Pressure." *Journal of Early Adolescence, 6,* 1986: 47–55.

10 S. Kassin, *Psychology.* Englewood Cliffs, NJ: Prentice-Hall, 1998; Gerald D. Winter and Eugene M. Nuss, *The Young Adult: Identity and Awareness.* Glenview: Scott, Foresman and Company, 1969; Edward A. Dreyfus, *Youth: A Search for Meaning.* Columbus: Merrill, 1972.

11 Jean Piaget, *Six Psychological Studies.* New York: Random House, 1967; *The Growth of Logical Thinking from Childhood to Adolescence.* New York: Basic Books, 1958; T. Revenson and D. Singer, *A Piaget Primer: How a Child Thinks.* New York, Plume, 1978; David Elkind, *Children and Adolescents: Interpretive*

Essays on Jean Piaget. New York: Oxford University Press, 1974; B. Inhelder and J. Piaget, *The Growth of Logical Thinking from Childhood to Adolescence.* New York: Basic Books, 1958; Lawrence Kohlberg, *Essays on Moral Development.* San Francisco: Harper and Row, 1981; *The Psychology of Moral Development: The Nature and Validity of Moral Stages.* San Francisco: Harper and Row, 1984; *Child Psychology and Childhood Education: A Cognitive-Developmental View.* New York: Longman, 1987.

12   J.M. Tanner, "Physical Growth." In P. H. Mussen (Editor), *Carmichael's Manual of Child Psychology* (3rd Edition, Volume I). New York: Wiley, 1970.

13   On this point, see Carol Gilligan, *In a Different Voice: Psychological Theory and Women's Development.* Cambridge, MA: Harvard University Press, 1982.

14   On this topic, see J. J. Conger and N. L. Galambos, *Adolescence and Youth: Psychological Development in a Changing World.* New York: Longman, 1997; R. Larson and C. Johnson, "Anorexia Nervosa in Context of Daily Living." *Journal of Youth and Adolescence, 10*, 1981: 455–471; Avis Rumney, *Dying to Please: Anorexia Nervosa and Its Cure.* Jefferson, NC: McFarland, 1983; Joan Jacobs Brumberg, *Fasting Girls: The Emergence of Anorexia Nervosa as a Modern Disease.* Cambridge, MA: Harvard University Press, 1988; Maud Ellmann, *The Hunger Artists: Starving, Writing, and Imprisonment.* Cambridge, MA: Harvard University Press, 1993; K.M. Pirke and D. Ploog (Editors), *The Psychobiology of Anorexia Nervosa.* New York: Springer, 1984; Rudolph M. Bell, *Holy Anorexia.* Chicago: University of Chicago Press, 1985; Helm Stierlin and Gunthard Weber, *Unlocking the Family Door: A Systemic Approach to the Understanding and Treatment of Anorexia Nervosa.* New York: Brunner/Mazel, 1989; and Hilde Bruch, *The Golden Cage: The Enigma of Anorexia Nervosa.* Cambridge, MA: Harvard University Press, 1978.

15   See Salvador Minuchin, *Families and Family Therapy.* Cambridge, MA: Harvard University Press, 1974; and Joseph A. Micucci, *The Adolescent in Family Therapy.* New York: Guilford, 2000.

16   Salvador Minuchin, Bernice L. Rosman, and Lester Baker, *Psychosomatic Families: Anorexia Nervosa in Context.* Cambridge, MA: Harvard University Press, 1978. See also H. Chubb, "Looking at Systems as Process." *Family Process,* 1990, *29*: 109–175; and M. Walters, B. Carter, P. Papp and O. Silverstein, "Toward a Feminist Perspective in Family Therapy." In *The Invisible Web: Gender Patterns in Family Relationships.* New York: Guilford, 1988: 15–30.

17   Salvador Minuchin et al., *Psychosomatic Families: Anorexia Nervosa in Context,* op. cit., page 93.

18   See J. D. Hunt, "The Family and the War." In A. Skolnick and J. Skolnick (Editors), (8th Edition). New York: HarperCollins, 1994: 537–547.

19   John Dewey, *How We Think.* Amherst, NY: Prometheus, 1991; and *The Sources of a Science of Education.* New York: Liveright, 1929; See also, R. Archambault (Editor), *John Dewey on Education: Selected Writings.* New York: Random House, 1964.

20   Erik H. Erikson, *Identity, Youth and Crisis*. New York: Norton, 1968, page 177.

21   Erich Fromm, *Escape from Freedom*. New York: Farrar and Rinehart, 1941.

22   Heinz Kohut, *Search for the Self*. Volume 2. Paul Ornstein (Editor). New York: International Universities, 1978.

23   On a related point, see John Bowlby, *Attachment and Loss,* New York: Basic, 1980; and Jerome M. Seidman, *The Adolescent.* New York: Holt, Rinehart and Winston, 1960.

24   Felton Earls and Mary Carlson, "Towards Sustainable Development for American Families." In America's Childhood, *Daedalus,* Winter, 1993, *122*: 93–122.

25   On a related point, see P. Noller and M. A. Fitzpatrick, *Communication in Family Relationships*. Englewood Cliffs, N.J.: Prentice-Hall, 1993.

26   Cited in *Lear's*, February, 1991, page 21.

27   "Serious Times, Trivial Politics." *The New York Times,* March 25, 1990: E18.

28   *Democracy in America*. New Rochelle, NY: Arlington House, 1966.

29   March 7, 1991.

30   Thomas Merton, *New Seeds of Contemplation*. NY: Norton (revised edition), 1974. I am grateful to Thomas O'Toole for bringing this citation to my attention.

31   John Kotre, *White Gloves: How We Create Ourselves Through Memory*. New York: The Free Press, 1995.

32   Sigmund Freud, *A General Introduction to Psycho-Analysis*. New York: Liveright, 1935.

33   See Neil Postman, *Amusing Ourselves to Death: Public Discourse in the Age of Show Business*. New York: Penguin, 1986.

34   See Harold Garfinkle, *Studies in Ethnomethodology*. Englewood Cliffs, NJ: Prentice-Hall, 1967; and Erving Goffman, *The Presentation of Self in Everyday Life*. Garden City, NY: Anchor, 1959.

35   Karen A. Callaghan (Editor), *Ideals of Feminine Beauty*. Westport, CT: Greenwood, 1994.

36   See E. Esman, *Adolescence and Culture*. New York: Columbia University Press, 1990.

37   Christopher Lasch, "Beyond Sentimentalism, A Review of Feminism without Illusions: A Critique of Individualism," by Elizabeth Fox-Genovese. *The New Republic,* February 18, 1991: 58.

38   See Norman Kiell, *The Universal Experience of Adolescence*. London: University of London Press, 1969.

Chapter 2

The Noise of Distraction

The Attractions of Life

Even this early in our discussion, we are beginning to see how confounding and often insidious this business of distraction can be. Already some readers, I imagine, are beginning to think what some of my students must think: If this man is asking me to question everything I do and think and the way I do it and think it, I'm going to stop reading altogether and rent a video. Alas, we now recognize this impulse, too, is a form of distractive thinking. Let me repeat what I have said thus far about distraction.

Whether it is our attention being diverted, the experience of conflict, boredom, confusion, or even a felt sense of madness, pursuing distraction involves how we examine, perceive, and reflect on the world and our being in the world.[1] It involves as well the sorts of conversations we have with ourselves and the outside world, the conversations in which we seek to understand these worlds as well as our own feelings about them. Although personal reflections and actions ultimately are shaped by our societies and cultures, our thinking also has the power to shape these same societies and cultures. Personal reflection, in other words, is dialectical in nature:[2] The culture shapes the adolescent's personal ruminations, but these ruminations shape the culture as well; high school teachers know this to be true.

And here is something else: Part of the work of constituting adolescent consciousness, distracted or not, involves the adolescent's commitment to critical thinking and moral responsibility although we already see that a distracted mind provides a weakened foundation for both critical and moral reasoning.[3] Indeed, this is one of the major lessons teachers seek to impart to adolescents. When the mathematician admonishes her students to show their work, she is looking for the logic or illogic in calculations. Emotional self-reflection reveals similar sorts of logical and illogical pathways, which adolescents gradually come to understand and appreciate.[4] Herein are a few simple illustrations.

Most of us perceive our own newborn baby to be the most beautiful thing in the world. Can anyone, however, be objective about the faces of newborns? Do they not appear comically wrinkled, mushed up, dangerously flushed, often bruised, and anything but beautiful? In the eyes of little children, all babies look alike. However, *our* baby is exquisite and unlike any other baby that has ever been born or ever will be born! In a word, our consciousness renders our own babies perfect.

Adolescents undertake similar actions in judging themselves. They hold in their consciousness a picture of themselves as attractive, intelligent, moral and kind, if the adults raising them safeguard what psychologists call healthy self-esteem or narcissism.[5] If their self-esteem is low, adolescents think of themselves as homely, stupid, and unkind, and in the case of all too many girls, overweight as well. "But no," we plead with that intelligent and lovely young man or woman, "you *can't* think this way about yourself. You're beautiful; people love you. How can you perceive yourself so incorrectly?"[6]

As another example, adolescents often wonder why rich, famous and successful people would commit suicide. They had everything, they argue. Why is it that adolescents would deny that something profoundly troubling might exist in the consciousness of a celebrity to cause him to take his life? The adolescent might comment about a classmate who has committed suicide, "He's the last person in the world I ever thought would do it. He had everything!" Is it possible, adolescents begin to wonder, that some people just come out of the womb "wired" to commit suicide at some time in their lives or are at least unwilling to live with the sort of pain that leads them to commit suicide? And might they themselves be among these "mis-wired" people?

In asking these questions, adolescents are confronting their own consciousness. Distracted or not, in every moment of their lives, adolescents confront one deceptively simple question: Do I go on, or do I stop? At every moment, with every step, adolescents for the first time in their lives, begin to wonder about themselves. They may imagine that something has gone wrong or that in some fashion they are defective.[7] Perhaps there are problems in the ways they re-encounter the past, confront present circumstances, or anticipate the future. Perhaps they dread what lies before them, or that death might arrive prematurely and hence all their plans and aspirations will be for naught.[8] Perhaps they feel they can control neither their thoughts nor emotions; they feel overwhelmed by an inability to soothe themselves. Whatever the content of their conversations with the outer as well as inner worlds, their consciousness remains their focus; self-reflection and personal exploration are at work. As the psychologist Carol Tavris wrote: ". . . it is not so much what happens to people but how they interpret and explain what happens to them that determines their emotional well being, their actions, their hopes, their ability to recover from adversity."[9] Adolescence is itself perhaps, all in the thinking, all in the fields of the mind, which leads us to another matter.

When adolescents live in a distracted state of consciousness, as wittingly or unwittingly American culture foists upon its young, they commence leading what the psychoanalyst Alice Miller called the inauthentic life, a life "bound to lose its meaning."[10] For Aristotle and more recently, Robert Nozick, the inauthentic life is the life unexamined,[11] but for Buddhists it is a life in which one willingly rejects emptiness or, even more precisely, selflessness. As we have observed, the distracted mind and, hence, the distracted life without focus, become a major part of our story of adolescence, as a focused mind can find, in Mihaly Csikszentmihalyi's words, the intrinsic pleasure of human activity,[12] whereas the unfocused mind cannot. This may be one of the most difficult messages adolescents are forced to confront.

If, as we have suggested, the culture through its various activities and products competes for the attention of consciousness, ultimately causing adolescents to be drawn away from some particular focus or making them feel as if they were crazed, then adolescents grow increasingly unable to concentrate on a single item, thought, task, or feeling. Over time, many adolescents find themselves barely able to sit still for five minutes and read a book or enjoy a meal. They slump in front of the computer or television set with remote control unit, attempting to watch six different programs simultaneously or play video games at lightning speeds. The tempo of the activity cannot be fast enough to keep up with the (search) engines of consciousness. Adolescents are themselves at times walking television sets, all of them allowing the viewing of more than one station simultaneously; they are themselves pictures within pictures. The human mind, seemingly, has become a tube with a picture . . . in a picture . . . in a picture. . . . As Sven Birkerts noted,[13] like the rest of us, adolescents seem to skim over the surface of screens rather than immerse themselves in anything for significant periods of time. Not only that, it is our impression that they insert so many things and so much noise between themselves and the so-called real or natural world, they barely afford themselves the opportunity of connecting with anything. Are these not examples

of distraction as diverted attention, confusion, conflict, madness, and perhaps boredom as well?

While seeking ways to gain control or understanding of their consciousness, adolescents live out for the rest of us, and for each other, the crazed
madness, conflict, and feeling of thoughts being diverted seemingly every
other second.[14] And herein lie two fundamental ingredients of adolescent
development in a culture of distraction. Adolescent consciousness may be
said to survive in a military theater of operations in which two major
battles rage. First, is the battle among the culture merchants, public relations campaigners, politicians, and entertainers, all of them practically
crashing into one another to gain the attention of the adolescent. The
second is fought among those forces already installed within the adolescent consciousness. There is no peace, no chance for a settlement, and
nobody knows yet whether anyone is willing to surrender, or give up
some hard-earned real estate.

Given this incredible madness, how can any sense of focus or enduring
attention develop in the adolescent's mind? How can adolescents even
think of ridding their minds of all these stimuli and concentrate on a
single topic, a single pursuit, a single course assignment for any stretch of
time (or, if in a meditation on no topic whatsoever) other than by employing additional distractive devices meant to take their minds off the noise
of their own consciousness, which, in fact, is caused by distractive devices
in the first place? If this sounds convoluted, then think of what adolescents are attempting to accomplish when they order drinks to ward off
feelings of depression. Through experience, adolescents have learned that
alcohol is a depressive substance, and yet many of them constantly, and
rather early on, turn to it in order to dissipate their depression or feelings
of sadness.[15] Distraction works much the same way, as each distractive
component in the culture yields a characteristic feeling (or felt sense) of
distraction in its wake, which is to say, in the mind of the adolescent.

The first definition of distraction, the reader will recall, was the turning
away or diverting of thoughts. This involves the notion we sought to
capture in the image of night vision; rather than look directly at an object,
we are obliged to divert our gaze. With distraction, the mind's vision no
longer remains focused on the genuine or authentic object. We have diverted our gaze, which means that our focus falls upon the inauthentic or
ingenuine. The feeling with which we are left is the familiar one of boredom or what we will learn is actually the felt sense of our minds being
enslaved.

The conflict feature of distraction, in which various components of consciousness compete for the attention of the adolescent, not unlike an army of political candidates demanding votes or television networks urging their audiences to watch a war on their stations, eventually leaves adolescents with the felt sense of agitation.[16] Not only do they grow bored, they become jumpy, unnerved, unable to relax and enjoy whatever they have planned for themselves if, in fact, they can even make plans. It seems as if these adolescents are suffering with attention deficit hyperactivity disorder (ADHD).[17] They appear so distracted that they can barely settle on a movie for the evening. They sit uncomfortably on their couches, compulsively clicking the remote control as if imagining they could stumble on an inner serenity channel. They eat and sleep too much, exercise too little, and find that no relationship or endeavor seems to endure. When they're working, they tell themselves they should be playing; when they're playing, they chastise themselves for the lost working hours.

As adolescents grow older, they often find themselves falling into the same distractive traps as their elders. Even on vacation they may have difficulty settling into the luxury of free time and few responsibilities. Modeling themselves after their parents, they hunt for the solution to the problem of emotional and cognitive distraction by exploring still-newer distractions. So there they are on vacation, watching the people around them making restaurant, snorkeling, diving, golf, and tennis reservations and jogging, swimming, walking, and exercising with the same militant intensity and compulsiveness they experience in their daily work lives. And invariably they hear these fateful words—"We really have to do this more often."

Make no mistake, I wish for everyone to travel and enjoy the world's treasures. Yet if the adolescent isn't careful, he or she may end up following the pattern of the culture, which is to employ the vacation trip, the tour, cruise, the time share, the golf or tennis excursion as the antidote to distraction when these activities may only provide people with further distractions. The vacation adolescents genuinely seek, the serenity they wish to discover somewhere on their cable band or on the perfect Caribbean isle, ultimately can be found only in their consciousness, but they must learn to create it, or at least make room for it, and nurture it—for it requires a front row chair in the theater of their consciousness. Better yet, it may mean emptying the theater of the mind altogether. Somewhere along the line, adolescents have been convinced by the culture that this chair can be purchased.[18] Suffice it to say, it is in the fields of the mind where we genuinely master the possibilities, or even let them disappear for a while.

Finally, the fourth definition of distraction—the felt sense of being crazed or outright madness—can be experienced by adolescents as a state of agitation or anxiety.[19] Perhaps it is caused by the force with which the various components of the adolescent's consciousness impose themselves on the young person or, as Americans are fond saying, "impacts" them. Perhaps like heated molecules in a confined space, these stimuli bump into one another and stir up the adolescent. Perhaps the adolescent is unable to control these molecules or slow them down to the point that he or she can focus on one issue, object, idea, task, or nothing at all for that matter, and work with it, embrace it, and be engrossed in it.[20]

Whatever it is, adolescents often feel as if they are overwhelmed by conflict, that the world has gone mad, or they themselves are unraveling. They feel as though they are losing it, coming unglued, going crazy, passing around the bend, heading for the funny farm or loony bin. (Interesting, that even the young have more words for describing getting drunk or feeling madness than they do for expressing love!) Benjamin Barber described the sensation this way: "Indeed, our current intellectual world is one in which the products of consciousness outrun consciousness itself. . . ."[21] And still the adolescent's solution for this felt sense of madness, once again caused in great measure by being distracted, is to hunt for newer forms of distraction.

No one properly can characterize an entire culture by employing purely psychological concepts although there is something intriguing about the notion of "national character."[22] After examining the various feelings one derives from the four descriptions of distracted consciousness, it is tempting to describe America in terms of an omnipresent sensation of anxiety, depression, and agitation. Perhaps the culture itself breeds the infamous attention deficit hyperactivity disorder.[23] Not coincidentally, one notes the huge quantities of psychotropic or mood-altering drugs as well as so-called "focusing" drugs administered to people in order to lift their spirits, reduce their anxiety and agitation, and help them to concentrate and think clearly. The enormous success of wonder drugs like Prozac, Zoloft, Paxil, Atavan, Aderol, and, especially, Ritalin seems to have hit the psychological and financial jackpots with their capacity to attack all three emotional states, states we allege to be part of the adolescent's cultural world. In one sense, all of the aforementioned medications might properly be called "antidistractives."

Let me linger for a moment on this subject of distraction and its role in the greater culture and, more specifically, on the relatively new yet familiar phenomena of attention deficit disorder (ADD)[24] and attention deficit hyperactivity disorder (ADHD).

Attention deficit disorder appears to be quite common among children and adolescents, typically revealing itself by age six or seven. Exactly as its name suggests, ADD renders a person barely able to attend to any task for more than a few minutes at a time. ADHD has the additional component of hyperactivity, with the symptom of children described as literally bouncing off walls, unable to gain control of their physical and mental actions.

I raise the specters of ADD and ADHD because their symptoms tend to resemble the state of distraction many adolescents who have no psychological disorders regularly experience. Both disorders could turn out to be a function of the culture's mercantile and media dynamics impinging on the learning, perceptual and organizing systems of the brains of certain children *and* adults who are genetically predisposed, perhaps, to ADD or ADHD or, for that matter, not genetically predisposed at all. In fact, there are already some suggestive studies supporting this hypothesis.[25]

Consider for example, the excessive motor activity of the ADHD child, and his or her inability to focus attention, which, in turn, makes constant work or performance of any sort nigh impossible. Something else about ADHD catches the eye of someone intrigued by distraction: The ADHD child has been known to struggle with the problem of not being able to perform a task one day that he or she accomplished with relative ease on the previous one. The child experiencing the impact of ADD resembles many of us who would not technically be considered ADD cases but who, nonetheless, exhibit many of these same symptoms. One is tempted to suggest that the impact of distraction on the human mind has led an entire nation to the brink of ADD, making the entertainment, fashion, sports, advertising, media, public relations, and consulting businesses jump with joy. Simply put, "There's gold in them thar ills!" Equally significant, children and, especially, adolescents become easy targets for a host of companies producing products of distraction.[26]

In a less clinically severe context, the pediatrician Penelope Leach makes a provocative statement in one of her guidebooks for parents.[27] One cannot discipline little children, she avers, one cannot actually make them do anything they don't wish to do. No matter what you try they just shout "NO!" So instead of ordering and demanding, Leach recommends that

parents attempt to distract children. The trick for parents is to get children to do something that will relieve the anxiety or lessen the boredom
or agitation, while at the same time convincing them that this is what
they wanted to do all along. In Ellen Langer's term, the children become
"otherwise engaged."[28] Oh, you can browbeat a child into becoming toilet trained, but you and the child will probably experience the repercus-
sions of this action for the rest of your lives. The same may be true when
working with adolescents. It is often difficult to know when young persons are ready to undertake a particular task, even a cognitive one. The
trick is to find a way to get adolescents to feel that they are good and
ready. At very least, we want to do all we can to get young people to know
that even if they are not quite ready for some activity, they are still good
and lovable persons.

Most of us recognize that the process at work here is socialization,[29]
which has at least two components. First, implore people to do what you
want them to do; second, convince them that they have come to these
decisions, such as what language they should learn, on their own. Socialization requires a degree of power as well as a degree of focusing of the
conscious world, which, in part, is why many adolescents often resist the
socializing lessons at hand. The adolescent simmering with boredom is
struggling to find some focus. In response, we limit the stimuli or discover
the precise stimulus that might thoroughly engage him or her for that
instant. Momentarily, the adolescent's consciousness seems unable to focus on anything; the internal distractions have become overwhelming.
What is required, therefore, is the reduction of external *and* internal stimuli.
Socially and privately, all persons need to find a place of serenity.

The issue for the adolescent is no different, it seems to me, than for the
adult: How does one control one's consciousness and, in a sense, gain
power over it? Again, the answer Americans have chosen is to pursue
newer distractions. We move every which way to avoid the truth, avoid
the here and now, avoid the messages of the consciousness (as well as
those from the unconscious), avoid internal stimuli, and try to mask everything or muffle the noise with some new form of external activity,
investment, or distraction. Conversely, we learn new distractive devices
for coping with distractions. And if this sounds redundant and self-defeat-
ing, it is meant to.

What we observe in adolescents are the ways in which distraction—the
drawing away of thought, conflict, and madness—tend to pull young people
away from the here and now as well as from the immediate and significant
matters competing for attention in their consciousness. Distractive forces

cause them to focus on everything *but* the here and now and then disconnect the here and now from all that preceded it and all that will follow.

The noises of distraction are deafening. Combined, they produce a sensate (or sensual) boom in the mind. The degree to which adolescents engage in distractive devices suggests that some of them must feel shell shocked. Nothing coming at them in these times is on a human scale; everything must be perceived in the way that one views a movie: larger than life, or adolescents pay little heed to it. They only see the movies that are the greatest, the most extraordinary. Everything, seemingly, must be sensation-al, or "super." The minds of adolescents literally are assaulted by facts, items, bits and bytes, none of which constitute anything resembling genuine knowledge, and still they clamor for more information, more consciousness input, more noise, and the culture is delighted to provide all they can handle and more!

Our (depersonalized) technological and communications society, the likes of which history never has witnessed, places a more oppressive and exhausting burden on the minds of adolescents than anyone possibly could imagine. Surely it causes adolescents to feel fatigued if not depressed. There isn't a place in this country anymore, it seems, where the adolescent can escape the assault to his or her senses, even though adolescents claim there is nothing more exciting than this very assault. Where does one go to escape the sounds of the radio? Lavatories, doctors' waiting rooms, elevators, gyms, coffee shops, malls, salons, warehouses, taxicabs, buses, first-aid stations, beaches, airplanes, newspaper kiosks, everywhere you go you hear noise, intended, I am advised, to be comforting, but noise nevertheless.[30] Noise has even become a weapon of the military. In the last few years, Panama, Iraq, and the Branch Davidian fortress in Waco, Texas, all received heavy doses of heavy metal music.

The result of this onslaught to the senses is captured in adolescents' responses to commercials on television and "elevator music": They see and they don't see; they hear and they don't hear; they focus and they don't focus. Living in a state of quasi-ADD, therefore, becomes an almost appropriate and healthy adaptation to the culture. Adolescents *have* to have ADD! They surprise themselves by knowing things they never realized were stored in their consciousness. They may not have been aware of having attended to these messages; evidently they have not focused on them, they just sneaked into the mind fields, joining all the stuff already accumulated. (As a teenager, I was never able to convince my father I didn't spend hours memorizing baseball statistics; somehow they just found their way into my brain. He always wondered why it was that mathematics didn't make it there in the same way.) Adolescents cannot keep out the noise and the images; they don't appear to want to. Quite the opposite; the more noise, the more activity, the more normal life becomes.

Americans properly decry the weight of junk mail they receive every day and the endless telephone marketing calls—designated courtesy calls, no less—in which one is urged to buy something. These unwanted intrusions symbolize the junk being shoved every day into the consciousness of adolescents, which, like most of the junk mail, the young person sorts through just in case there may be something he or she wishes to retain. Adults continually wonder about the adolescent who insists on doing his homework with the Walkman plugged into his ears or the one who can only complete her social studies sitting in front of a television set. "You couldn't possibly be concentrating with the TV on," we declare imperiously, but she just stares at us. Don't parents realize, she seems to be saying, that consciousness only kicks in (like a drug) when "Friends" is on? Don't parents realize that neurological molecules require the simultaneous experiencing of social studies homework, "South Park," and innumerable telephone calls? Don't parents realize that focusing on social studies is not the point? The point is to have a million billion stimuli buzzing around so that one may simultaneously focus on all and none of them.[31] Silence, apparently, is terrifying to some young people. It is as if adolescents live their lives according to what Don DeLillo calls the "hum" of human existence. "No," we parents respond. "We don't understand any of this. Honey, fix me another drink, will you?"

The columnist Michael Kelly conveyed well this noise and hum of modern existence when he wrote:

> Every hour, a new self-help tract is published. Every 30 minutes, a new gourmet food item is discovered and, simultaneously, a diet is invented. Every 15 minutes, a star is born, and every eight minutes, a star enters rehab. Every four minutes, a pundit speaks, mostly on cable. Every two minutes, federal researchers identify a trend, and every 60 seconds, a trend passes.[32]

The purpose of distraction, as we observed earlier, is not only to take us away from something, to divert our attention, but to place us in a world possessing no logical purpose or meaning whatsoever. Adolescents clearly would reject the idea of a theater of the absurd as being, well, absurd. Many probably feel they already live within a theater of the absurd, so why pay good money for a ticket? The rock concert, movie, television program, or ball game provides them intense excitement, which, in effect, represents the essence of sensationalism; that's the name and purpose of the game.[33] When a game is dull we want our money back. Some people cannot stand a pitcher's duel in baseball; like a meditation, it seems too empty of excitement. Far better to have home runs flying out of the park every five minutes. In a sensational culture like ours, the home run and slam-dunk contests are more interesting than the actual all-star Games that follow them. College and professional basketball require that a player shoot for the basket within an allotted period of time. There is something symbolic about the stipulation that teams no longer can stall; the audience clamors for action and noise, defined as scoring hundreds of points every game. Although John Dewey[34] warned us to slow down (our thinking), we despise any delay of any game. Those who would delay are served a penalty. We must keep going, keep on trucking, trudge on. When action fades, so, too, does our attention, and in a manner of speaking, so do we.

All of this, presumably, stands in contrast to the boredom and dullness of every other part of our days and nights. Many students will report that school is deemed boring because it cannot measure up to the standards and practices of the world of entertainment, of which athletics is merely a branch. Yet boredom and dullness, as we noted earlier, are also products of distraction. Adolescents crave excitement, action, something wild (as in go "wilding"), not only because essential parts of their lives must seem dull and uninteresting, but because these are the logical and predictable reactions to and enactment of the wilding extant in our consciousness. The opening scene of television's "Monday Night Football" reveals a rock band yelling out the question, "ARE YOU READY TO PARTY?" Boxing matches are preceded by "LET'S GET READY TO RUMBLE!" (Dare I even mention that professional wrestlers seem unable to speak at normal decibel levels?) The screaming and acting-out are legitimate, if not *de rigueur*, at events like rock concerts, wrestling matches, and ball games (in contrast to classical music concerts, plays, and museum and library visits). They are the symbolic representations of the adolescent's felt sense of consciousness. Adolescents are taught to find comfort in watching the big games, the big award shows, the big events on big television sets capable of pumping up the volume.

Each person in the viewing audience, of which adolescents are a prime component, is another stimulus, the audience reaction becoming as important as the activity on the stage. Arena scoreboards flash the message: "LET'S MAKE NOISE!" Basketball teams refer to their fans as the "sixth man," and rock concerts are as much a display of fandom as a particular artist. Watching a sporting event or awards show on television is more thrilling if people are clustered around the television set, although, interestingly, some people admit to finding the commercials more preposterous in collective settings. Apparently the social context of viewing causes us to see the unabashed materialism and often absurd (and pernicious) messages which then are described as affronts to one's intelligence (and consciousness).

Sports and entertainment externalize the deepest sensations of adolescents. There seems to be no way for classical art to compete with this war of sounds and images, impulses and action. A conservative professor friend once remarked that rock and roll cannot be art simply because it makes too much noise. Yet most adolescents will tell you that the whole point of these activities is to feel the excitement, the senses being jostled and pushed to extreme (literally sensation-al) levels. The mind fields of contemporary America are represented by the roller coaster ride: The more terrifying, the more adolescents love it or at least are intrigued by it, for they know they ought to be able to overcome any fear, any noise, any warning from their consciousness. The quiet and calm ascent of the roller coaster remains tolerable only because adolescents recognize that action and fright lie just around the bend. Young people line up for blocks to see the most frightening movies as they did during the summer of 1993 when *Jurassic Park* broke all opening weekend box office records. Involvement with horror, as David J. Skal has written, allows adolescents to become entangled with the forbidden, repressed, and everything about their, and our, society and themselves they seek to forget.[35] Stephen King has emerged as literally god-like, and the grotesque is worshipped. Pity the high school English teacher escorting her class to the local museum's exhibition of line drawings by Gauguin. Neither she nor Gauguin will "make it" unless, of course, the students are permitted to listen to their Walkmans in the galleries.

The Gauguin show loses its appeal for at least one important reason: It is seen as sensationally stagnant, immobile, quiet, and, ironically, enduring. Adolescents cannot always see their way out of the immediate museum circumstances. American consciousness in a culture of distraction cannot abide by any of these criteria. Instead, adolescents crave constant change, novelty, turnover, motion, action. Maybe something lasts a week for them, two at the most. A so-called "classic" rock song remains number one on the chart four weeks, tops. (There was even talk about how long Americans would stay interested in the Gulf War if it went on "too long.") Movie and television plots must veer suddenly and frequently but, nonetheless, contain instantaneous resolutions.[36] Better yet, like every television soap opera or the movie *Magnolia*, American consciousness prefers several stories that evolve simultaneously. Performing "artists" (an overworked term) regularly reinvent themselves, their prior personae wearing thin in the minds of their audiences. In a culture of sensation, moreover, singers must produce videos; sound alone no longer suffices. The very existence of MTV, an adolescent staple, requires sensation of all varieties. Movies mustn't stay at the local cinemas too many weeks; television images must not remain on the screen for more than a few seconds.[37] Adolescent consciousness, apparently, hungers for visual excitation and special effects; its appetite seems insatiable. Watch an adolescent's face drop when his teacher proposes he read a 300-page book. Two words rise at once in his mind: Cliff Notes.

If the society provides constant change and excitation and bets much of its economic resources on this need for (and insistence that adolescents feel) change and excitation, then adolescents' own psychologies have been conditioned to demand it as well. Many feel themselves to be losers if they are the same today as they were, say, a year ago. Adolescents stress the constant change portion of Erikson's identity equation rather than continuing sameness.[38] Modern consciousness adores personal reinvention, which often is vexing for the adolescent in the throes of establishing something that might be called a baseline identity. They see their parents having to make more money than *their* parents, buying costlier clothes and fancier cars, improving their appearance but definitely not concluding the year where they commenced it, as if they could. If nothing else, adolescents learn they can always change their hair style, get a tattoo, or pierce some piece of their body. The need to alter one's existence, despite the often-frightening ramifications of such action, is observed in the behavior surrounding New Year's Eve celebrations. A person would be un-American not to celebrate the arrival of a new year or make a resolution that this year he or she is going to change nothing at all. Adolescents learn quickly that on New Year's Eve, and every other day for that matter, they must not orient themselves around the concept of merely being when the entire culture screams for doing and becoming.

All of this is part of the noise: Turn yourself into something new, the adolescent learns, reinvent yourself. Never settle for what you have been nor rest on laurels. Celebrate ambition; never feel satisfied or that dreaded word, bred by familiarity, content! You must (force yourself to) keep changing, and keep feeling excited. When you run out of ideas for personal change, redecorate your bedroom or your consciousness. After all, the adolescent learns, when you stop changing you're as good as dead! If you aren't changing, you are merely enduring.

Adolescents spend an inordinate amount of time and energy checking out, as they would say, every facet of our changing culture to make certain they are not missing out on something, and always they know what the richer and more famous people are doing that appears to set them apart.[39] Always there is something else to shoot for (an interesting idiom). The "other-directed" orientation advanced 50 years ago by David Riesman in The Lonely Crowd,[40] in which people employ social antennae in order to direct their lives through the actions of others, now has changed somewhat. Now people incorporate television antennae as well as radio broadcasts, magazine picture stories, and of course, the Internet to orient their worlds. The media may not explicitly direct the lives of adolescents, but implicitly they do. In the furious pace of their productivity, they both generate and satisfy the moods, tempi, senses as well as the excitation thresholds and appetites of adolescent consciousness.

In commenting on the political furor arising out of the initial appointment by President Clinton of Lani Guinier to a cabinet position followed by the abrupt rescinding of that appointment, columnist Ellen Goodman captured the hastened tempo and hunt for constant stimuli not only of our modern living and decision making but of the quality and nature of our thinking and perceiving. Her observations seem relevant to the world of adolescents:

> We fast-forward through the dull parts, certainly through obscured footnoted legal journals, in search of the highlights. We channel surf for the defining or the distorting moment. . . . The speed with which things happen is not all deliberate speed. It's no-time-for-deliberation speed. [41]

The result for adolescents is an increasing pressure to shape their lives according to the patterns established by the most noisy, visible, and outrageous persons in the culture, those presumably, with the biggest hum.[42] (If the cultural dictates are to be believed, adolescents perpetually stand ready to make their consciousness rumble.) Some Americans claim to despise the transgressions of televangelists, politicians, actors, athletes, and rock stars, yet many of us never cease watching these folks. Little wonder that we have become a nation of lookers, and adolescents have joined in the action. If one can't look good or act good (according to the latest trends), at least he or she wants a good look. Adolescents are taught to adore beautiful faces and thin bodies and fame in whatever form it may take; at least it provides a modicum of recognition.[43] And if the famous provide adolescents with a good look, they will pay obeisance to the media hounds and public relations cadres they otherwise claim to distrust. Like their elders, some adolescents are fascinated with despicable people, those they love to hate; these people are just part of the noise and stimuli adolescents ask their consciousness to digest.

Television magazine shows are the best example of the culture's seeming adoration of the sensational aspects of criminals and criminal activities.[44] Adolescents have learned that these are the people, the stars of the world in any and all fields, carrying the biggest hum. Increasingly, adolescents consume the technical products of the Internet and television as well as the glossy photographs of the *paparazzi*. Americans, and others of course, keep an eye on the celebrated; accordingly we stand prepared to pay for the privilege. Courtrooms, ball games, rock concerts, award shows, any location may be a place to ogle the famous, for America and its adolescents continue to worship the god Amor: We all just love to look. Adolescents window-shop the society just as they window-shop the malls. Everywhere adolescents play show and tell; it is the most important lesson they have learned from television and the Internet. No one can live without the hum and noise, without the stimuli, without the look, least of all distracted adolescents who have learned this from their elders.

Distraction and the Avoidance of Death

There is another aspect of the story of adolescents and distraction, another purpose to distraction, so to speak, that we will be commenting on throughout our discussion.

If we conjure up the image of distracted adolescents seeking all varieties of devices and products that might divert their attention and take them away from daily problems, we recognize young people working hard or at least spending a great deal of energy making certain their consciousness is brimming over with stimuli. It makes one believe that adolescents do this in order to make certain not only that they are alive—as too few stimuli, it has been decided, are tantamount to death—but that something else more grand will follow. Left to their own nondistractive ways, they run the risk, they imagine, of an empty conscious state, which implies that nothing will ever again come to fill it up. Distraction, in other words, becomes a way of warding off death or at least protecting them from a conscious emptiness that some adolescents imagine is the felt sense of death. If they don't continually make things happen, if they don't continue their pursuit of distraction, they imagine they will die! Suddenly, life itself is born in and defined by distraction. (In this regard, it is interesting that some theorists contend that a major sign of the healthy family is the capacity to let all of its members experience their own emptiness and fill it on their own or leave it just that way.)[45]

The sentiment has been expressed succinctly in a wholly different context. In an article written before the commencement of the ground war in the Persian Gulf and published four days before the end of the war, Philip Caputo asserted that ". . . some of our political and military leaders may be encouraging us to deceive ourselves, partly because they are themselves victims of self-deception, partly because they know we may not yet be emotionally ready for what may be coming."[46]

It is that last phrase referring to an emotional unreadiness for the future that strikes me as a significant feature of distraction, particularly as it affects the world of adolescents. That from which adolescents wish to divert their mind, that which causes them anxiety, agitation, and conflict, that which on occasion causes them to feel as if they had gone mad is the future, or more precisely, their own construction of events that "live" in the future. In war, as in all aspects of life, that event, of course, is death. Caputo's notion of self-deception is peculiarly relevant. Distraction requires self-deception, some entrance into a game requiring every player to recognize that what is called reality is not reality at all. Because adolescents have agreed, however, to falsify reality, which they do when they enter in to distractive realms, what harm, they reason, may result from their periodic diversions and distractions? If they wish to pretend they are not afraid of the future or of the agents of death surrounding them, then who dares to step forward and spoil their game?[47]

In pursuing distraction, adolescents are pursuing an (imagined) antidote to their most terrifying apprehension. Adolescents are frequently accused of believing in invincibility, immortality. Expressing dismay at this inconceivable mind state, their elders nonetheless imagine that if they dress young, act young, exercise, and get into rock 'n roll and antioxidants, who knows, they, the elders, may live forever. That regimen, however, is yet to be proven; all we do know is that every aspect of it makes someone a great deal of money. Despite our fantasies about and personal constructions of the adolescent world, adolescents themselves know only too well that they are mere mortals. They have confronted or contemplated death all too often to conclude otherwise. In the development of the adolescent identity, death can be neither avoided nor ignored.

In the end, the adolescent pursuit of distraction may turn out to be an assortment of paths chosen not only to quiet normal adolescent con-

sciousness and still the terror born in the first recognition of finitude, but
to avoid the authentic messages of consciousness and eventually mask
the fact that adolescents, as young as they may be, have already begun to
lose a sense of reality as well as a sense of themselves. Goals are envisioned even as the means are explored. A final product is imagined even
as the first pieces of an adult foundation are laid down; the end, or the
sight of it anyway, arrives with the beginning. At some level, adolescents
remain wholly aware of this. It is this awareness of their (existential) anxiety[48] and the root of it that frequently drives them toward the paths of
their own distraction in the first place.

It may have sounded strange during the Persian Gulf War to hear com-
mentators speak of the war's "cleansing" nature. At very least, these observers suggested, the military incursion caused Americans to confront
the seriousness of a national situation head on. Life and death were on
the table, and Americans clamored for the truth, for once accepting no
deceptions, no distractions. Others, however, felt the war provided yet
another arena or battlefield, if you will, for pursuing distraction. It made
some viewers feel as if they lived among perfectly truthful accounts and
reports, but all the while obvious deceptions abounded.

The same may be said about normal adolescent development in the
context of a distracting culture. Some experiences, normally those of the
greatest significance, cause the adolescent to shun deception and the
usual repertoire of conceits. There simply are moments when, as the
song suggests, there's no one to run to, nowhere to hide. The perfect
example, sadly, is the death of an adolescent in a car accident, a suicide,
or the murder of young people in their schools. Nothing calls the adolescent up short like these hideous occurrences, and despite the scenes of
shocked young people weeping, many observers of the young continue to
perpetuate the notion that adolescents live with the idea of their own
invincibility.

The specter of death in school brings forth yet another example of
distraction confronted by adolescents. Serious trauma naturally brings
out professionals trained to help the young cope with their lingering feelings in the aftermath of tragedies. In this orientation of coping, one assumes that the object with which one must cope, death perhaps, ineluctably remains in place and inviolate. All too often, however, it does not. In
focusing on adapting, adjusting and coping, we divert our gaze from the
authentic realities of our consciousness.

Why not, in contrast, suggest that death, as best as anyone young or
old can "know" it, is merely a state of mind, yet another construct or

product of consciousness or, in the present discussion, a construct of the adolescent mind? As no one has ever reported what death is like, why not aver that finality is that which every moment our consciousness "determines" that it is? Rather than focus on death as a state of mind, however, adolescents somehow are taught to focus instead on the felt sense of that which remains in their minds after they have attempted to focus on death. Understandably, they then seek a way to avoid the situation by distracting themselves from that very same state of mind. Yet it is precisely that utterly normal, human state of mind that offers adolescents the possibility of dealing with the realities of their existence—its beginnings, middles, and ends—and diverts them from their inevitably unproductive pursuits of distraction and unreality.

I do not digress when I quote from a 1991 SyberVision systems catalogue in which one finds an advertisement for a program by Bettie B. Youngs entitled "Helping Your Child Manage Stress, Pressure and Anxiety." Beneath the program title are the words: "Understand your child's stress—and teach him/her how to manage it." Look closely at the catalogue's message and note again that, whether we acknowledge it or not, our mind fields are being diverted, distracted, made to focus on managing the stress rather than rooting out the source of the stress and obliterating it. Adolescents would be far better served to have information about suicide broadcast on television than they are by having reporters swoop down on their schools after a suicide.

No culture on earth is probably more uncomfortable with death and dying than our own. We know this to be true merely by noting how frequently and absurdly (that is, untruthfully) death is revealed and handled on television and in the movies, like it or not, prime teaching agents of the young. As viewers imagine themselves delving into this topic almost every waking second, they may be attempting simultaneously to avoid it altogether. In doing so, we, adolescents and adults alike, leave ourselves unable to mourn or even talk with mourners or deal with the dying (who inevitably are labeled patients rather than people). Like many adults, adolescents too, are barely able to bring themselves to read about death or watch death on television, unless, of course, they are assured that it is make-believe death, at which point they eagerly watch thousands of deaths each year while publicly decrying the amount of violence portrayed on television. Some Americans objected strenuously to the graphic footage shown during the Gulf War, when in fact during the actual ground campaign the only televised footage involved interviews with several wounded soldiers, all of whom revealed their uncritical medical status. At that point,

American audiences actually had not yet seen one dead American soldier. The reality of dead Iraqis was something else altogether, but this is just more fodder for our discussion of how reality comes to be constructed.

Many adolescents tend to turn to religion when someone close to them dies, and hence they come to believe, perhaps, that religion's primary value is found in helping people deal with death. Some young people cannot bring themselves to say the dreaded "D" word but speak instead in terms of "losing" someone, or someone "passing." At the same time, some of their elders worry more about exposing children to the deaths of grandparents, parents, or even pets than about exposing children and adolescents to abandonment, homelessness, neglect, physical abuse, and poverty.

To summarize, every day it seems the young employ distractive devices to avoid even thinking about death, which at some level means they may also feel uncomfortable thinking about the future even in a profoundly future-oriented culture. To look too closely into the future is ultimately to see, that is, to imagine one's own demise. Distraction, adolescents conclude, draws them away from the conflict, confusion, and madness caused by imagining that they no longer exist. The future, in other words, evokes little more than dread, and hence all eyes must be on the present, which means, adolescents reason, that all the powers of their being must be devoted to immediate sensation and making certain to fill every seat in the theater of their consciousness.

Contrast this conception, shared, actually, by adults with James Carroll's poetic vision of the future, really of thinking about the future, containing as it does nothing of dread or despair but the goodness and warmth of summer itself. His words may well constitute the antidote to adolescent anxiety and the dread of that which is to come:

> The very intensity of your longing is the great teacher; the future is built into the present as the source of your self-surpassing. The future is what creates you. The future draws you out. The future keeps you going. The future saves you. One day, perhaps, you will learn that the future has a name. You will recognize the future as having been your only absolute. And you will know that you were right to love it since being young.[49]

Notes

1. Martin Heidegger, *Being and Time*. Translation by Joan Stambaugh. Albany: State University of New York Press, 1966.

2. Stephen Kemmis, "Action Research and the Politics of Reflection." In David Boud, Rosemary Keough, and David Walker (Editors), *Reflection: Turning Experience into Learning*. London: Kogan Page, 1985: 139–163.

3. Howard Gardner, *The Unschooled Mind: How Children Think and How Schools Should Teach*. New York: Basic Books, 1991.

4. See B. Inhelder and J. Piaget, *The Growth of Logical Thinking from Childhood to Adolescence*. New York: Basic Books, 1958.

5. See Ralph Gemelli, *Normal Child and Adolescent Development*. Washington, DC: American Psychiatric Press, 1996; and D. Schave and B. Schave, "Characteristic Behaviors of Early Adolescents." In D. Schave and B. Schave, *Early Adolescence and the Search for Self: A Developmental Perspective*. New York: Praeger, 1989: 1–16.

6. See Mary Pipher, *Reviving Ophelia: Saving the Selves of Adolescent Girls*. New York: Ballantine, 1994; and H. Smith, *Unhappy Children: Reasons and Remedies*. New York: Free Association Books, 1995, Chapter 5.

7. On this point, see Heinz Kohut, *The Restoration of the Self*. New York: International Universities Press, 1977.

8. See Heinz Kohut, *Search for Self,* Volume 2, edited by Paul Ornstein. New York: International Universities Press, 1978.

9. See her review of *Flow: The Psychology of Optimal Experience* by Mihaly Csikszentmihalyi. *The New York Times Book Review.* March 18, 1990: 7.

10. Alice Miller, *The Drama of the Gifted Child,* translated by Ruth Ward. New York: Basic Books, 1981.

11. Robert Nozick, *The Examined Life: Philosophical Meditations.* New York: Simon and Schuster, 1989.

12. See Mihaly Csikszentmihalyi, *Flow: The Psychology of Optimal Experience.* New York: HarperCollins, 1990.

13. Sven Birkerts, *Readings.* New York: Graywolf, 1999.

14. Alan E. Kazdin, "Adolescent Mental Health: Prevention and Treatment Programs." *American Psychologist, 48,* 2: 127–141.

15. See D. B. Kandel, "Socialization and Adolescent Drinking," in O. Jeanneret (Editor), *Child Health and Development: Volume 2, Alcohol and Youth*. Basel:

Karger, 1983: 66–75; and B. A. Christiansen et al, "Development of Alcohol-Related Expectancies in Adolescents." *Journal of Consulting and Clinical Psychology, 50*, 1982: 336–344.

16   On a similar point, see Peter Marris, "The Social Construction of Uncertainty." In C. M. Parkes, J. Stevenson-Hinde, and P. Marris, *Attachment Across the Life Cycle.* London: Tavistock/Routledge, 1991, Chapter 5.

17   See Edward Hallowell and John Ratey, *Driven to Distraction.* New York: Pantheon, 1994; Karen Zelan, *The Risks of Knowing: Developmental Impediments to School Learning.* New York: Plenum, 1991; William Bender, *Learning Disabilities: Characteristics, Identification, and Teaching Strategies.* Boston: Allyn and Bacon, 1998; Roa Lynn, *Learning Disabilities: An Overview of Theories, Approaches, and Politics.* New York: Free Press, 1979; and Larry B. Silver, *The Assessments of Learning Disabilities: Pre-School Through Adulthood.* Boston: Little, Brown, 1989.

18   On a related point, see M. E. Colton and S. Gore (Editors), *Adolescent Stress.* New York: De Gruyter, Inc. 1991.

19   A. Jersild, *The Psychology of Adolescence.* New York: Macmillan, 1957.

20   Ellen J. Langer, *Mindfulness.* Reading, MA: Addison-Wesley, 1989.

21   Benjamin Barber, "Brave New World," review of three volumes by Manuel Castells. *The Los Angeles Times*, May 23, 1999: 6.

22   See Alex Inkeles, *National Character: A Psychosocial Perspective,* with contributions by Daniel J. Levinson. New Brunswick, NJ: Transaction, 1997; *One World Emerging? Convergence and Divergence in Industrial Societies.* Boulder, CO: Westview, 1998; *Exploring Individual Modernity,* with contributions by David H. Smith. New York: Columbia University Press, 1983.

23   Edward Hallowell and John Ratey, *Driven to Distraction,* op. cit.

24   See for example, *Challenge, A Newsletter on Attention Deficit Disorder, 1,* 1, February, 1987: l.

25   On this point, see Sam Goldstein, *Managing Attention Deficit Disorder in Children.* New York: Wiley, 1990; L. H. Diller, "The Run on Ritalin: Attention Deficit Disorder and Stimulant Treatment in the 1990's." Hastings Center Report, March-April, 1996: 12–18; Sari Solden, *Women with ADD.* Grass Valley: California: Underwood, 1995; Kathleen Nosek, *The Dyslexic Scholar.* Dallas: Taylor, 1995; Larry B. Silver *Attention Deficit Hyperactivity Disorder.* Washington, DC: American Psychiatric Press, 1992; R. A. Barkley, *Attention Deficit Hyperactivity Disorder: A Handbook for Diagnosis and Treatment.* New York: Guilford Press, 1990; and S. Zentall, "Research on the Educational Implications of Attention Deficit Hyperactivity Disorder." *Exceptional Children, 60,* 2, 1993: 143–153.

26   See "Teens: Here Comes the Biggest Wave Yet." *Business Week*, April 11, 1994: 76–86.

27 Penelope Leach, *Your Growing Child: From Babyhood Through Adolescence.* New York: Knopf, 1986.

28 Ellen Langer, *The Power of Mindful Learning.* Reading, MA: Perseus, 1997.

29 J. C. Coleman (Editor), *The School Years: Current Issues in the Socialization of Young People.* London: Routledge, 1992.

30 See S. Frith, *Sound Effects: Youth, Leisure, and the Politics of Rock 'n Roll.* New York: Pantheon, 1981.

31 L. A. Tucker, "Television, Teenagers, and Health." *Journal of Youth and Adolescence, 16,* 1987: 415–425.

32 Michael Kelly, "Class of '99, Listen Up." *The Boston Globe,* June 3, 1999: A23.

33 See P. M. Greenfield, L. Bruzzone, K. Koyamatsu, W. Satuloff, K. Nixon, M. Brodie and D. Klingsdale, "What Is Rock Music Doing to the Minds of Our Youth? A First Experimental Look at the Effects of Rock Music Lyrics and Music Videos." *Journal of Early Adolescence, 7,* 1987: 315–329.

34 John Dewey, *How We Think.* Amherst, New York: Prometheus, 1991.

35 David J. Skal, *A Cultural History of Horror.* New York: Norton, 1993.

36 George Leonard makes this point in *Education and Ecstasy.* New York: Delacorte, 1968. See also his *The Transformation: A Guide to the Inevitable Changes in Humankind.* New York: Delacorte, 1972.

37 See Postman, op. cit.

38 The notion was advanced by Martin Heidegger in *Being and Time,* op. cit.

39 On a related point, see D. K. Lapsley, "Egocentrism Theory and the 'New Look' at the Imaginary Audience and Personal Fable in Adolescence." In R. M. Lerner, A. C. Petersen, and J. Brooks-Gunn (Editors), *Encyclopedia of Adolescence* (Volume 1). New York: Garland, 1991.

40 See David Riesman, *The Lonely Crowd,* New Haven, CT: Yale University Press, 1950.

41 Ellen Goodman, "Here They Come, There They Go." *The Boston Globe,* June 9, 1993: 15.

42 On a related point, see J. J. Conger, "Hostages to the Future: Youth, Values, and the Public Interest." *American Psychologist, 43,* 1988: 291–300.

43 See Kathleen E. Musa and Mary Ellen Roach, "Adolescent Appearance and Self Concept," *Adolescence, 8:* Fall, 1973: 385–394.

44 Stacy Davis and Marie Louise Mares, "Effects of Talk Show Viewing on Adolescents." *Journal of Communication, 48,* Summer, 1998: 69–86.

45 See, for example, Michael P. Nichols and Richard C. Schwartz, *Family Therapy: Concepts and Methods.* Needham Heights, MA: Allyn and Bacon, 1991; and C. L. Shannon, *The Politics of the Family.* New York: Lang, 1989.

46 See "War Torn" by Philip Caputo. *The New York Times,* February 24, 1991: 34ff.

47 See Ernest Becker, *Denial of Death.* New York: Free Press, 1973; see also Phyllis R. Silverman, *Never Too Young to Know: Death in Children's Lives.* New York: Oxford University Press, 1999.

48 See Rollo May, *The Meaning of Anxiety.* New York: Norton, 1977.

49 James Carroll, "That Knot of Longing That Strikes in Early June." *The Boston Globe*, June 15, 1999: A27.

PART II

THE FIELDS OF ADOLESCENCE

Chapter 3

The Construction of Independence and Intimacy

Social Constructions

Among the more popular theories found in sociological literature is that of social construction.[1] On the surface, the social construction of knowledge seems a rather straightforward idea: Groups of people, as for example, races, sexes, and for that matter adolescence as well, are little more than what the powerful forces of a culture define them as being. One's knowledge about these groups, in other words, is constructed,[2] and hence one's definitions of them derive from this (socially constructed) knowledge. In turn, the groups define themselves in terms of these same social constructions. The reality of adolescence, therefore, is found in what Hervé Varenne and Ray McDermott call "cultural facts,"[3] which, again, constitute nothing more than socially constructed knowledge.

Whether we choose to examine individual adolescents or the systems in which they function,[4] their accomplishments or deficits, their intelligences or disorders, our perspectives represent social constructions, which means that adolescents will define themselves according to these same constructions. Mara Sapon-Shevin describes a social construct "as a way of thinking and describing that exists in the eyes of the definers."[5] Definers, moreover, as Jay Shafritz[6] points out, normally gain legitimacy by the power of their special knowledge or expertise and thereby gain superior status to those whose identities they construct. David Steiner makes the same point when he observes that "The elite are not the elite because they have learned to speak a special language fixed in time and in principle available to all, but because they speak a language that will continue to be redesigned to preserve barriers to entry."[7] How possibly could an adolescent refute the word of a teacher, parent, minister, or any adult for that matter who, well, just knows better?

One hardly need mention that every space of an adolescent's life except perhaps his or her bedroom sanctuary is filled with norms, expectations, values, edicts, ideologies, rules, conventions, rituals, each meant to direct behavior and thinking and each a social construction, a sort of construction site, that could, in the beat of a heart, be profoundly altered. If we wanted, and most adolescents would subscribe to this, we could determine that schools open each morning at precisely 12 P.M., except on Thursdays, when they open at 2 P.M. in order to let students sleep late.

Sociological literature also contains descriptions of the defined group protesting the social constructions of the defining group,[8] the people at the bottom opposing those at the top, the people on the margins grappling with those at the center.[9] At stake is nothing short of human freedom, a fact that hardly escapes the adolescent, whose fundamental work is the construction of a self, a personal narrative or identity carved not wholly from expectations to conform. The fundamental purpose of the adolescent's self-construction is to gain freedom from the constructions of him or her made by the culture.[10]

Of course the adolescent rebels; rebellion represents the logical response to overwhelming social constructions of which a child is not yet aware. In fact the first recognition of social constructions in the lives of people normally signifies the commencement of adolescence. Equally important, not only for those sharing their lives with adolescents but for everyone in the culture, is that social constructions ultimately limit the freedom not only of the defined but of the definers. All Americans, Martin Luther King wrote, "are tied in a single garment of destiny."[11]

Hardly arbitrary, the components of social construction at times appear almost mythic although we perceive them often as distractions. Our focus in this chapter is on two such components, independence and intimacy, wholly real in the emerging narratives of adolescents but social constructions nonetheless. We begin with one of the more powerful ideals constructed for adolescents by the culture, an ideal that turns out to be somewhat of a distraction—the belief that young people are meant to become totally independent and self-sufficient human beings. Independence has become such a rudimentary criterion of adolescent mental health many in the society have made it, along with self-sufficiency, the core of modern (or is it popular?) psychology.

Self-reliance and Self-sufficiency

Born in the home and nurtured in school, the concepts of independence and self-sufficiency are rarely questioned. That one can be neither independent nor self-sufficient apparently concerns only philosophers. The rest of us have no time to think through the meaning of these concepts or many of the other expectations we hold for adolescents. That the culture accepts these expectations as either inborn or immutable reflects still another facet of human distraction to which adolescents will subscribe.[12] An example will clarify this point.

When I give a lecture, my students presumably expect me to speak from a so-called independent position. Neither they nor the university's administration dictate what I can say or how I must say it. So there I am, standing in front of 75 students, speaking my piece, carrying on about some matter regarding adolescence, a vision of exquisite independence.

Now behold the distractive devil lurking in this image. In truth, my mere presence at the podium is made possible by the physical efforts of probably hundreds of people who funded, constructed, and maintain the lecture hall. Then there are all the drivers I encountered on my way to class; one of them goofs, and I'm splattered on the highway.

Then there are the students. If they are not present and I stand in a perfectly empty classroom saying exactly what I would say to a crowded classroom, I am immediately labeled psychotic and probably transported to a nearby hospital emergency room. So in those moments, the mere existence of the class, irrespective of student assessments of me, publicly determines the state of my mental health

Now something of a practical nature: If my wife or any of our children or grandchildren becomes ill, I will cancel the lecture. They come first; it's not noble, merely a matter of necessity, but it means that I am also dependent on the health of several people as I stand before my class extolling the virtues of independence. Plato was right: We deceive ourselves if we believe that any one of us is self-sufficient.

Reinforcing the (fallacious) concept of adolescent independence is the pejorative quality that enshrouds the concept of dependence. Few adolescents would dare admit to their dependence on anybody, or on any substance for that matter. Physical and especially emotional dependence inevitably is perceived as deleterious. Is it not possible, however, that when an adolescent confesses an emotional dependence on a friend, he or she may be revealing a strong and healthy attachment if not devotion? Apparently not in our culture!

One reason dependence has taken on a pejorative connotation and a good illustration of how history and culture affect personal conceptions involve America's position in the international world of geopolitics. The nation's self-conception that creeps into the stories of individual adolescents' self-conceptions, is that of a superpower, an international police officer, a global patriarch, a totally self-sufficient family unto itself. In fact honoring our geographical relationships with Canada and Mexico, we should properly refer to ourselves as *North* Americans.

Safeguarding the idea that because we are so huge (which we are) and so geographically isolated (which we are not) we need not learn all that much about other countries or their histories; they will have to learn about us. Moreover, we don't seem to need to learn their languages; they will have to learn ours. Need one mention the number of people America sends abroad as representatives and ambassadors who do not speak the native language. Our flawed political and historical perspectives cause us to believe that we truly are the greatest nation in the world, reliant on no one.

A false premise, independent freedom leads not just to the notion that whatever you do in your own mind is permissible but that whatever you do in the privacy of your own home is permissible, which historically has led to among other things, overlooking domestic violence, rape, and molestation. "Go for it," the culture instructs adolescents, thereby implying that it's no one's business to intrude on other people's comings and goings, even if curfews and regulations are required for civilized action. "Individuality, Alex Beam wrote, "is the opium of the 20th-century masses."[13]

Whenever adolescents are taught the false notions of independent action and gratification of instincts at all costs, preposterous and dangerous conditions ensue. These ideologies and rituals are partly predicated on the (distracted) notion of independence if not human isolation. In contrast, if early on children were taught cooperation and care[14] and the virtues of trust, friendship, and healthy dependence on and responsibility for other human beings as well as the natural environment, a wholly different culture of adolescence would emerge.

Given the many children and adolescents who live their lives at peril,[15] it may be that a study of adolescence in an age of distraction requires us to question our very way of life. Perhaps we should question those products that although yielding colossal profits, have turned out not to benefit children at all. One of the profitable areas has been in child rearing, where regularly one hears the unquestioned virtues of autonomy, independence and self-sufficiency. Strange that experts would invent all sorts of (profitable) new technologies for raising children, when, as Felton Earls and Mary Carlson[16] have stated, the needs of children and adolescents haven't changed for centuries!

Individualism and Competition

The push for competition and independence, it is normally asserted, is essential if adolescents are to "make it" in modern society.[17] That is, if our narrative of the world requires fierce independence and fearless competition, we are obliged to raise our children to be able to play in these arenas. Conversely, if our story of child rearing contains the belief that children contribute to the *construction* of the world as much as they are constructed by it, then we free ourselves to raise children according to wholly different values and competencies. This is what Fromm meant when he said that we possess a choice of whether to build our culture on life (biophilous) forces or death (necrophilous) forces.[18]

To fear that the noncompetitive adolescent will lose out on opportunities is merely another story founded on distraction. Economic in nature, the premise of the story alleges competition to be inherently good. Admittedly, it takes courage to argue against the ultimate value of competition; a free enterprise system lives and dies with people's ability to thrive on or at least adapt to the realities and spirit of competition. Competition demands that adolescents never rest satisfied with what they have, never act complacent in the face of victory; there is always the next deal, the next game, the next opportunity, another mountain to be climbed. If no one is around with whom to compete, the adolescent is taught, then compete with yourself. In the old days, questioning the intrinsic goodness of competition practically opened one to the charge of being a communist. Yet if we examine competition closely, we discover that it often precludes other motives and dynamics, other stories equally valuable, from taking root in the adolescent's mind and becoming part of the adolescent's self. Let me illustrate this point.

For years it was standard operating procedure to demand that students do their own schoolwork. Typically, they were instructed not to converse with fellow classmates and most definitely not to consult with one another on homework. The admonitions seemed sensible, even if few of my generation obeyed them. Of course we conversed and consulted with each other about homework; school nights were defined by these consulting telephone calls. What is more, we were smart; we telephoned experts: Mimi knew the English, Paul the math, Susie knew French, Tony the chemistry, and Jimmy, the talking, walking encyclopedia, knew everything about everything.

We reacted as well to another facet of the educational system's adherence to standards of individualism and competition. Constantly hearing the words, "Just do the best you can and don't worry what anybody else does," we nonetheless worshipped percentile scores, learning precisely where we stood on every test we ever took. And, of course, we engaged in the ritual known as "Whadjeget?" The instant the examination was passed back, we turned, as a reflexive action, to anyone who happened to be standing nearby and uttered: "Whadjeget?" Significantly, their response put our performance in perspective.

Nowadays, however, it turns out that students who work together, share material, and divide the labors of scholarship perform better academically than students who choose to work alone.[19] The once-inviolate classroom principle has shifted 180 degrees, and students now are questioned as to why they prefer *not* to work with classmates. Independent work, the diadem in the academic crown, has been thrown out, and children are openly encouraged to teach one another, which everyone knows is the best way to learn. In this less competitive and more collegial environment, the anxious "Whadjeget?" has been transformed into the solicitous, "Djegetit?"

In the process of encouraging cooperative rather than independent and competitive learning, the parent-child relationship will also be transformed. Now parents will be discouraged and moved to action by their adolescent's unhappiness and not merely by his or her poor school performance. Similarly, parents may celebrate nothing less than their adolescent's continuously emerging self,[20] not his or her periodic accomplishments or performance.

The transformations made by adolescents from independence to dependence and competition to cooperation inevitably are affected by economic and political institutions. Public situations define our public actions as well as our private ones; they influence emotions as well. Political events, after all, shape the substance of dreams,[21] as we know from the reports of frightened children during times of war[22] and natural disasters. Even adolescents hold on to security blankets and stuffed animals, what Donald Winnicott[23] called transitional objects.

Observe students at a basketball game played between rival schools in rural, urban, or suburban communities. One can feel the tension in the gymnasium, a tension that often erupts in fights in which serious injury, even death, may result. These are just young people living mere streets from one another, but now, because of the competitive nature of the culture, they are willing to cause harm over the matter of who is number one on a basketball court.

Given the effects on the mind of the media and, especially, television, our vision of these gymnasium tensions characteristically focuses on the infamous "inner city" and, more specifically, urban gangs and their deadly serious notions of boundaries and turf. Independence and competition seem to rule these young men, many of them fatherless if not familyless. They call themselves "home boys," indicating thereby that the turf they defend so zealously is their true home. Some would call their behavior extreme,[24] aberrant even, yet what these young men act out sometimes in menacing fashion is what millions of Americans act out in more genteel ways for everyone to see.

Observing closely the boys on Wall Street, the car manufacturers, politicians, and attorneys as well as the show biz types known as sharks and barracudas play their deadly games, one sees that the personal stories of adolescents contain aspects of these games. Listen to the linguistic patterns and observe closely the habits: Gang boys aren't the only ones speaking about kicking butt, busting balls, knocking off enemies. There's a whole other world of competitive folks employing expressions like strangling companies, engaging in hostile takeovers, cutting throats, and prosecuting wars.

We're Number One!

A recently stated goal of American education is to become number one in the world in mathematics. Millions of adults in this country can neither read nor compute numbers at a third grade level, but the goal is to be number one in the world. Notice the priorities: It is not that we seek to revamp our educational system; we're focusing on attaining preeminent stature in the world. Notice, too, our preoccupation with the concept of priorities; we're always prioritizing. It is possible, after all, to make a list of things to do and designate none of the items number one. This is the way we treat our children, isn't it?

Being number one is captured in the image of the athlete waving to the camera after he has scored a touchdown and flashing his finger at us as he mouths, "Hi, Mom" (rarely "Hi, Dad") or in students chanting the message, "We're number one! We're number one!" It's the essence of the American competitive spirit: We must win; there's no room at the top for anyone else. The late football coach Vince Lombardi is known to have said that "Winning isn't everything; it's the only thing!"

In our need to win, we refuse to allow ties. Ties mean a playoff or sudden death, and everyone knows that expression that likens a tie to kissing one's sister. Students of all ages are known for the way they compete with one another—it is said it's "in their blood"—and all of this finds its roots in the adolescent's learned pursuit of independence and self-sufficiency. Driving styles reveal the adolescents' competitive urges: They must get there ahead of anyone else, and death to those causing traffic jams that keep the young from getting where they need to go, causing the newly minted disorder known as road rage.

Competition carries with it the notion that the other person has no place other than beneath us: "Knock 'em down and keep 'em down." We alone must make it to the summit, and once there, maintain our position as king of the mountain, not incidentally, the name of a game played by children in which everyone wrestles their way to the top of the heap, the winner being the last one standing. One wonders whether schools offer queen of the mountain, or don't girls have these same independent and competitive drives pushing—and punishing them—through life?[25]

The danger facing all standing kings, even adolescent ones, is that although they view everyone as serfs or subjects, they fear that pretenders to the throne plot to overthrow them. This, in turn, means they must be vigilant in maintaining their armor and exclusivity. In time, king of the mountain becomes a story of being the richest, smartest, most famous, or the one able to live the lavish styles of the rich and famous. Athletic departments play down the meaning of team rankings but make no mistake about their desire to be number one. King or queen of the mountain or not, the rest of us cannot designate any activity successful without everyone knowing once and for all who is the best!

Everywhere people are publishing reports, honor rolls, and class rankings, making it incontrovertibly clear who is the best of the best, the richest, the most handsome, the most well known, the sexiest in the world. Adolescents sit on the edge of their seats viewing MTV awards, Oscars, Golden Globes, Emmys, Grammys, Peoples Choice Awards ceremonies. They watch celebrities bask in their glory, caring not at all that nominations and awards are a multimillion-dollar public relations business. They witness awards handed out to the prettiest teenager in America, the prettiest teenager in the world, the prettiest woman in America, and finally the prettiest woman in the universe. They watch men's and women's body-building competitions and pairs body building competitions, individual, pairs, and team aerobic workout competitions and individual, pairs, and team cheerleading competitions. Every other day adolescents acknowledge someone earning a first-place award. Winners always thank hordes of others, but award shows are only about winners. They are occasions to celebrate the nature of competition, the re-emergence of individualism, and the apotheosis of being numero uno!

Award shows, as the journalist Ed Siegel observed,[26] also reaffirm celebrities as the quintessential archetypes of modern culture, which worships anyone experiencing even a moment of notoriety. Siegel is also right to say that celebrity worship is fundamentally an archetype of adolescence as it appears to resolve youthful concerns about American identity formation. Just the sound of the name of the winner accords that person immediate identity, fame, recognition, wealth, success, and, who knows, immortality as well. Adolescents adore the winners' look of shock, their tears of joy and disbelief, for they are acting out the adolescent's own emotions that would erupt had only he or she been publicly anointed number one. Of course adolescents are stunned when award winners commit suicide. How is it that fame and wealth fail to immunize a person against the personal demons of one's mind fields?

Award shows accomplish something else: they placate adolescents' anxiety associated with the need to be number one, though they fail to answer the question of why we need to know, or, for that matter, be number one? What underlying psychological matter is actually being settled for adolescents by the award show, final standings, or championship game?

Vulnerability to distraction places adolescents in the role of passive child or audience member as opposed to adult actor and critic (of self). Award shows represent transitory public confirmations of whether adolescents' own preferences for cultural stimuli jibe with the selections made by the experts, the cultural definers. In their way, these shows, like the recent spate of lavish television game shows reveal to adolescents how intelligent, "with it," current, hip, turned on, they are. If I don't know the name of the award-winning artist or the song or the answer to the $100 question, I'm out of it! And no one wants to be out of it, excluded, overlooked, surpassed, eclipsed, rejected, omitted, unintelligent, a loser.

On award-show nights, as on all other nights, no adolescent wishes to be invisible. Only naturally they are profoundly disappointed when "their" song or movie, "their" play or athlete, "their" hero or favorite pageant contestant is not chosen number one. Adolescents aren't easily fooled: Nominations lose their glitter the moment the winner's name is called. It's not enough to be nominated. Not winning means that the adolescent is not part of the "in" crowd; he or she is missing out on the powerful currents and currencies, sentiments and experiences of the culture. The result may be a defective (sense of) self.

If award shows help resolve adolescents' anxieties about their lack of a solid and stable identity or enduring relationships that, they have learned, ward off their dread of separation and loneliness,[27] then the shows also provide adolescents an answer to the most important question they have for their parents: Am I the most beautiful and intelligent? Am I your favorite? Am I number one?

Precisely because in many respects popular culture is the perpetuation of high school social life (but now for profit) the powers of conformity, rebellion, and idealism gain especial prominence in the lives of adolescents.[28] One must be like the others, act like the others, derive one's public and possibly, too, private identity in part from being identical to the others.[29] Finally, whether or not it comes with a particular brand of ideology, adolescent idealism requires that a person act with courage and bravery in the face of adult responsibilities and obligations. Most of all, one has to be included, "with it," connected, approved of, and popular, highly popular.

Within these contexts, adolescents seek personal and public significance; they wish to make a name for themselves, be known, recognized. One has to "make a difference." Presumably this is the opposite of "making sameness," leaving the world precisely as it was when one entered it, which means one's presence has made no difference whatsoever. Although the concept of identity formation for Erikson[30] was comprised of these two components, continuing sameness and constant change, the adolescent achieves both by not only being part of the school or the culture's popular and elite groups but by reaching the top of those groups. The point is illustrated by one student:

> In my mind, we had this ladder. There were a lot of people on the top, and even more on the bottom. I fit somewhere on the middle. Every day I moved up or down, or even stayed on the same rung. When I was in junior high, the thing I wanted most was to climb to the top of that ladder. That is where all of the "popular" people were. In junior high, I was not popular. I don't even think I was noticed. Now when I look back on it, I'll bet other kids felt the same way that I did.[31]

Ironically, the word "award" derives in part from the French word meaning "to guard," which, in turn, means to keep safe from harm, watch over and protect, defend, shield.[32] Without the award and the protection it affords, therefore, adolescents may be forced to spend the rest of their lives sitting in front of television sets waiting to learn who is number one in all the world's categories; individual qualifications and criteria appear to matter very little. As an invisible, anonymous, and possibly frightened member of the audience and hence ineligible for the competition, the young person, for the moment, is obliged to remain satisfied with the knowledge that someone (else) has been chosen number one. Although perhaps not pure illusion, all of this is the product of individual stories, individual human constructions. Award shows, competition, the need to know who is number one derive directly from the way individuals think and what they choose to think about. Knowledge itself is being socially constructed.

Adolescent competition is, of course, a double-edged sword. Independence, ambition, and competition bring out the best in some young people, although no research demonstrates that this is true for most young people. Some adolescents collapse at the thought of stiff competition. Some choke when, as they say, the money's on the table. Some adolescents demure, claiming they're lovers not fighters. Some are thrown off teams because they are unable to go for the jugular.

Many adolescents, apparently, don't possess what athletes call the "killer instinct." They lack those inimitable resources owned by the great boxer: The fire in the belly and the eye of the tiger. Many adolescent boys, apparently revealing a yellow streak, feel too compassionate; they actually feel sorry for the losers.[33] They root for underdogs with whom they identify, because bringing down top dogs is thrilling. And always they remain aware of the import of popular words used for popular people like "superstar" and "megastar." Self-sufficient, independent, able to care for themselves, the name of the adolescent game often appears to be rely on no one, despite an intense desire to do just the opposite.

The spirit of independence is never more in evidence than when young people earn their driver's licenses. If ever there was a feeling of independence, it's the moment the adolescent takes his or her seat behind the wheel of the family car, which long ago the adolescent feels should have been traded in for a fancier model. Driving as the supreme symbol of independence is pure myth. The adolescent driver is as dependent on seen and unseen people as I am standing in that classroom droning on about adolescence.[34]

The road of independence and self-sufficiency walked by the adolescent is often false and distracting. Adolescents imagine independence; they are taught independence; they pretend independence and write it into their personal narratives, but it remains unattainable, sheer fantasy.

God must be looking down at adolescents and their elders in utter dismay. Putting scientific theories of evolution aside, how long, really, was Adam going to garden alone? If nothing else, the man needed distraction.

Independence or Abandonment?

Every one of us, probably, has questioned a friend about the possibility of being stranded on a desert island. How would you live? Who would you ideally want to be with? For years, millions watched a television show, "Gilligan's Island," which transformed these terrors into allegedly comedic situations. We make light of the desert island scene because it distracts us from unthinkable fears of aloneness and abandonment and reveals how unrealistic are the notions of self-sufficiency and independence. Many fear they would die all too quickly on a desert island as they wouldn't know any more survival techniques than a two-day-old baby would. No wonder so many people have been attracted to the television program "Survivor."

The desert island hypothesis bespeaks a fundamental terror of being alone and friendless, of the self abandoned by itself. The myth of independence provides protection against the fear of dying *and* living alone.[35] After all the jokes about desert islands subside, what is it that lovers tell each other? "I don't want to be on this earth without you." My father had been dead only a few minutes before I watched my mother bend down and kiss his forehead. Then, looking at him through tears, I heard her say, "I'll join you soon."

Indeed, we are joined to the hips of others, connected, united, attached, wedded, tied, stuck. Some adolescents never recover from the loss of a friend or family member. They recognize that someone once attached to them is gone and has taken a part of them with him or her. The poet advised us that it is better to have loved and lost than never to have loved at all. It is true but not as satisfying as having loved and won! The myth of independence masks the reality that the adolescent's life force turns out to consist of all the others in his or her life. Why would one want to go on without these special people? Without friends there is no intimacy, there is no one on whom one may try out his or her latest version of self.[36]

Adding to the myth of independence has been the growing need for self-sufficiency in the so-called baby boomer family. Baby boomer children learned early on the utter necessity of being able to live on one's own; parents working outside the home simply weren't going to be around that often. From all indications, children of this generation got the message they had to compete with other people and other activities for the attention and time of their parents. There were the careers, friends, social engagements, evening meetings, community doings, vacations sometimes taken without children, and divorce. The statistic indicating that 76 percent of American children wish they could spend more time with their parents speaks volumes.[37]

Baby boomer children grew up steeped in the ideas of America's worship of independence, which they experienced as the independence of parents from one another as well as parents from children. Boomer parents taught their children to be able to play, spend time, work, study, entertain themselves on their own as early as possible. Literally or symbolically latch-key children, a generation of adolescents grew up believing that being on one's own was tantamount to a healthy sense of individualism and esteem. Only logically, parents insisted that independence was essential for survival even though their assertion was open to all sorts of questions.

Like self-esteem, survival seems to be on the lips of many adolescents. People recounting stories of personal unhappiness on television invariably refer to themselves as survivors.[38] At first hearing, the word strikes one as melodramatic, but it is meant to capture this phenomenon of battling the world on one's own while desperately desiring the assistance of others, particularly those who have abandoned, abused, or betrayed you. The word "battling" is not an exaggeration, for clearly these people feel that life and death are in the balance. The Darwinian notion of survival has come to encompass a generation of people who early on learned they would not be closely safeguarded but would have to make it on their own, as if anybody can. They must feel as if they have escaped the abyss of deception and death and survived. They return to us from a desert island of emotional and/or physical desertion.[39]

Millions of adolescents tell stories of having been left on their own to fend for themselves. We are not surprised by the finding that 50 percent of America's eleven-year-old children return from school to an empty home. Placed in the care of others or obliged to care for siblings, the six-year-old tends the three-year-old, both of them frightened, the older one more so, perhaps, because he or she must assume the care-taking responsibilities. A (distracted) culture that glorifies independence must also believe that children are more mature than their chronological age would indicate and hence their need for supervision less severe. All children, and especially care-taking girls, are labeled precocious; they are always nine going on twenty-eight.[40] Earls and Carlson[41] have it right: Adults may transform the technologies of parenting, yet children require adults to nurture, guide, and supervise them. Truth be told, many adolescents find the notion of an independent self an anathema.

The commencement of independence and autonomy[42] is marked by the infamous stage of toilet training. In an effort to induce independence, parents may prematurely initiate natural physical and psychological processes.[43] They need the child trained because of the independence that will result, but the child has 50 ways of saying, "I don't like this seat!" Successful toilet training allows parents to be independent, if not children; if parents don't have the time, they have to, well, push early toilet training.

Not long after toilet training, children, even those children who are never left alone except at night in bed, enter a stage of night terrors.[44] Hearing their wailing, parents rush to their rooms as the weeping children describe the monsters under the bed and the ghosts in the closet. If children in average, predictable home environments are terrified of aloneness, what must be going through the minds of adolescents who will ultimately label themselves survivors but presently live these night terrors every day without ever being comforted?

Though I have no verification of the notion, I tend to believe that adolescents' preoccupation with the horror films and terrifying movies that they go to in droves, their faces buried in their arms during the ghastly scenes, are emotional rehearsals for or more likely replications of the physical and emotional terrors they experience. If emotions can be mastered in darkened movie theaters by viewing films over and over again—actually a sound behavioral therapy technique—then the adolescent may develop the strength to get through the everyday terrors experienced in aloneness, abandonment, and abuse.

The myth of independence plays still another role in the lives of adolescents. Imbuing young people with (false) independence presumably prepares them for separations, detachments, or divorces—divorces, incidentally, that many adolescents refer to as nightmares.[45] Best adolescents not depend too strongly on people if there is any possibility they may leave. The only one going to be there forever, the adolescent concludes, is myself, so I will look out for number one.[46] As Soren Kierkegaard counseled, the genuine lover "has comprehended the deep secret that also in loving another person one must be sufficient unto oneself."[47]

Divorce need not strike one's own home to develop a dread of it. The moment young people come into contact with divorce,[48] they begin to wonder about the marital status of their parents. Suddenly, children examine more closely than ever before Mom and Dad's treatment of one another, or consider the nature of their lives in homes where there has never been a mother or a father. They worry about parental competition, the absence of devotion, the possibility that they will live with only one parent. Adolescents, especially, examine parental avoidance, disinterest, abandonment, selfishness, and turn these issues into their personal stories and constructions of selves.

In the spirit of independence, some parents advance the notion that curfew laws instituted during adolescence preclude the development of a sense of independence. Impose too many regulations on adolescents, it is alleged, and one detracts from their power to make good judgments on their own. So young people wander about the streets scoffing at friends who must be home by ten or are required to telephone their parents if they anticipate being late. Beyond establishing boundaries for adolescents, the curfew stands as a reminder that parents do care about children. How is an adolescent to know, for example, that independence is not to be interpreted as disinterest?[49] Hold in mind that permissiveness typically is perceived by adolescents as disinterest, which, in turn, leads to them growing up disliking themselves. Hold in mind as well, Fromm's notion that when parents withdraw from children, the children become destructive. (Similarly, when parents act destructively toward children, Fromm theorized, children withdraw.[50])

Most adolescents dislike the notion of (false) independence that parents seek to instill in them. Think of all the popular song lyrics devoted to the pain of separation and the need for attachment.[51] Obliged to "act" independently, many adolescents mourn the loss of attachments so vital to their development of self, yet remain unable to speak about these matters except to one another, and even then they may do so with shame and a sense of having betrayed their families. They act in public as if all attachments to their family were normal, so that the public will perceive their family and them as normal;[52] it is the nature and style of attachments to family members that the public employs to assess "normality" in the first place. The one time, perhaps, adolescents seek a reasonable facsimile of independence is when they react to overbearing, smothering parents, but this is but a survival technique to protect them from being swallowed up by parental neediness.

Granted, most adolescents demand independence and act as if they were living free and clear of parents, but in the development of a unique self, this action proves essential; eventually all of us must go off on our own.[53] Besides, it is practice for the future when one lives independently from one's parents. So, like children on roller skates unable to skate backward, adolescents push against the walls of their parents, thereby propelling themselves in some direction.[54] When they get to the next wall, they merely turn around and push off all over again. Take the walls away, and the adolescent is frightened if not altogether stymied.

So parent and adolescent dance the independence sham, in which parents complain of rebellion, and children complain of oppressive attachment, while secretly, in healthy families at least, parents enjoy their adolescent's attempt to stand on his or her own feet, and children remain thankful they don't have to pay room and board,[55] and that Mom and Dad aren't going anywhere.

When adolescents are told by their parents (and country) that they are meant to stand alone, to be independent, their first impulse often is to make an unconscious philosophical and psychological leap: They separate themselves from everyone in the universe. Committed to independence, they fear attaching themselves to anyone; hence, they grow up with the notion that there must be a separation between themselves and everyone else.[56] No one has explicitly told them this; they deduce it from the nature and character of their family's relationships. No matter how intense their relationships may be with those they choose as intimates, there is always that space in their constructed self, the space created by false or pseudo-independence. Often, adolescents will reveal this space by becoming involved with the "wrong" people, those with whom they know they could never be intimate but with whom they simultaneously act out (pseudo) intimacy and independence.

The presumably independent adolescent has been discouraged from trusting. Indeed, the lack of trust in anyone becomes *the* source of his or her (independent) actions and ideals. As no one is permitted to get close, no one is allowed to receive the adolescent's inner world as a gift. With all this armor in the name of independence, one cannot love or be loved, and, hence, a competitive world is probably not a bad playing field, except for the fact that many adolescents are ill equipped to compete. If one is separated from others, there can be no intimacy; no one need care for anyone. Life becomes a war of all against all, one person's impulses warring against those of another. Everyone gets to "do their own thing."

In their distractions, adolescents may well imagine this ideal to be the precursor of freedom, but it yields only libertine ventures. Of course one values the adolescent adventurer, the firebrand, the marginal person exhibiting courage through his or her independent stance, but these people are rare. Most adolescents are taught a mixed message: Do your own thing but conform. This philosophy hardly serves as a stable foundation from which to author a consolidated self.

In *Escape from Freedom*,[57] Fromm spoke of the conflict caused by our paradoxical pursuit of both genuine independence and freedom and of comforting security, something adolescents evince again and again. They run from the group, conventions, rituals, attachments, only to discover that their newly found sense of individuality or independence causes them to feel insecure, lonely, insignificant, alienated.[58] The "successful" result of their strivings for independence frequently leaves them feeling frightened, alone, isolated. To restore an almost childlike sense of meaning and the feeling that they belong, they attempt to reunite, reattach, even get swallowed up by another person through their work or, best of all, through sexuality and intimacy.[59]

Adolescents often attempt to regain security by erasing differences between themselves and others, by becoming exactly like their peers, conforming to their styles, costumes, appetites, linguistic traits, and requests. Parents often wonder whether these behaviors imply that the adolescent has sacrificed his or her personality—the genuine self—for the sake of inclusion and security.

The story could be worse, however, as Americans have discovered in recent years. As Fromm observed, adolescents may adopt authoritarian mechanisms for regaining security and avoiding shame, as they reveal in subscribing to Nazism, and masochistic, sadistic, and even nihilistic strivings and by their advocacy of "proactive aggressive" people who enjoy seeing others suffering, and outright destructiveness.[60] Many of these adolescents even advance the goal of eliminating people—fellow students, teachers, and parents—and destroying homes and schools. Might these be the young people Kohut had in mind when he wrote that "narcissistic rage is directed at selfobjects (sic) who threaten or have damaged the self."[61]

A Performance Problem for Boys

Another problem emanating from the expectation of adolescents, and especially boys, to be independent is captured in the word, "expectation." Boys more than girls grow up steeped in the philosophy that expectation is everything. In composing their unique narratives, boys forever struggle to rid themselves of those expectations others have of them which they now have internalized.[62] Dominated by expectation, adolescents feel that the essence of life perpetually resides beyond them, never where they presently stand. How can they ever enjoy the present moment when each moment must be employed to shape future moments? This is, after all, the essence of an expectation.[63]

There is another aspect to the marriage of expectation, independence, and competition: When performance ends, adolescents lose because they often cannot find anything substantial to fall back upon. All of life, seemingly, is predicated on doing rather than being, on instrumental action with a discrete purpose rather than seemingly purposeless reflection. Recall the question that is still asked more of boys than girls: "What are you going to do when you grow up?" If young men are challenged for their inability to commit to someone or be intimate or sensitive, then let us understand these phenomena as the results of a calculated form of socialization.[64] These are the selves the society wants to construct in its young men. If they are raised in the same manner as boys, girls, too, will reveal the same difficulties with intimacy and commitment. Little wonder that so many young people derive pleasure from "doing" absolutely nothing but what they call "hanging out." It seems the only viable antidote to the oppressive expectations of adolescence.

Inadvertently, adolescent boys have been taught the dynamics of chauvinism. In being obliged to dance the independence sham, young men often find themselves not only uncomfortable with their need for intimacy, they may perceive women as threatening because women seem so at ease with intimacy. Then again, as Fromm[65] theorized, when parents withdraw, children tend to become destructive, especially with those with whom they seek closeness, those who evoke the pain of a life free of genuine attachments.

In the middle and upper classes, where for good and bad, psychological theories have taken root, young people are labeled narcissists, meaning intensively self-loving.[66] Narcissists perceive the world strictly in terms of how it treats them. So now we find young people allegedly interested only in themselves, not only feeling superior to others whom they distrust but unable to love at all, except perhaps their fellow chauvinists and narcissists.

Yet it is not precisely narcissism that causes these problems as much as it is a *damaged* narcissism that so many adolescents experience.[67] When they are taught that they are little more than the sum of their moment-to-moment performance and, accordingly, must orient their identities around future preparations (the inevitable expectations), how do they ever reach the point where they can love themselves for who they are or accept themselves without public proclamations to improve? All they are able to love is the illusion of their performance. And it *is* illusion because these performances are not genuinely their own; they derive from other people's narratives.[68]

Adolescents know what they are doing. Boys especially seek out someone with whom they need not perform, someone to whom they may reveal their true self even as it is being constructed. Hoping to rid themselves of the armor which precludes intimacy, they seek assurance that not only are they loved and lovable but that this love evolves from their mere being rather than their capacity to meet the culture's omnipresent expectations. Being oneself, creating one's own narrative is thrown into conflict with the culture's constant imposition of expectations; it is the quintessential dialectic of adolescence. Rewards come from performance, not from showing drafts of a still-incomplete self-story.

The danger is that if love and intimacy remain contingent on performance and if all of life is predicated on expectation, then when does the adolescent ever hear that he or she has performed well or at last met the culture's expectations? Does the culture fear that by stripping adolescence of performance rewards, young people might stop performing at all? Rewarding adolescents, apparently, is risky business; it addresses the possibility that they will see the illusions of independence and competition before their own performance energy has been completely exhausted. That a culture embraces the idea of "conditional love" speaks to the frequently absurd expectations and reward rituals imposed on young people. Everyone knows that loved and respected children and adolescents tend to perform better just as they know that some of the most rewarding aspects of life require no performance whatsoever. So why would anyone ever withhold love or make it conditional?

Adolescents constantly hunt for signs and signals that they are lovable and loved and not defective although their hunt is often secretive and inconspicuous.[69] One begins to wonder whether "playing it cool" is little more than working hard at not revealing one's need to be lovable and loved or the fear that perhaps one is defective. Granted, coolness may be affectlessness, but it may also be a sign of an already damaged narcissism. Adolescents must always assume that posture of success, casualness, being under control, despite the endless cultural expectations and classroom assignments.

David Mamet's play, *Glengarry Glen Ross,* is a powerful statement of precisely these issues. Although the characters are tough, performance-driven salesmen, the messages pertain to adolescents. There is no love in Mamet's offices, no sense of possibility, nothing but souls wrecked by a cultural dynamic that renders these men impotent, unsuccessful, emasculated. How telling is it that the play reveals not one woman, not one moment of intimacy, only men struggling to maintain a sense of independence, competitiveness, manliness even though everyone can see the barrenness of their lives.

Glengarry Glen Ross portrays quintessential distraction. All these characters require is the closing of the deal and they will be satisfied, sanctified even. The metaphor is sexual, symbolic, and, in the end, utterly real. It is the same message many learn during adolescence: Close big deals, get high grades, enter prestigious colleges, obtain good jobs, meet every expectation, show that you are a great prospect, perhaps even get your name recognized, and you will gain entry into adulthood.

When the young woman's armor and the young man's armor crash against each other in moments that are meant to be intimate, it is most likely anxiety, fright, insecurity, dependencies, and hurt that come into play although adolescents may not immediately recognize their own true emotions. Reprisals, revenge, defiance, and resentment practically asphyxiate the young couple, but it is insecurity, and the lack of nurturance and intimacy that lurk in their quarrels. Anxiety is generated by the fact that when adolescents are stripped of performance criteria, when they are told to come forth with their pure, inner self even if it is not yet ready for prime time, they are left feeling armorless. Although frightened, deep down both know that it is this armor that has suffocated them. As William Butler Yeats wrote: "We make out of the quarrel with others, rhetoric, but of the quarrel with ourselves, poetry."

What adolescents desire of one another in genuine intimacy is precisely what they require of themselves but remain unable to admit to needing and wanting.[70] On those special nights with those special people, at long last they make their admissions and reveal the products of their personal narratives. Safe with a true companion, a sharer of selves, they no longer are embarrassed by their nakedness and sexuality. In the armorless darkness, when they choose to face the truths of themselves without distraction, experiencing only self-generated expectations, they come face to face with the soul they have worked so hard to construct. "In the jungle of human existence," Erikson wrote, "there is no feeling of being alive without a sense of identity."[71]

Then comes the light of the following day, and discomfort once again revisits them. It is not, however, because they were armorless the previous evening; rather, they have returned to their unself-reflective forms. They are back in the school's corridors, acting properly, independently, dutifully self-sufficiently exactly as their parents, teachers, camp counselors, and coaches want them to be, expect them to be. They stand in front of their mirrors checking their hair, their skin, the cut of their clothes, their collars or makeup. All is right: narcissism in place, armor in place, distractions in place. Looking good, the young man or young woman is ready to close a deal somewhere.

Notes

1 See James A. Banks, "The Social Construction of Difference and the Quest for Educational Equality." In *Education in a New Era: ASCD Yearbook 2000*, Ronald S. Brandt (Editor). Alexandria, VA: Association for Supervision and Curriculum Development, 2000. I am grateful to Arthur Beane for this citation.

2 P. L. Berger and T. Luckman, *The Social Construction of Reality: A Treatise in the Sociology of Knowledge*. New York: Anchor, 1966.

3 H. Varenne and R. McDermott, *Successful Failure: The School America Builds*. Boulder: Westview, 1998.

4 On this point, see J. R. Mercer, *Labeling the Mentally Retarded*. Berkeley, CA: University of California Press, 1973.

5 Mara Sapon-Shevin, *Playing Favorites: Gifted Education and the Disruption of Community*. Albany: State University of New York Press, 1994.

6 Jay M. Shafritz, *The Dorsey Dictionary of American Government and Politics*. Chicago: Dorsey, 1988.

7 David Steiner, "Retreat from Judgment." Unpublished manuscript, Boston University, 2000.

8 See James A. Banks, *Multicultural Education, Transformative Knowledge, and Action: Historical and Contemporary Perspectives*. New York: Teachers College, 1996.

9 See G. Y. Okihiro, *Margins and Mainstreams: Asians in American History and Culture*. Seattle, WA: University of Washington Press, 1994.

10 On this point, see Thomas Hine, *The Rise and Fall of the American Teenager*. New York: Bard/Avon, 1999.

11 Martin Luther King, *Letter from the Birmingham Jail*. New York: HarperCollins, 1994, page 3.

12 See J. L. Stone and J. Church, *Childhood and Adolescence: A Psychology of the Growing Person*. New York: Random House, 1973.

13 Alex Beam, "If You're Dull You'll Be Dull on the Web Too." *The Boston Globe*, May 5, 1999: F1.

14 Carol Gilligan, *In a Different Voice: Psychological Theory and Women's Development*. Cambridge, MA: Harvard University Press, 1982.

15 See Thomas J. Cottle, *At Peril: Stories of Injustice*. Amherst: University of Massachusetts Press, 2001; and Roberta Wollons, *Children at Risk in America: History, Concepts, and Public Policy*. Albany: State University of New York Press, 1993.

16   Felton Earls and Mary Carlson, "Towards Sustainable Development for American Families." In America's Childhood, *Daedalus*. Winter, 1, *122*, 1993: 93–122; Frances K. Goldscheider and Linda Waite, "The Future of the Home in the Twenty-First Century," in *New Families, No Families? The Transformation of the American Home*. Berkeley: University of California Press, 1991, pages 193–209; and E. S. Cromwell, *Quality Child Care*. Boston: Allyn and Bacon, 1994.

17   See James E. Marcia, "Identity and Self-Development." In R. M. Lerner, A. C. Peterson and J. Brooks-Gunn (Editors), *Encyclopedia of Adolescence*. New York: Garland, 1991.

18   Erich Fromm, *Escape from Freedom*. New York: Farrar & Rinehart, 1941.

19   R. Slavin, "Cooperative Learning and Student Achievement." In R. Slavin (Editor), *School and Classroom Organization*. Hillsdale, NJ: Erlbaum, 1989.

20   Barbara Schave and Douglas Schave, *Early Adolescence and the Search for the Self: A Developmental Perspective*. New York: Praeger, 1989.

21   On this point, see Fred Weinstein and Gerald Platt *The Wish to Be Free*. Berkeley: University of California Press, 1969.

22   Roger Rosenblatt, *Children of War*. Garden City, NJ: Anchor, 1983.

23   Donald W. Winnicott, *Home Is Where We Start From*. Compiled by Clare Winnicott, Ray Shepard, and Madeline Davis. New York: Norton, 1986; and *The Family and Individual Development*. New York: Basic Books, 1965.

24   See Herbert Bloch, *The Gang: A Study in Adolescent Behavior*. New York: Philosophical Library, 1958.

25   Harold Marchant and Helen M. Smith, *Adolescent Girls at Risk*. New York: Pergamon, 1977.

26   E. Siegel, "Life, Celebrity and the Pursuit of Happiness," *The Boston Globe*, December 13, 1998: C1.

27   L. Stern, "Conceptions of Separation and Connection in Female Adolescents." In C. Gilligan, N. Lyons and T. Hanmer (Editors), *Making Connections*. Cambridge, MA: Harvard University Press, 1990.

28   On a related point, see Gary Schwartz, *Beyond Conformity or Rebellion*. Chicago: University of Chicago Press, 1987.

29   One is reminded in this context of the notion often put forth by psychologists as a motivation for young girls to have babies. Besides having someone love them, the baby is intended to be physically identical to them. The child, in other words, is the symbol of conformity and identicality. In general terms, see G. R. Adams, T. P. Gulotta, and R. Montemayor (Editors), *Adolescent Identity Formation*. Newbury Park, CA: Sage, 1992; A. S. Waterman (Editor), *Identity in Adolescence: Processes and Contents*. San Francisco: Jossey-Bass, 1985; and J. LaVoie, "Ego Identity Formation in Early Adolescence." *Journal of Youth and Adolescence*, 5, 1976: 371–385.

30 Erik Erikson, *Identity, Youth and Crisis.* New York: Norton, 1968.

31 "Leanne's Story," cited in Kathleen Bennett and Margaret D. LeCompte, *The Way Schools Work: A Sociological Analysis of Education.* White Plains, NY: Longman, 1990.

32 *Webster's New World Dictionary of the American Language.* New York: World, 1960.

33 See William Pollock, *Real Boys: Rescuing Our Sons from the Myths of Boyhood.* New York: Random House, 1998; and Dan Kindlon and Michael Thompson, *Raising Cain: Protecting the Emotional Life of Boys.* New York: Ballantine, 2000.

34 R. Josselson, "Identity and Relatedness in the Life Cycle." In H. A. Bosma, T. L. G. Graafsma, H. D. Grotevant, and D. J. De Levita (Editors), *Identity and Development.* Newbury Park, CA: Sage, 1994; and H. S. Bernard, "Identity Formation in Late Adolescence: A Review of Some Empirical Findings." *Adolescence, 16,* 1981: 349–358.

35 Robert S. Weiss, *Loneliness: The Experience of Emotional and Social Isolation.* Cambridge, MA: MIT Press, 1973; J. De Jong-Gierveld, "Developing and Testing a Model of Loneliness. *Journal of Personality and Social Psychology.*" 1987, *53:* 119–128.

36 R. M. Ryan and J. H. Lynch, "Emotional Autonomy Versus Detachment: Revisiting the Vicissitudes of Adolescence and Young Adulthood." *Child Development, 60,* 1989: 340–356; R. R. Kobak and A. Sceery, "Attachment in Late Adolescence: Working Models, Affect Regulation, and Representations of Self and Others." *Child Development, 59,* 1988: 135–146.

37 G. Armsden and M. T. Greenberg, "The Inventory of Parents and Peer Attachment: Individual Differences and Their Relationship to Psychological Well Being in Adolescence." *Journal of Youth and Adolescence, 16,* 1987: 427–454.

38 On a related point, see K. Kemper, "Constructing a True Story: The Moral Autobiography of a Survivor." *Thresholds-in-Education,* 3, *22,* 1996: 23–26.

39 On this point, see John Bowlby, *Attachment and Loss,* Volume 3, *Loss, Sadness and Depression.* New York: Basic Books, 1980.

40 David Elkind, *The Hurried Child.* Reading, MA: Addison-Wesley, 1981; Nicole Peradotto, "Little Women: A New Generation of Girls Growing Up Before Their Time." *The Buffalo News.* January 26, 1997: F1.

41 Earls and Carlson, op. cit.

42 See J. P. Allen, S. T. Hauser, K. L. Bell, and T. G. O'Connor, "Longitudinal Assessment of Autonomy and Relatedness in Adolescent-Family Interactions as Predictors of Adolescent Ego Development and Self Esteem." *Child Development, 65,* 1994: 179–194.

43 On this and related points, see David Elkind, *The Hurried Child.* Reading, MA: Addison-Wesley, 1981.

44   John Mack, *Nightmares and Human Conflict*. Boston: Little, Brown, 1970.

45   E. M. Cummings and P. Davies, *Children and Marital Conflict: The Impact of Family Dispute and Resolution*. New York: Guilford, 1994.

46   A Boston television station (WCVB-TV) reported that as of January 1991, around 30% of men owing alimony and child support payments make these payments, and of this 30%, about one half pay the full amount as ordered by the courts.

47   Soren Kierkegaard, *Fear and Trembling*, translation by Walter Lowrie. New York: Doubleday, 1954: 55.

48   See Judith S. Wallerstein, "Children of Divorce: The Psychological Tasks of the Child." In *Annual Progress of Child Psychiatry and Child Development*, Stella Chess and Alexander Thomas (Editors). New York: Brunner/Mazel, 1984; Judith S. Wallerstein and Joan Berlin Kelly, *Surviving the Breakup: How Parents and Children Cope with Divorce*. New York: Basic Books, 1980. See also E.M. Hetherington and J. Arasteh (Editors), *Impact of Divorce, Single Parenting, and Stepparenting on Children*. Hillsdale, NJ: Erlbaum, 1988; E. M. Hetherington, E. R. Anderson, and M. S. Hagan, "Divorce: Effects on Adolescents." In R. M. Lerner, A. C. Petersen, and J. Brooks-Gunn op. cit.; and N. Kalter, *Growing Up with Divorce*. New York: Free Press, 1990.

49   For whatever relevance it may have to this discussion, one notes that putting primates used in laboratory research in cages by themselves makes them more agitated and "less happy" than putting them together in groups. See Tina Adler, "Put Primates in Groups, A Scientist Recommends," *The APA Monitor*, February 1991, *22*, No. 2: 10.

50   Erich Fromm, *Escape from Freedom*, op. cit.

51   J. P. Hill and G. N. Holmbeck, "Attachment and Autonomy During Adolescence." *Annals of Child Development*, *3*, 1986: 145–189.

52   Thomas J. Cottle, *Children's Secrets*. Reading, MA: Addison-Wesley, 1990.

53   Sigmund E. Dragastin and Glen H. Elder, Jr. (Editors), *Adolescence in the Life Cycle: Psychological Change and Social Context*. New York: Halsted, 1975; Gerald Caplan and Serge Lebovici (Editors), *Adolescence: Psychosocial Perspectives*. New York, Basic Books, 1969; and Louise J. Kaplan, *Adolescence, the Farewell to Childhood*. New York: Simon and Schuster, 1984.

54   See Peter Blos, *On Adolescence: A Psychoanalytic Interpretation*. New York: The Free Press of Glencoe, 1962; and Peter Blos, *The Adolescent Passage*. New York: International Universities Press, 1979.

55   On this and related points, see Thomas J. Cottle, *Children's Secrets*, op. cit.; and K. W. Allison and R. M. Lerner, "Adolescents and the Family." In R .M. Lerner (Editor), *Early Adolescence*. Hillsdale, NJ: Erlbaum, 1993.

56   See Rolf E. Muuss, *Theories of Adolescence*. New York: Random House, 1968; Daniel Offer, *The Psychological World of the Teenager*. New York: Basic Books,

1969; Judith E. Gallatin, *Adolescence and Individuality: A Conceptual Approach to Adolescent Psychology.* New York, Harper & Row, 1974.

57 Erich Fromm, *Escape from Freedom,* op. cit.

58 James G. Kelly (Editor), *Adolescent Boys in High School: A Psychological Study of Coping and Adaptation.* Hillsdale, NJ: Erlbaum, 1979.

59 E. E. Werner and R. S. Smith, *Vulnerable but Invincible.* New York: McGraw-Hill, 1982, see especially chapters 13 and 14; and James Youniss and Jacqueline Smollar, "Self Through Relationship Development." In *Coping and Self-Concept in Adolescence,* Harke Bosma and Sandy Jackson (Editors). Berlin: Springer-Verlag, 1990.

60 Janet Shucksmith, *Health Issues and Adolescents: Growing Up, Speaking Out.* New York: Routledge, 1998.

61 Ernest Wolf, *Treating the Self: Elements of Clinical Self Psychology.* New York: Guilford, 1988: 78.

62 On this point, see Jerald G. Bachman, Patrick M. O'Malley, and Jerome Johnston, *Adolescence to Adulthood : Change and Stability in the Lives of Young Men.* Ann Arbor, MI: Institute for Social Research, University of Michigan, 1987.

63 On this point, see Jane Kroger, *Identity in Adolescence: The Balance Between Self and Other.* New York: Routledge, 1989.

64 William Pollock, *Real Boys,* op. cit.; Paul Smith (Editor), *Boys: Masculinities in Contemporary Culture.* Boulder: Westview, 1996.

65 Erich Fromm, *Escape from Freedom,* op. cit.

66 See J. Broughton, "The Cognitive Developmental Theory of Adolescent Self and Identity." In B. Lee and G. Noam (Editors), *Developmental Approaches to Self.* New York: Plenum, 1983.

67 See Alice Miller, *The Drama of the Gifted Child,* translated by Ruth Ward. New York: Basic Books, 1981.

68 See Lynne Layton and Barbara Ann Schapiro (Editors), *Narcissism and the Text: Studies in Literature and the Psychology of Self.* New York: New York University Press, 1986.

69 Heinz Kohut, *Search for the Self,* volume 2, Paul Ornstein (Editor). New York: International Universities Press, 1978.

70 See James Marcia, "Representational Thought in Ego Identity, Psychotherapy, and Psychosocial Developmental Theory." In I. E. Sigel (Editor), *Development of Mental Representation: Theories and Applications.* Mahwah, NJ: Erlbaum, 1999: 391–414; John Coleman and Leo Hendry, *The Nature of Adolescence.* New York: Routledge, 1990; Israel Rosenfield, "Memory and Identity." *New Literary History.* Winter 1995: 197–204; J. Wellwood, "Intimate Relationship as Path." *Journal of Transpersonal Psychology, 22,* 1, 1990: 51–58; and

E. Berscheid, M .Snyder, and A. M. Omoto, "Issues in Studying Close Relationships." In C. Hendrick (Editor), *Close Relationships*. Newbury Park, CA: Sage, 1989.

71   Erik H. Erikson, *Childhood and Society*. New York: Norton, 1950: 130.

Chapter 4

The Construction of Recognition and Attachment

The Role of Recognition

Given the evolution of popular culture in America, it is little wonder that so many adolescents would wish to be Michael Jordan or Bill Cosby, Miss America, Celine Dion, Tiger Woods, or any number of rock stars, actors, or athletes. Not only do these people represent the culture's elite—defined these days as the rich and famous—but their very being substitutes for the adolescent's internally formulated conception of an ideal self. Increasingly one hears adolescents coming forth with a peculiar new response to that age-old question: "What do you want to be when you grow up?" The young person knows well the answer to this one. "I want to be a star!" Adolescents and adults alike are performing artists as well as audiences in what Neal Gabler calls "The Republic of Entertainment" in America.[1]

While much of adolescent hero worship seems normal enough, some of it is a manifestation of distraction. Throughout this discussion, we will be considering the manner in which adolescents' attention is not only drawn away or diverted but the manner in which their sense of self is being drawn away or diverted, leading them to define themselves in distracted forms.

It appears as if actors, rock stars, and popular culture figures in general become for the adolescent living representations if not of the world, then of the self. In effect, they become embodiments of the entire culture, and eventually, because of the felt sense of proximity to stars made possible by technological equipment, the culture for the adolescent becomes one in which celebrity, stardom, recognition, status, wealth, power, and visibility become significant ingredients of the adolescent's ego and emerging identity. It is not that adolescents imagine that police officers and lawyers, doctors, journalists, and even ex-convicts are identical to the ones seen on television. More precisely, the real and pretend lives of stars and athletes come to form a part of the adolescent's sense of himself or herself as well as his or her (distracted) reading and ultimate rendering of the world. And somewhere along the way, the same media that create stardom have designated these people to be role models.

Psychoanalysts might allege that stars now fill the empty spaces in the adolescent's developing ego. Stardom oozes its way into the conscious and unconscious worlds of adolescents, along with the star's (imagined) manner of dealing with emptiness and loneliness, life and death. The boundaries, as Gabler noted, between the real and the unreal have almost completely faded away just as they do in cases of family enmeshment. Faced with an emptiness that the adolescent may not be able to articulate, he or she has at least two psychic roads to travel: Turn *to* the celebrity's life, and the real or imagined role played by that celebrity, or turn *into* the celebrity. Either way, distraction triumphs.

Why might a culture's adolescents be prone to this emptiness and so vulnerable to this diversion and to being drawn away from one's own self? Why are so many adolescents seemingly able to fill their psychic emptiness, indeed shape their psyches, with the distraction provided them by "larger-than-life" celebrities? Why should anyone be unaware or even afraid of the real activities, mysteries, and the genuineness of "life-size" beings? Although these processes presumably unravel in the unconscious, we still may ask, why settle for the substitute, the compensatory, fantasized, or *ersatz* existence? Why might an adolescent elevate a celebrity to the level of icon and ideal self? Why are all these well-known people called role models? And why, furthermore, would an adolescent establish such intense attachments between untouchable star and immediately touchable being? Gabler answered many of these questions.

> The celebrity archetype addressed social fears extant in modern America: the anxiety of losing one's identity or never finding it at all; the terror of having too little amid plenty; the dread of anonymity; the awful suspicion that some were blessed and some were not and that most Americans were among the latter.[2]

Is it possible that adolescents absorb celebrities and follow their every step as if it were their own, because in a sense it is their own? Have some adolescents turned their lives over to these artificial demigods? And might the reason for this be found in the concept of attachment?[3]

To answer these questions, we hunt through child developmental processes for fundamental aspects of attachment and recognition that continue to live in the mind fields of adolescents. In recognition, for example, we literally re-cognize something or someone; we know again this something or someone, readjusting not only our sights on the object but now reestablishing it in a familiar if not intimate context. As Aristotle suggested when he wrote that in learning material is called up in us, so too does the action of recognition require something being called up in us.

Joan Erikson believed the birth of recognition occurred in those moments when the mother looks down at her baby. Psychologist Jerome Kagan[4] later would document that this "I know you" phenomenon requires the mother to be looking full face at the child, something Erikson knew instinctively. Seeing this full face peering down at them, most babies not only smile, their bodies may convulse slightly. Their little arms and legs jump off the mattress as they reveal patterns of primitive recognition. In that instant, they are as excited to see and be seen as adolescents in a school corridor, at a prom, ball game, mall, or on television.

Recognition has another and more familiar meaning: It suggests superior status. One gains recognition, which is to say we place a person on some higher level, perhaps on a pedestal. Recognition in this context is granted and received, thereby connoting a social status. Personal and social recognitions constantly are taking place for the adolescent. Young people will be seen, then re-seen in new contexts, and in this way will end up being something different than what they were moments before. The moment of recognition, therefore, not only marks a notable moment on an old clock, it launches a new clock as well, thereby confirming one's old being while simultaneously launching a new being. In this way, recognition becomes central to Erik Erikson's[5] definition of adolescent identity: A sense of sameness coupled with the awareness of constant change.

Adolescents reveal another aspect of recognition, one appearing in their complicated ambivalence about being seen or noticed. One often hears adolescents claiming to enjoy looking at people, but isn't it the case that being seen is the hidden reward of people watching? Students walk through school unaware of what is making them self-conscious. Is it that they are looking at someone and fearing that they may be caught in the act? Are they perhaps fearing (or wishing) that a certain someone will look at them, and then, awesome, know their name? Many young people offer complicated reasons for not liking their names, and although some of these accounts bespeak their struggles with parents, family origins, identity formation,[6] esteem, and heaven knows what else, they reveal as well a foundation of recognition. When someone knows my name, I am recognized.

The great teacher recognizes her students and not merely their work or efforts. She hugs and honors them, makes them feel special, and, most especially, respects them.[7] By their early teenage years, children barely are able to articulate what they may be feeling about this respect-laden recognition. But at eight or nine and then again in high school, there is no holding back the young person. Adolescents are more than quick to recount the joy they feel in having a teacher recognize them. Part of the privilege of being an adolescent is being able to grumble, "It doesn't matter." Another part is being able to tell one's parents how much one really *loves* Mrs. Cottle.

When teachers allow adolescents to look deep within themselves and let go of some of those internally protected secrets, a form of recognition takes place. Adolescents are performing the act of re-knowing themselves, which provides them yet another opportunity to develop new feelings about themselves or at least establish new and transitory selves, all part of the formation of identity.[8] Tomorrow, when more of one's inner world, one's inner caves will be explored, the process of re-knowing, recognition, and, we hope, re-loving oneself commences all over again.

In this regard, amusement and entertainment and, hence, actors and rock stars do not carry the day. Partly, they fail because too little of the self is explored, too little resembling recognition has taken place. The adolescent is only being diverted or having something evoked that is quickly dismissed in favor of yet another diversion. Albeit pleasurable when it is not alienating, diversion rarely provides the adolescent paths to genuine and joyful recognition of self because self-reflection has been ignored. Missing here is that rare opportunity not only to rediscover, re-contextualize or re-create oneself, something adolescents constantly are doing, but the possibility of falling in love with oneself, ideally, all over again. Good families, good schools and communities, good teachers, coaches, and friends allow adolescents the opportunity to fall in love with themselves or at very least respect themselves.

Psychoanalysts call this the evolution of healthy narcissism.[9] When young persons learn that nothing about them is lovable, nothing they do allows them to generate a love or respect for themselves or, in Erikson's[10] terms, feel fidelity towards themselves, then ultimately one suspects their life becomes a joyless pursuit of empty tasks or accomplishments. If, on the other hand, adolescents are able to examine their own image in that mythic pool and not fall in and drown, as was the fate of poor Narcissus, but decide instead that the image is lovable, they are on their way to self-recognition and, one hopes, joyous recognition and a supreme sense of fidelity to others.[11]

What's in a (young person's) name? Nothing less than the commencement of the capacity to be recognized. "How'd you know my name?" one student asks another, partly bemused, partly curious, but mainly enthralled.[12] Why collect an autograph or have a friend write in one's yearbook if a handwritten name is not a slice of human recognition. The adolescent is now in touch with someone, which means he or she has been touched by the author of the autograph, the autograph symbolizing a personal connection between two people, at least the adolescent thinks that it is, and joyous recognition spills all over it.[13]

The Recognition of Celebrities

By definition, celebrity worship is a recognition of so-called larger-than-life people. (And if all these people are larger than life, then by definition, adolescents are smaller than life, which means that they remain in some sense, an audience of unrecognized, unfulfilled, undeveloped people, enslaved by the rules of appetite, sense, caprice, and immediate circumstance.[14]) It is an action, moreover, that celebrities have refined and perpetuated as they engage in their frequent award ceremonies in which they publicly recognize themselves, ceremonies, moreover, that most adolescents adore precisely because they have been conceived and produced for adolescents, the prime consumers of celebrity.

Traditionally, nearly all cultures have ceremonies and rituals in which public recognition is granted to certain people, typically the culture's elder citizens. A person is publicly recognized simply for having made it to an age that the culture deems venerable. Some cultures actually find the wisdom of their elderly citizens valuable. Americans, however, do not subscribe to this. Fearing death and cursing aging, we pay lip service to the wisdom of our elders but then proceed to worship (and simultaneously resent) the young and youthful behavior.[15] Perhaps we are too impatient (or too unself-reflective) to wait for people to grow old before granting them recognition. Or perhaps we need to experience change so often in our lives—what has come to be called reinventing ourselves—we are willing to recognize anyone able to give the present moment a special sparkle, be that person a child or adult. We are far more excited by Oscar winners than Nobel Prize winners.

To study closely those to whom adolescents grant special recognition is to learn the sorts of personalities our culture first manufactures, then values, and finally imposes on the young. We love, for example, independent, autonomous, powerful, and wealthy people. In fact, we have become so worshipful of independence and autonomy, we forget or overlook the fact that each of us is utterly dependent on myriad people and institutions for our survival. Nonetheless, we bestow recognition on the "totally independent" person who appears to "have it all." Too regularly, adolescents indiscriminately digest this message.

More intriguing is the idea that recognition may become its own reward; we even honor outrageous people merely because we're so eager, apparently, to grant recognition to anyone who can make a name for himself or herself. As someone remarked, some people are famous merely for being famous. We find nothing wrong in granting recognition to people we dislike. The media may scorn a public figure, but that person's recognition factor only increases. The name of the Milwaukee mass murderer is better known to adolescents than most all members of the president's Cabinet, and Charles Manson is still known to more young people than the beautiful young actress he murdered. That we even speak of something called a *recognition factor* testifies to the proposition that recognition looms as important if not more important than the accomplishment or deed that brought recognition in the first place. This too, is taught to adolescents. As long as recognition is granted to people, as long as the culture celebrates these people being seen, heard, and known, it doesn't seem to matter whether the culture as a whole approves of these people or even likes them.

In granting recognition, moreover, we honor the product of a person more than the person or perhaps the construct (ours or theirs) of the person more than the person. This too, becomes an important message heard by adolescents. Our country honors fame more than effort; this is precisely what the culture teaches adolescents they should receive for their efforts. Some people spend their lifetime seeking recognition, a search typically begun in adolescence; it seems the only thing they desire. In contemporary America, we have fashioned all sorts of ways to grant these people the recognition they crave.[16] It cannot come as a surprise therefore, that many adolescents would aspire to stardom, whatever that term means, with only minimal thought given to how this stardom might be achieved or what costs might accompany it. In contemporary culture, recognition is superior, albeit a distracted goal, to reputation. It's not enough that our parents gave us our name; now we must "make" something of it.

In a world of (name) recognition, adolescents learn, a person's character no longer need refer to anything of substance nor any special moral quality. America's new notion of character, not that it enjoys the same status as celebrity, involves what sociologist C. Wright Mills called "emotional morality."[17] If enough people have sufficiently strong feelings about someone, like the football or field hockey captain, that someone may be bound for recognition, even stardom. Emotional morality also helps us understand why adolescents find so many people so utterly charismatic but only for short periods of time,[18] and why they speak of people "giving off vibes." If the adolescent feels something, culture teaches, it must be real, and it must be honored; it's called, "going with your gut." As long as the adolescent feels something about someone, he or she needs no further rational or reasoned proof of the person's value.

In olden days when we spoke of enduring heroes, recognition came to be focused not only on how persons seemed to be but on their contribution to the culture or their definition of living. Now, however, recognition focuses on the public persona, the personality, the entertaining character, the star. Public opinions, fads, marketable commodities, fashions, and a momentous public relations machinery shape what adolescents presently call "personalities" as well as their perceptions of them. We have even labeled an entire occupation "television personalities." Saying nothing about what these people actually do, the term suggests that their function is less significant than the recognition and personality attributes they are able to achieve by dint of their presence on the screen. Adolescents speak, furthermore, of the media influencing their lives, but no one is perfectly certain of who or what "the media" are, or how, precisely, "they" shape or define the adolescent. In the end, however, none of this seems to matter, for many young persons just keep on hunting for the latest personality, celebrity, star, icon or "living legend," an apt term at that.

A fascinating aspect of those to whom adolescents grant recognition—the so-called "recognizenti"—is the ostensibly changeable nature of their personalities. More than flexible, malleable, or labile people, they appear almost egoless. In their desire, presumably, to grant recognition to certain people, adolescents have come to treasure those personalities who can fill any role, assume any position, or change themselves into almost anything they wish them to be, no matter how inconsistent, contradictory, or outrageous their actions. It is almost as though the personalities adolescents cherish most personify the roles listed in an actor's credits.

As a result, the power of the person is the power of his or her personality. Indeed, the young often appear to deal more in "inter-personality relations" than in interpersonal relations. In a visual world, moreover, personalities require a public response and, in the case of celebrities, special rights and status. The powerful personality earns money by dint of the force of his or her personality and has the "right" to skirt normal social conventions and laws, the ideal situation in the minds of some adolescents. To be granted recognition therefore, is to be rewarded a special status and morality all one's own, often by dint of little more than one's personality or persona. Ours is often perceived to be a culture, in other words, that operates much in the manner of the popularity contests inherent in high school interactions. Come to think of it, much of popular culture seems to operate as if it were little more than an extension of high school, something else, one suspects, adolescents have discovered.

It is hardly surprising that many adolescents no longer embrace genuine heroes who have done something truly valuable, such as Nelson Mandela and Martin Luther King. Men like these pale in the world of rock stars, actors, and athletes. Little wonder too, that many people feel entitled to recognition merely because circumstances or gestures have made them famous. Adolescents look to personal acts, personal products, personal politics, personal endorsements, personal experiences and recognition as proof of the successful life. The personality-driven life, the young have also learned, warrants the highest remuneration.

However harmless this recent evolution may seem, eventually it leaves many adolescents unhappy and spiritually barren. For one thing, there cannot possibly be sufficient public recognition to satisfy each new facet of one's personality. For another, adolescents appear not to linger with any one facet of their personality for a long time. Even worse, a culture that grants recognition to people merely because of their personalities or views recognition as its own reward and expects its young to do the same will begin to see large-scale erosion of its most important institutions, values, and moral precepts, something that will directly affect young people. Indeed, the erosion has begun to occur.

Adolescents often become unable to discern realities because the so-called "truth tellers" earn their credentials not through the acquisition of knowledge but through visibility alone, which, in turn, translates into recognition, which, in turn, translates into likeability and popularity, which, in turn, translate into credibility, which, in turn, translates into knowledge, expertise, and authority. It is often not the correct or thoughtful response we crave but rather the familiar, palatable, or pleasant one as stated by a familiar, palatable, and pleasant personality, a phenomenon all too familiar to the young. Successful presidential candidates, as Gabler observed,[19] run the risk of presenting themselves to the public almost as actors auditioning for a game show host or variety show emcee. Which, of course, transforms the rest of us, young and old alike, into the audience.

Given what we have learned from popular culture and the dissemination of information, it is evident that if adolescents wish to learn something, they will turn more frequently to the Internet, television, and commercial films than to books and documentaries, more frequently to entertainment media, as Postman[20] suggested, than to traditional educational media. They will turn, moreover, to the world of celebrities to learn about "relevant" social and political matters, as, for example, the material presented in so-called "movies of the week," which explore psychological trauma and social ills.

In the end, however, the celebrity factor often destroys the search for knowledge precisely because it supplies safe distraction. However enlightening the presentation, a safety valve constituted of celebrity and fiction prevents us from authentic experience. This phenomenon rarely takes place for adolescents when they view, for example, documentary footage of concentration camps. The grainy black and white images seem unrelenting not only because of the horror documented but because the person has nothing to insert as a protective veil; these images truly seem real. No longer can adolescents tell themselves that they are looking at actors performing make-believe. When watching such documentaries, adolescents have nothing to shield them from their own raw vulnerability (and self-reflection), a state that represents the quintessential opposite of as well as possible antidote to distraction.

Apparently what adolescents crave in the presence of certain realities is a sort of fictionalized comfort zone of the type that loving and protective parents are meant to provide. I remember when I was young and found myself terrified by a television program, my mother comforted me by doing two things. First, she pretended to be scared, too. More importantly, however, she lessened the terror by reminding me that there were all kinds of lights and cameras and people standing about on the set with the actors. That was the veil I required, the reminder that there was an acceptable cognitive action I could take to alter the state of my consciousness and hence distract myself from the fright of the program, which ironically, was meant to be distracting. Unfortunately, there are no comforting words to utter when viewing Holocaust documentaries.

If fiction and the celebrity factor reveal our distractive approach to certain social problems and personal matters, then adolescents learn as well that financial priorities remain the best indication of the extremes to which the society is willing to go to remain distracted. Adolescents hardly need to be told that an actor's fee for one movie may exceed the annual budget of all the academic departments in their high school. I am not opposed to movies or television programs of this sort. Indeed, in our postliterate entertainment-oriented society—what someone labeled "electronic tribalism"—it is important that Hollywood producers choose significant subjects. Still, the momentary result of these products for the adolescent often is pure distraction. Many adolescents will settle for a raised consciousness and let it stand as knowledge, perhaps even social action as well. An actor or rock star may be glorified, but America will not necessarily move in the direction of valuing knowledge either for its practical uses or its own sake.

It is neither truth nor knowledge that we ask the adolescent to consider nor even reasonable facsimiles of them. Unwittingly perhaps, we distract adolescents from knowledge that can be gained only by personal discovery and disciplined study.[21] We often provide them packages of information that, although emotionally and intellectually comfortable as well as entertaining, do not necessarily make it possible for adolescents to understand their own lives or the lives of other people. The package, in other words, is all and all. What matters in these instances of *faux* education, is the satisfaction of a sense or an appetite.

If actors turn into experts, then genuine experts run the risk of turning into actors or imagine they must "play the part" of experts. All too many teachers discover that their courses tend to be evaluated by students on the basis of performance and entertainment values rather than the courses' intellectual content and didactic strategies. If they are not careful, teachers, ministers, and physicians, men and women with the best intentions, run the risk of falling into the entertainment/performance/celebrity trap, or believe they are being pushed in that direction.

The notion of performance is especially relevant to the personal and educational experiences of adolescents. It is one thing for a teacher to make academic fare understandable but not overly simplistic or free of any demands for serious thought and self-reflection.[22] The model for the presentation of the material suddenly becomes popular (visual) culture. Like the celebrities themselves, the material and more precisely its presentation, must appear palatable, if not outright pleasant. Valuable criteria to be certain, they hardly represent the criteria of scholarship. Think, for example, of the hours adolescents spend on their computers developing PowerPoint graphics for their classroom presentations. Can a classroom even be considered "up to date" if it doesn't contain a television set,

VCR, and access to the Internet! Who cares if the great books, however defined, are not being read?

The Role of Identification and Attachment

During childhood, and again during adolescence, young people hunger for attachment, a process David Ausubel calls resatellization,[23] or seek a form of play or work that might ward off the pain of loss and at the same time offer them a taste of feeling genuinely competent. They tend to find not only symbolic representations to fill the emptiness but models with which they identify. Early in life, when children identify with someone or something, in fact they render themselves psychologically identical with that someone or something and hence make these objects their own. It may even be that such identifications constitute the self.[24]

Not surprisingly, we discover the same Latin root (*idem*, the same) of three important words: Identification, identity and identical.[25] Thus, when I identify with you, I become identical to you, and you are now a part of my identity. In this manner, adolescents come to be comprised of connections, relationships, all of which live in their minds, something Heidegger noted when he wrote that it is not so much that we *have* relationships as much as we *are* relationships.[26] Again, the process begins with attachment, tangible or imagined. The models with whom adolescents identify, moreover, reveal something about the emptiness they feel and now seek to fill.[27]

Students of child behavior are familiar with these notions. Every day, for example, they observe that when playing baseball, children almost instinctively pretend to be some famous athlete who, by definition of the identification, becomes a heroic figure. In this context, the hero is not precisely someone the child wishes to be like but someone deep in his or her private sense of self, anyway, the child already is. And all the children of the world may identify with the same hero. For when human imagination and the world of instincts are simultaneously at work and play, when genuine identification and attachments and with them identities are taking root, there is plenty of (psychic) room for everyone. Identification knows no exclusivity, just as it knows no boundaries, especially between the self and the model.[28]

Identifications are normal, predictable, and mysterious dynamics of the child's and adolescent's ego development. Still, some young people reveal such intense attachments to popular culture's celebrities, it makes one wonder whether these people have any genuine attachments to anyone, including themselves, in their real, nondistracted lives. One imagines that every one of the adolescent's wishes may be fulfilled, every request for personal confirmation granted, through his or her identifications with the heroes of the moment.

Let me admit to my biases here. Because I love certain sports teams, I become so nervous watching them that I barely enjoy the game. My own childish behavior clearly bespeaks classical identification processes. Yet it must be a broken coupling somewhere or perhaps the continuing experience of a broken coupling that would make adolescents turn their lives over to cultural demigods. Something (or someone) momentous must have fallen away in order for them, through distractive devices, to devote their lives to following the daily and nightly routines of rock stars, actors, and athletes. The intensity of the feelings shown and the identifications made with these celebrities are frequently somewhat frightening; the celebrities are often frightened as well. The attachments bespeak what psychoanalysts call *cathexis*,[29] the instinctual investment one makes in objects such as one's father's watch or mother's brooch or even human stars. Observing some young people as they connect with their heroes makes one believe that in the concept of attachment one discovers a life (defining) force, or more simply that it is the reason some adolescents choose to remain alive. Distraction in the form of celebrity worship or investment in teams may well operate in a life-saving manner, albeit a somewhat inauthentic one.

To find the psychological essence of attachment, we look to the opposite concept: namely, the feelings associated with detachment or decoupling. Although distractions may be pleasing, they rarely yield genuine peace and serenity. Games, concerts, and movies bring exciting and necessary joys to our lives, but the proof that they fail to satisfy genuine hunger or ease the hurt in certain people is confirmed by the speed with which these people return again and again to the same distractions. No matter how intensely adolescents invest in the attraction, be it an event or a person, they continue to remain decoupled from something or someone. They cannot get close enough.

Consider teenage girls screaming at the stage at a rock concert. Many of them hyperventilate; others properly may be called hysterical. Tears roll down their faces as they scream and reach up their arms toward the performers as if they wished to be lifted up and embraced. In observing these young women, one feels nothing could bring them comfort other than their being physically entwined with the young men they clearly worship. The scene moves well beyond what Erikson[30] referred to as normal identification, an essential component in the formation of identity. It spills over to what Erikson called fanaticism, a developmental hitch or setback.

In writing about the adolescent stage of development, Erikson theorized that the fundamental conflict confronting people was the matter of "identity cohesion," the integrated personality as it were, versus "role confusion," typically related to sense of self, career, and ideology. Successful resolution of the conflict, Erikson asserted, led to what he called the "basic strength" of fidelity.[31] A maldevelopment at this time, conversely, led to fanatic behavior. Lost in the search for oneself, in other words, the young person becomes fanatically involved with another person, an icon, a celebrity, even an ideology.

The young women at the rock concert would call the spectacle awesome, but something causes one to sense a desperation about these people. One sees in these faces too often the expressions not of ecstasy but of despair, stemming perhaps from loss, the severing of relationships, or the need to reconnect somewhere or to someone. One imagines these audience members—most concertgoers are not affected to this degree—have taken the unfinished emotional business from home, school, or intimate relationships and deposited it at the feet of stars. Some imagine, perhaps, that sexuality will solve all concerns of intimacy and thereby erase all previous decouplings. We know this to be true of many unwed teenage mothers who look to their babies, not their families or boyfriends, as the source of human connection, intimacy, and love.[32] For other rock star worshippers, brief contact, a mere touch would send them into a veritable swoon. Yet, as they cluster together in this wailing mob, each imagining herself to be the one and only lover of this guitarist or that drummer, one also imagines them standing utterly alone and in mourning.

Entertainment impresarios thrive on the knowledge that young people will see a movie or rock band many times—the young always keep a precise count. There are foods and personal images, what John Dewey called appetites,[33] of which some adolescents cannot get enough and to which they cannot attach themselves securely enough. Yet adolescents' attachment to celebrities, the need to see the same rock band ten times in eleven days, and the incorporation of celebrities, music, and games into their psyches, reveal an abiding dependence on a multibillion dollar (distraction) industry. In psychological terms, they reveal something of the ways in which adolescents attach themselves to someone who will, as they say, take them away from all this.

When celebrities speak, adolescents tend to listen. Corporations invest millions of dollars in magazines and newspapers to report daily the words and deeds, real and manufactured, of celebrities because they know consumers, many of them young, will spend millions of dollars to read the gossip. Americans, who once believed anything if told by people with an accent but who then grew sophisticated and decided to trust people with the word "Doctor" (or retired General) before their name, now want life explained to them by the rich and the famous, and that includes athletes who, truth be told, are often held in the highest ambivalence.

At the same time that some adolescents attach themselves to athletes, others express their resentment and envy of these same athletes. The culture provides athletes a unique ride; it starts before they reach their teens and lasts until the moment (we decide) their bodies have failed them, and us too apparently, whereupon we drop them as if they were hot rocks. Like school children with notes from their mothers, athletes may be excused from classroom obligations and any variety of human responsibility as long as they perform on the field. As long as athletes are successful, adolescents and adults alike tolerate their inevitable human flaws.

When athletes perform admirably, they are often more important to some adolescents than anything else happening in the country or, presumably, in their own lives. It is not hyperbole to suggest that athletes distract some adolescents from their own mortality. Their feats, after all, seem superhuman. The young even use that word ("super") to describe them. When athletes fade or their prowess recedes, adolescents latch on to newer, which usually means younger ones. There is always a new super human simmering somewhere on America's playing fields, basketball courts, and ice rinks. Playing before screaming fans and urged on by scoreboard messages reading, "MAKE NOISE!," athletes possess the mysterious power to quiet the terror of death. When our team has lost and our children appear teary eyed, we console them with the words, "It's hardly life or death; it's only a game." Assured that the children seem comforted, we wonder whether they know we have lied.

Given this extraordinary psychological investment in athletes, along with the financial and entertainment value of their talent, it hardly surprises anyone that on average they earn more than anyone else in the culture. They have become our number-one priority, and we, adolescents and adults alike, their (psychological) owners, accede to their every demand, while somewhere in our minds remaining utterly mystified by the dramatic illusions we and they together perform.

To label student athletes unintelligent and emotionally immature, as is done on occasion even by their fellow students, excuses our own misplaced idolatry and eases our ambivalence. Diagnosing athletes as mentally unstable or unintelligent may represent good old-fashioned elitism or, in some instances, racism.[34] Yet there is another identificatory matter to contend with as well.

It must confuse some adolescents and adults that allegedly illiterate poor young men should attain such public status and income. It also must distress some young people to know that immoral behavior in schools occasionally is overlooked so that teams may field the best athletic products available. So, as the young revere, they may resent; as they fawn, they may derogate. In a distracted manner, this is the way we deal with our complicated identification with and recognition of people about whom we hold deeply complex feelings. And what, one wonders, do adolescents make of those coaches who stalk the sidelines of athletic events, barely maintaining their sanity.

For adolescents, athletes are also important models in the sense that they utilize one of many human intelligences, in this case what Howard Gardner[35] called kinesthetic intelligence. The great ones, adolescents learn, whose performances are witnessed by the public, possess a God-given talent that must be nurtured and disciplined. Athletes are no different from the outstanding pianists, painters, dancers, and mathematicians who, also blessed with gifts, work to hone these gifts or at least care for them as one would valuable pieces of art. Throwing a baseball with speed and accuracy, the maturing young person recognizes, involves a complex and perfectly noble form of intelligence. Fair enough, yet what adolescents often react to is the fact that this form of intelligence should be ranked more valuable than the ability to paint "The Nightwatch," compose *Parsifal*, or write *Buddenbrooks*.

The games and their players take adolescents away from their lives. Even high school sports become show business and, hence, turn into distraction. When work isn't play for the adolescent, it becomes unbearable. To recast a line from Bertolt Brecht: He who is cheering (Brecht said "laughing") obviously hasn't heard the horrible news.

Young people often cannot meet athletes on a human scale. They may tremble upon meeting these rare specimens and react with surprise that athletes possess the same traits they do. Some adolescents perceive athletes as bigger, stronger, and more beautiful than themselves or anyone else they have ever observed; they may place athletes on pedestals.

Conversely, when athletes fail them, they may wish to club athletes with the very same pedestals. The disappearance of heroes has been greatly exaggerated; they are found in locker rooms everywhere.

The country is about making money; this too, adolescents know and seem to accept. Life-size values have been trampled by larger-than-life-size values, and no one personifies the latter more than athletes. Their stock has become part of the adolescent's spiritual and psychological portfolio; their triumphs and breakdowns, moments of perfection and premature departures become ours as well. Through some magical identification, we seek to own them, transform them into ourselves.

Regularly, athletes appear to assume greater role modeling power for a child than the child's own parent. That an athlete probably cannot influence a young person except in matters of spending is a matter we rarely confront. It just feels better, somehow, imagining that athletes are gods and let it go at that. If their endorsements of products yield windfalls for corporations, why question the (distractive) nature of their power in shaping the psychological lives of the young.

The worship of and identification with athletes as well as the investments of all sorts made in them reveal a great deal about the adolescent's definition of an ideal culture. It is extraordinary to contemplate that on every night of the baseball season, one of America's major league parks will be filled with the same number of fans as there are children in the world who will, that same night, die from malnutrition.

The great athlete of this era must not only perform on the field but, in addition, be able to satisfy an essential commandment of popular culture: Thou shall not bore! This point is crucial for understanding adolescents' involvement with celebrities and the world of entertainment generally. For whatever the reasons, many young people find their lives to be utterly boring. Athlete worshippers must constantly find ways to kill the hours before the next sporting event. Ironically, it is in these times of deprivation, denial, and loss that adolescents move closer to discovering the unalloyed truths of their existence, as for example, that under some circumstances, they may break down. In American culture, however, which bases so much of its economic power on the art of distraction, adolescents find themselves pushed back from the precipice of personal discovery. It is as though they are being taught they must never allow the suspension of disbelief to dissipate, which, in part, is what the worshipping of celebrity is all about.

Adolescents continue to keep an eye on the "grand personalities"; their faces and behavior are studied and critiqued by the young, themselves wondering whether they can ever be content pursuing the culture's less visible and hence less remarkable careers as "faceless" workers. It is "a time," Tom Engelhardt wrote, "when democracy seems to have increasingly little to do with ordinary life."[36]

A public relations image-consciousness culture seduces the young into watching people they deem magical. Without even recognizing their own exquisite personal transformations, adolescents come to believe in the new realities created by a distracted culture. Dewey was right: When one's senses, appetites and reactions to immediate circumstances dominate one's thinking (or lack of it), one slides dangerously far away from self-reflection and self-awareness, two qualities that actually characterize adolescent development.[37]

All of this makes me think that perhaps television cameras should pan on audiences at sporting events more frequently. And when they do, rather than wave hysterically when *we* become the image on the tube, we might do better to stand perfectly still and examine the faces and souls the cameras record.

The Glory of Revelation

Whether they are aware of it or not, interviewers of celebrities often find themselves caught in an interesting intellectual dilemma. Interviewers may claim they want to explore the *inner* world of the celebrity, but more often it is the *private* world that is sought and gobbled up by a hungry public. The distinction has relevance for the development of adolescents. The private world refers to the stuff we know about ourselves, our families and friends and would perhaps just as soon not talk about; it is what we call gossip. More importantly, it represents what a distracted culture craves as much as any form of information. Adolescents recognize that people wish to know about their comings and goings, partly because others genuinely care about them and partly in order that others may better know how to assess themselves in relation to one another.[38]

The point is summarized, indeed it was predicted by the poet W. H. Auden years ago. "Reason," Auden prophesied, "will be replaced by revelation."[39] It is true; ultimate knowledge presently is synonymous with revelation, which, in turn, is assessed purely in terms of its believability. Again, it is not the message that is evaluated, but the messenger, which, in part, accounts for the heightened significance of celebrities. The revelation of private worlds has become a powerful commodity in a distracted world. Consider as illustration, this passage from a *Newsweek* review by Ellis Cose of Jill Nelson's book *Volunteer Slavery: My Authentic Negro Experience*:[40]

> . . . Nelson's memoir is as unsparing of herself as of other (Washington) *Post* personalities. It is so unsparing that at points Nelson comes across as a vengeful, self-indulgent, sex-obsessed neurotic. Yet the same brutal honesty allows her figuratively to strip herself naked also makes her *credible* (emphasis added).

One should be more charitable here. Any conversation, be it on television or in the school cafeteria, offers the possibility of learning something and having feelings evoked. One way into the truth of our own lives is to first hear it and recognize it in the life of another person. In this regard, television performs an extraordinary service by allowing us to approach our own lives through a sort of side door—the personal accounts of other people. We hear and see celebrities, but we don't (have to) meet them or, for that matter, ourselves. Television exposes us to them but, at the same time, keeps us immune from them. We never leave our living room; they never truly enter it. Able to walk away from an experience that only appears intimate, we are freed of certain psychological constraints by not being direct participants, which may distract us or, conversely, open that side door into ourselves.

For adolescents, the danger of all this is the tightrope walk they must master between intimacy and identification, gossip and genuine inquiry, and information as titillation or enlightenment. The danger, as Postman, Gabler,[41] and others have pointed out, is the glamorously triumphant exposition of celebrities precisely because their very being signifies larger-than-life success. Adolescents must separate the celebrity from their own narratives if they are to remain undistracted by that celebrity's story. Would they even consider the words had they not been uttered by the celebrity? Do adolescents, furthermore, fantasize that their own inner explorations will transpire as they did for the celebrity and yield them not merely insight but insight wrapped in fame? Do adolescents identify with the story being told, the story's teller, or both?

Although not always able to recognize it, adolescents often are confused by their heroes' confessions of pain and tribulation. It helps, perhaps, to learn that one's idol has struggled as one presently does, but how is the adolescent to know whether fame and public recognition ultimately have caused or alleviated the problem? In the adolescent's mind, grand success may solve just about everything, exactly as a certain American ethic would have us believe. Yet if this is true, the young person reasons, what happens to me if I don't become famous? Will I stay troubled forever? Adolescents know that Americans are not so much interested in so-called human interest stories as they are fascinated by *super*human interest stories.

The press, too, becomes confused by its periodic inability or outright refusal to differentiate private worlds from inner ones, and hence gossip from news. If an event or statement involves a celebrity, then inquiring minds, as they say, want to know. The scenario hardly changes even when a situation takes on precarious social and political overtones. A case in point is what has come to be called "outing," a process wherein homosexuals choosing to keep their sexual orientations private are publicly named as they are in many high schools. With all the ideological rhetoric and alleged political justification of this action, the fact remains that, at some level, outing is nothing more than invasive gossip. In the inevitable pursuit of distraction, the cry goes out that outing is legitimate. How ironic, as Roger Rosenblatt pointed out,[42] that gays should reserve the right to private choice but not, according to the "outists," private lives.

What is it then about the lives of adolescents that makes celebrity gossip part of their blood? Some observers of the culture claim adolescents have no heroes; others say that heroes are people who, upon reaching celebrity status, are brought to ruin through self-imposed or externally caused tragedy. Is this perhaps why some adolescents secretly delight in the tragic news about celebrities? Are celebrities weeping more appealing—that is, human—than celebrities laughing? Do some young people dwell on their lavish life styles, the houses, boats, planes, and parties because these are the standards and practices of American success? Or do some adolescents, out of their own ambivalence about or concern for their own personal, social, and financial success, maintain some perverse need to witness the scandals, sadness, and ultimate downfalls of celebrities? Is this the young person's expression of fear that he or she may not achieve success?

The celebrity's tragedy remains the grand leavener. Supposedly tragedy renders everyone equal and human, but tragedy does more: It transforms the have's into the have-not's. For a while adolescents may be content but only until the next celebrity reveals his or her own rich and famous lifestyle, about which the young are both admiring and envious. In their own minds at least, the famous person has both set the new standard and, in their fantasies, replaced the old standards.

Civility rests on constraint. In all of our significant relationships, we are forever capable of hurting if not destroying people by divulging what we know about them. The social psychologist Georg Simmel once remarked that relationships are predicated on what I know about you that you don't know I know, and what you know about me that I don't know you know. Although his words could very well launch a vaudeville routine, they are true. Palpable human boundaries permit relationships to flourish.[43] Demarcations of the private from the public, the intimate from the sexual, the discrete from the indiscreet, sustain friendship, civility, and probably, too, civilization.[44] Boundaries also edge us away from our distracted existence.

Lives are not necessarily meant to be open books, even when these books are those of famous people. It is not incumbent upon anyone, young or old, to open their life books; everyone is perfectly free to kiss without telling. Nor is it proper for others to pry us open—yet another lesson ideally learned during adolescence. Psychoanalysis reveals the normal process of resisting opening oneself to another even in psychotherapy, when revelation would seem to be the central purpose of the endeavor. Some of the most unsuccessful books are the ones in which people tell all. They are rivaled only by those works in which ersatz biographers tear open the unopenable.

The message to the young is complicated: When one opens one's inner world to another, one risks rejection of the self, for revelation brings the self as product or object to another for consideration and validation.[45] In its deepest sense, revelation is not to be employed as fodder for gossip, but for the social confirmation of the self leading to the ultimate consolidation of the ego. Apparently this is best accomplished when one person promises to safeguard forever as a secret the inner world, (the self as object as Kohut[46] might say,) of another person. In other words, consolidation of the self is constructed in the work of intimacy wherein adolescents discover they can exchange, as it were, their inner selves, or at least their ongoing conceptions of their inner selves with another.[47] As Yeats said, it is a time when young people are capable of "Dying each other's life, living each other's death."[48] When this material is publicized, as it is in gossip, the self feels an assault, for in destroying trust and intimacy, gossip threatens the adolescent's hoped-for consolidation of his or her self.

The frequently proffered justification, therefore, that a look at the private world offers us insight into the human condition rings false. The human condition, the self as object seen by itself—surely an act made possible by intimacy—is revealed to adolescents through studied and reflective examination of their *inner* lives and the confrontations of these lives with history, circumstance and luck, or the absence of it. The *pri-*

vate life, conversely, offers adolescents insight primarily into the profitable commodity market of gossip, which, in turn, provides the perfect combination of appetite gratification and appeal to immediate circumstance. Adolescents learn that cheating on a friend is but one form of infidelity. An equally egregious form is to reveal what has been told in confidence. The adolescent would claim that his or her reputation has been harmed, but it is even more grave: The adolescent's grip on his or her self has been threatened.

Healthy persons take charge of their lives or at least know how to solicit help;[49] the healthy society need not invade a citizen's privacy for mere appetite or profit on what passes as news. The social good is at stake along with the health of the individual adolescent ego when anyone makes the decision to retreat from the boundary of decency. Granted, it is frustrating to be close to some titillating territory only to have to stop oneself at an invisible border. The reporter hot on the trail of gossip and unable to step back and question whether this action is appropriate is not unlike the panting teenage boy in the back seat of his parents' car dismissing the protestations and terrors of a young woman. The stories young men tell their friends about what happened on Saturday night, many of them fabricated, are not unlike actual date rape. On and on we go, unheeding the hurt of the innocent, their tears and pleading unable to restrain us.

In genuine intimacy, I draw from inner containers and share it with you, trusting that you will safeguard every bit of the contents.[50] In gossip, I revel in smashing every molecule of that same container, which is the self. Self-imposed constraint ought to remain in working order when human insights, freedoms, and life itself lie in the balance. The human heart must be as carefully protected by society, adolescents learn painfully, as it is by anatomy.

The Power of Role Models

In addressing the matter of certain celebrities as role models for adolescents, we tend to miss a rather important matter: There is no evidence to support the notion that celebrities have much influence on the behavior of young people who otherwise claim to worship these stars. In order to address the issue of the genuine role models of the world, consider one celebrity's predicament in a very precarious moment of his life.

Most readers will recall the boxing match in which Mike Tyson bit off a piece of Evander Holyfield's ear. In the press conference following the fight, Tyson expressed contrition and then, most interestingly, in reflecting on his childhood, said something to the effect that he never had the luxury of schools or, and then he paused, "people" who might have helped him.

It was that word, "people," that stayed with me. The word that should have been forthcoming, of course, is parents. Granted, we have all heard the argument that childhood deprivation cannot be held up as justification for boorish behavior or criminal action. Yet, Tyson was touching upon the matter of bonafide role models,[51] a central concern for adolescents.

Because of the power of television, movies, and the rock stage, anyone whose face is recognizable emerges as a potential role model for the young. Such persons need not be heroic; in truth they rarely are. All they need to be is recognizable, and suddenly they are in the schools advising students not to drop out, drink, get pregnant and to mind their manners, teachers, and parents. I am delighted that busy people with famous faces take the time to, as the expression goes, "give back to the community." I also read the reports and studies of drug and pregnancy programs in America's schools and learn that adolescents don't seem to be swayed by the parade of manufactured role models; adolescents generally are superb detectors of what is genuine.

Never in the history of this country have more famous faces appeared before the children of America's (mainly public) schools (mainly in poorer communities). And never in the history of this country have young people drunk more, taken more drugs, and got pregnant more often, and never have we observed these behaviors starting so early in a young person's life.[52]

In an article entitled "Towards Sustainable Development for American Families," Felton Earls and Mary Carlson introduced an intriguing and provocative definition of family.[53] For these authors, family is defined by the strategies adults and children together employ to deal with nurturance, security, and a sense of comfort with intimacy, a sense that inner selves can be shared and protected.

Three things to be observed here: First, no mention is made of any relationship other than parents and children. Second, the definition implies that children learn to nurture and make their parents feel secure in the same way that adults do with their children. Third, not one word has been uttered about love. The result of successful nurturing, security making and intimacy development—which combined constitute a rather lovely definition of love—is the opportunity for children and adolescents to grow up and engage in enduring relationships, nurture their own partners and children, and in turn feel nurtured by these partners and children.

Here, then, is a genuine definition of role models for adolescents, a far cry from the autograph feasts going on in schools, in which well-intentioned messages are going out to students. As I say, the messages aren't sticking, for messages of this significance have no reason to stick merely because they are uttered by the famous. Adolescents do model themselves after certain people, but something more profound takes place in authentic role modeling: Adolescents learn to identify themselves partly by identifying with (unconsciously becoming identical to) the role model as well as differentiating themselves from that same role model.

In working on the formation of their identities, their genuine inner selves, adolescents are becoming their own people. This is what is meant by the consolidation of the self. The young man wants to be exactly like his father but simultaneously distinct from him. Thus, the young man may experience conflicts with the very people he establishes as his personal (self-defining) heroes or models. Adolescents don't simply become these models; rather, they see themselves reflected in them, a fact that causes adolescents some relief as well as some tension.

Yet few of these actions in one's mind fields, these turnings of the self, pertain in the popular culture's conceptions of role models who properly should be called "performance models." In our culture, appearance has become performance—consider the burgeoning of the fashion industry. Adolescents grant recognition to famous persons for the way they look and for the way they perform. Look and performance can yield one the (false) status of hero. What young people crave, Herbert Hendin wrote, "is to restructure their own emotions, not to be themselves, but to live as some 'other.' What this 'other' is like and how it can be achieved cut to the center of the changing American psyche."[54] When adolescents examine the treasured photograph of a performance model, they perhaps see themselves in some wishful form, as if the image before them represents a fantasized outcome or state of being. For an instant transported, they can pretend to be that image. Staring at the photograph or poster, adolescents see themselves not as external image but as existing from the inside out. There is past and future in this image, their own and the performance model's as well. Perhaps too, the photograph and their attachment to it allows them to focus on the central threads and (internally held) images of their being. If the adolescent is transported by the performance model, it is in an inward direction.

Authentic role models turn out to be the persons who nurtured us, made us feel secure, comfortable with intimacy, which in our culture some still confuse with sexuality. Authentic role models conducted themselves in ways that not only offered a form of guidance but consecrated the nurturance and security we were feeling. Authentic role models are the ones we are moved to comfort when they are unable to care for themselves. Perpetual care and nurturance are natural results of what Earls and Carlson espouse as the essential feature and definition of family.

Ultimately, the nurtured, secure adolescent, comfortable with intimacy, finds joy living in enduring relationships not only with contemporaries but with parents as well.[55] Not surprisingly, the healthy family may be described as just a good place to be. Why then would one abandon people merely because they have grown old? Besides, no matter where these authentic role models now reside, we eternally carry them in our heads.

Only God knows how many times adolescents "have become" Michael Jordan, Ken Griffey, Junior, or Tiger Woods. Yet one wonders whether any of these men's names were invoked by young people when a significant moral issue was contemplated or an action of any consequence undertaken. That part was played, literally, by authentic role models who not only model behavior but make adolescents comfortable with the world that lives within.

When the young are drinking, carousing, or just cruising, when in an instant the answers on the test sheet of the smartest student in the class are suddenly visible, one seriously doubts the faces of Michael Jordan or Madonna appear in the mind fields of adolescents. Along with anxiety, excitement, and confusion are the words and conduct of genuine role models, the ones who didn't abandon or misguide, the ones who probably never spoke to any student body assembly, never appeared on television, nor signed autographs, nor defended the concept of "quality time." These are the ones Mike Tyson would have liked to recall, the ones who not only provided material protection and educational opportunities for us but, as the best of friends, safeguarded the mind fields in which our identities were explored and developed and our selves consecrated. These weren't just people, moreover; they were and are caretakers, mothers, fathers.

Notes

1   Neal Gabler, *Life the Movie: How Entertainment Conquered Reality.* New York: Knopf, 1998.

2   Cited in Ed Siegel, "Life, Celebrity and the Pursuit of Happiness," *The Boston Globe*, December 13, 1998: C4.

3   See R. R. Koback and A. Sceery, "Attachment in Late Adolescence: Working Models, Affect Regulation, and Representations of Self and Others." *Child Development, 59*, 1988: 135–146; G. Armsden and M. T. Greenberg, "The Inventory of Parent and Peer Attachment: Individual Differences and Their Relationship to Psychological Well-Being in Adolescence." *Journal of Youth and Adolescence, 16*, 1987: 427–454; and M. D. Blain, J. M. Thompson, and V. E. Whiffen, "Attachment and Perceived Social Support in Late Adolescence." *Journal of Adolescent Research, 8*, 1993: 226–241.

4   Jerome Kagan, *The First Two Years.* Cambridge, MA: Harvard University Press, 1981; and *The Growth of the Child.* New York: Norton, 1978.

5   Erik H. Erikson, *Identity, Youth and Crisis.* New York: Norton, 1968.

6   James E. Marcia, "The Empirical Study of Ego Development." In H. A. Bosma, T. L. G. Graafsma, H. D. Grottevant, and D. J. de Levita (Editors), *Identity and Development: An Interdisciplinary Approach.* Newbury Park, CA: Sage, 1994; and H. D. Grotevant and C. R. Cooper, "Patterns of Interaction in Family Relationships and the Development of Identity Exploration." *Child Development,* 1985, *56*: 415–428.

7   On this point, see Sara Lawrence-Lightfoot, *Respect.* Reading, MA: Perseus, 1999, especially the chapter entitled "Dialogue": 91–116.

8   See Erik H. Erikson, "Identity and the Life Cycle." *Psychological Issues, Monograph 1.* New York: International Universities, 1959.

9   Sigmund Freud, *The Basic Writings of Sigmund Freud*, translated and edited by A. A. Brill. New York: Modern Library, 1938; and Heinz Kohut, *Search for the Self*, Volume 2, Paul Ornstein (Editor). New York: International Universities Press, 1978.

10   Erik H. Erikson, *Childhood and Society.* New York: Norton, 1950.

11   On this point, see Heinz Kohut, *Search for the Self*, op. cit.

12   Then, again, there's the story of my three-year-old grandson in a Seattle park who, seeing no other children about, went up to a woman and said: "Hi, I'm Luke. What do you think of that name for a little boy?"

13 See Carol Gilligan et al. *Making Connections*. Cambridge, MA: Harvard University Press, 1990.

14 Siegel called the cult of celebrity "nothing more than child's play." See Siegel, op. cit.

15 Interestingly, the movie, *Saving Private Ryan,* which once again opened discussion of the culture's elderly citizens, was only latently about the lives of men who now would be considered old. In fact, the movie portrayed these men in their younger years.

16 On a similar point, see James Cote and Anbton Allahar, *Generation on Hold.* New York: New York University Press, 1994.

17 See C. Wright Mills, *Power, Politics and People.* New York: Oxford University Press, 1963.

18 On this point, see Max Weber, *On Charisma and Institution Building*, S. N. Eisenstadt (Editor). Chicago: University of Chicago Press, 1968.

19 Gabler, Life the Movie op. cit.

20 Neil Postman, *Amusing Ourselves to Death: Public Discourse in the Age of Show Business.* New York: Penguin, 1986.

21 On this and related points, see Edwin J. Delattre, "Civility and the Limits to the Tolerable." Unpublished manuscript, Boston University, 1999: 8.

22 See D. N. Perkins, E. Jay, and S. Tishman, "Beyond Abilities: A Dispositional Theory of Thinking." *Merrill-Palmer Quarterly, 39*, 1993: 1–21; R. H. Ennis, "Critical Thinking: Literature Review and Needed Research." In L. Idol and B. F. Jones (Editors), *Educational Values and Cognitive Instruction.* Hillsdale, New Jersey: Erlbaum, 1991; D. P. Keating, "Adolescent Thinking." In S. S. Feldman and G. R. Elliot (Editors), *At the Threshold: The Developing Adolescent.* Cambridge, MA: Harvard University Press, 1990; and L. B. Resnick, *Education and Learning to Think.* Washington, DC: National Academy Press, 1987.

23 David P. Ausubel, *Theory and Problems of Child Development.* New York: Grune and Stratton, 1958.

24 Sigmund Freud, *The Complete Introductory Lectures on Psycho-Analysis,* translation by James Strachey. New York: Norton, 1966.

25 A. Strachen and D. Jones, "Changes in Identification During Adolescence: A Personal Construct Theory Approach." *Journal of Personality Assessment, 46,* 1982: 139–148.

26 Martin Heidegger, *Being and Time*, translated by Joan Stambaugh. Albany: State University of New York Press, 1966.

27 On a similar point, see James Cote and Anbton Allahar, *Generation on Hold,* op. cit.

28   On a related point, see Harry Stack Sullivan, *The Interpersonal Theory of Psychiatry*, edited by Helen Swick Perry and Mary Ladd Gawel. New York: Norton, 1953.

29   Sigmund Freud, *The Complete Introductory Lectures on Psychoanalysis*, op. cit.; M. H. Erdelyi, *Psychoanalysis: Freud's Cognitive Psychology*. New York: W.H. Freeman, 1985.

30   Erik H. Erikson, *Identity, Youth and Crisis*. op. cit.

31   Interestingly, Erikson proposed that the maldevelopment evolving from role confusion was "repudiation," by which he meant the adolescent questioning or opposing almost everything in his or her life.

32   T. Field and E. Robertson (Editors), *Teenage Parents and Their Offspring*. New York: Grune and Stratton, 1981; M. H. Bornstein (Editor), *Children and Parenting* (Volume 3). Hillsdale, New Jersey: Erlbaum, 1995; Joy G. Dryfoos, *Adolescents at Risk: Prevalence and Prevention*. New York: Oxford University Press, 1990; and Lisbeth B. Schorr, *Within Our Reach*. New York: Anchor, 1989.

33   John Dewey, *How We Think*. Amherst, NY: Prometheus, 1991.

34   On a related point, see Howard Gardner, *Frames of Mind: The Theory of Multiple Intelligences*. New York: Basic, 1983.

35   Howard Gardner, op. cit.

36   Tom Engelhardt, review of *The Norton Book of American Biography*, Edited by Jay Parini. *Los Angeles Times Book Review*, April 4, 1999: 9.

37   See John Dewey, *How We Know*. op. cit; and John Dewey, *How We Think: A Restatement of the Relation of Reflective Thinking to the Educative Process*. Lexington, MA: D. C. Heath, 1933.

38   Harry Stack Sullivan, op. cit.; See also Mihaly Csikszentmihalyi and R. Larson, *Being Adolescent: Conflict and Growth in the Teenage Years*. New York: Basic, 1984

39   Cited in Robert Hughes, *Culture of Complaint: The Fraying of America*. New York: Oxford University Press, 1993: 3.

40   *Newsweek*, June 28, 1993: 54.

41   Neil Postman, *Amusing Ourselves to Death*, op. cit.; and Neal Gabler, op. cit.

42   Cited in Tom Goldstein, "It's Not Up to You," book review of *Queer in America* by Michelangelo Signorile. *The New York Times Book Review*, June 27, 1993: 15–16.

43   Salvador Minuchin, Wai-Yung Lee, and George M. Simon, *Mastering Family Therapy: Journeys of Growth and Transformation*. New York: Wiley, 1996.

44   Edwin J. Delattre, "Civility and the Limits to the Tolerable." Unpublished manuscript, Boston University, 1999, page 8.

45   Heinz Kohut, The Chicago Institute Lectures, Paul and Marian Tolpin (Editors). Hillsdale, Illinois: Analytic, 1996. Cited in Donald Palladino, Jr., "Poets to Come: Walt Whitman, Self Psychology and the Readers of the Future." Unpublished manuscript, 2000.

46   Heinz Kohut, *The Chicago Institute Lectures,* op. cit; and *Search for the Self,* volume 2, op. cit.

47   See D. Burnes, *Intimate Connections.* New York: William Morrow, 1985; H. G. Lerner, *The Dance of Intimacy: A Woman's Guide to Courageous Acts of Change in Key Relationships.* New York: Harper and Row, 1989; E. L. Paul and K. M. White, "The Development of Intimate Relationships in Late Adolescence." *Adolescence, 25,* 1990: 375–400; D. Buhrmestrer and W. Furman, "The Development of Companionship and Intimacy." *Child Development, 58,* 1987: 1101–1113.

48   William Butler Yeats, A Vision. New York: Macmillan, 1938: 72.

49   Robert Kegan, *The Evolving Self.* Cambridge, MA: Harvard University Press, 1982.

50   See Ruthellen Josselson, *The Space Between Us: Exploring the Dimensions of Human Relationships.* San Francisco: Jossey-Bass, 1992; R. J. Sternberg and M. L. Barnes (Editors), *Anatomy of Love.* New Haven, CT: Yale University Press, 1988; W. W. Hartup, "Friendships." In R. M. Lerner, A. C. Petersen, and J. Brooks-Gunn (Editors), *Encyclopedia of Adolescence* (Volume 1). New York: Garland, 1991; and W. K. Rawlins, *Friendship Matters.* Hawthorne, New York: Aldine, 1992.

51   It is interesting to consider, in this context, that approximately 50% of children brought into juvenile court never return. Of the half that do, one finds a panoply of problems like learning disorders, lower IQ scores, substance abuse, and physical and sexual abuse. In sum, it is the children with the weakest family structures who tend to show up in court again and again.

52   In a recently published survey, a number of fourth grade students reported drinking beer and wine coolers as well as sniffing inhalants. In addition, 4% of the fourth, fifth and sixth graders surveyed report having smoked cigarettes. Cited in *The Boston Globe,* April 8, 1999: A8.

53   Felton Earls and Mary Carlson "Towards Sustainable Development for American Families." *Daedalus,* Winter 1993, *122,* Number 1: 93–122.,

54   Herbert Hendin, *The Age of Sensation.* New York: Norton, 1975: 121.

55   See W. W. Hartup and R. Zubin, *Relationships and Development.* Hillsdale, New Jersey: Lawrence Erlbaum, 1986.

PART III

THE FIELDS OF THOUGHT

Chapter 5

Narratives and Reflections

Styles of Thinking

In this chapter we examine a form of cognitive activity in which a person is able to think about thinking. Psychologists call the activity "going meta" inasmuch as the activity involves the field of meta psychology.[1] Adolescents go meta all the time, as do younger children who undertake some rudimentary meta steps, which their parents typically find extraordinary. Going meta for adolescents is seen by some to be a preoccupation, an obsession even, but as we will see throughout this book, it is the cognitive action that makes possible much of the work of normal adolescent development.

According to the psychologist Jerome Bruner,[2] two fundamental modes of thought characterize the majority of an adolescent's conscious activities, *narrative* and *paradigmatic*. In narrative thinking, the mode most familiar to us even if we have never thought about thinking, we are essentially engaged in attempting to explain experiences to ourselves and to others. To a degree, this activity requires telling stories. When we ask a young person to tell us what is making her sad, we are actually inviting a story, a narrative of sadness, as it were, in which she attempts to recount her emotional state or capture her inner sense of self. As listeners, we may assess her account in terms of how detailed or insightful it was, how the various parts of her story cohere, or whether the story is typical of adolescent experiences. In fact, we often listen as teachers grading papers, for like any writing assignment, the story recounted reveals the mind (fields) in action. Whatever our reactions, we have just encountered the narrative mode of thinking.

In paradigmatic thinking, quite different cognitive forms are undertaken. In this mode, we begin to get a flavor of scientific reasoning. First, we are employing our skills of description and explanation, logic and analysis. If, as John Allen Paulos wrote,[3] the narrative approach, incorporating descriptions and gossip, involves the specific and personal, then paradigmatic thinking represents the world of the general and the detached. We are not interested here in telling the personal story as much as we wish to know how the various parts of the story fit together, whether the story makes sense and whether it appears valid or true. We want to know, moreover, how we might prove the story to be true, how, in other words, we could test or verify it. We listen closely for the words, hunting for inconsistencies and contradictions, the logical and illogical, because in paradigmatic thinking we are engaged in the business of establishing scientific propositions that others may attempt to test and replicate.

Philosophers like Richard Rorty[4] regularly debate the matter of what people want to know or should know and, hence, what mode of thinking they will choose to employ. The reader recognizes already that mathematicians and logicians are going to employ paradigmatic thinking, and novelists and dramatists will lean toward narrative thinking. One recognizes too, that the paradigmatic mode is what some authors refer to as left-brain thinking, whereas the narrative mode is typically called right-brain although neuroscientists are hardly certain about this allegedly clear-cut brain function differentiation called lateralization.

Said simply, if we wish to know how we can discern truth from falsehood in our lives, reality from "unreality," and adolescents are more than fascinated with these tasks, then, like it or not, we are going to have to employ paradigmatic thinking. If, on the other hand, we wish to know how it is that experiences like that of confronting one's self come to have meaning and what meaning they have for us, then we will rely on the narrative mode of thinking. Some illustrations of these points might prove helpful.

A group of community residents sit around a table listening to committee reports of a program devoted to assisting victims of crime. Among those present at the meeting are parents of murdered children whose deaths were once major stories in their city. One conclusion of the report is to introduce a violence curriculum into the schools. Children and adolescents, everyone agrees, must learn about violence. So far, everything seems reasonable enough for both the narrative and paradigmatic thinker.

Now, however, consider several statistics involving violence in America, and keep in mind that our focus here is not on violence *per se* but on how we think about it. First, by the time children enter middle school, they will have witnessed over 50,000 murders on television. Second, according to psychologist John P. Murray, "about five violent acts are committed during one hour of 'prime-time' evening television programming, and 20 to 25 violent acts occur during each hour of Saturday morning 'children's programs.'"[5] Third, according to sociologists Murray Strauss and Richard Gelles,[6] one in two American families *every year* *reports* some form of family violence. (I emphasize "reports" to suggest that the number of violent incidents may even be greater.)

Granted, narrative thinkers may be strongly affected by the emotional appeal of parents of murdered children and rarely bother to move intellectually beyond the powerful stories these people recount. They are reacting, in other words, to the sensational or evocative aspects of the accounts. Accordingly, they may never question the possible relationship between a violence curriculum and the reduction of violence nor choose to address the matter of how one would reliably assess this relationship. They are focusing almost exclusively on the story of immediate events and circumstances.

The significant question remains: Will a violence curriculum in a school reduce violence in that community? It seems a reasonable question, yet surprisingly few people have investigated the reasons why, with all the drug and alcohol education programs in schools throughout the country, substance abuse among high school students in many areas has increased![7] The numbers appear even more discouraging among middle school students. Still focusing on modes of thinking, we might wonder why few people choose to differentiate between alcohol and drugs, when alcohol itself is a rather potent drug. To undertake this investigation scientifically, paradigmatic thinking would have to be employed. It is not enough to be moved by a good story or anecdote, which may or may not purport to tell the truth; one has to make a scientific, systematic, and reasoned inquiry using a different mode of thought.

Much of television and radio, media that dominate the mind fields of adolescents, involves narrative thinking and asks the viewer or listener to respond in kind, that is, employ narrative thinking. Media outlets assume the engagement of a mode of thought intended to help us understand or make sense of the meaning of an experience like today's activity on Wall Street or a war. The emphasis in these accounts necessarily is placed on the telling of the story, what we call the report; hence, the story teller or reporter becomes an essential if not *the* essential feature of the story. Hold in mind that every television newscast has a star.

Importantly, the major ingredient of the story is the combination of words and pictures, both of which affect our consciousness. The point of the newscast is to transmit a story and evoke an emotion that spontaneously generates transformations in our mind fields that ultimately structure for us what is transpiring. At all times we are attempting to make meanings of these events, exactly as we do in our everyday lives.

Watching the nightly news (or more precisely the messenger of the news) causes some of us to question: How do I know this account to be true? How do I know for certain that what I am observing is verifiable fact? I have learned something from the story, and it *appears* credible, but how do I know that any of it bears any relation to the truth? Not so incidentally, when a journalist awaits confirmation of a story, he or she still is involved in narrative thinking, for it is not until abstractions, higher-order conceptualizations, and logical conclusions are brought into the discussion that we employ paradigmatic thinking. Hunting for the truth is not only a difficult task, adolescents learn, it often requires one to put aside emotions and feelings, provocations and evocations, and dig for verifiable and empirical explanations. As Bruner writes: "There is a heart-lessness to logic: one goes where one's premises and conclusions and observations take one, give or take some of the blindness that even logicians are prone to."[8]

In some degree, this too, is a concern of adolescents who constantly differentiate between what they choose to call the "facts" of their existence or their feelings about these facts. Narrative thinking dominates the explorations required in identity formation. The mind fields of the young are filled as much with internal experiences and reflection as they are with the processing of external events. At the end of the day, however, the concern of adolescents is whether their processing of experiences that form the basis of their developing selves is accurate. Constantly they hunt for the genuine, the authentic, so they can build it into the consolidated identity they are constructing. In thinking not only about their experiences, externally or internally driven, adolescents must also be thinking about their thinking—still more narrative reasoning. They must be watching themselves, becoming, as Kohut[9] suggested, objects of their own personal investigations.

In the investigations of their developing mind fields, the fields that give birth to identity, adolescents employ a process psychologists call "self speak." Simply put, they tell stories about themselves and others and offer accounts of personal experiences to themselves. They not only feel various emotions, they speak to themselves about these emotions; these matters too, are described and explained (to oneself and others) in the narrative mode. Young people are constantly thinking in terms of personal stories, accounts, narratives, as well as imagining how others might respond to these stories. Recall that some psychologists believe that we are nothing more, nothing less than the stories we tell (to others and ourselves).[10] We recall that Elie Wiesel has noted that perhaps we are constituted of nothing but memories, many of them profoundly sad. I wonder how adolescents would respond to this most provocative statement.

In normal everyday lives, the narrative mode is dominant. We nonscientists and philosophers are not usually in the business of employing the paradigmatic mode of thought, and, because we are not, we may be prone to all varieties of distractions. We are prone, for example, to dismiss logic from our thinking and discipline from our personal reflections; hence, what we adjudge to be perfectly reasonable relationships between notions or ideas which, under scientific investigation (paradigmatic thought), would immediately be recognized as illogical and false. How is one to react, for example, to this sign posted on the window of a Redding, California, restaurant? "This facility permits smoking, and tobacco is known to the State of California to cause cancer." The obvious inconsistencies in the sign's wording are no less significant than the notion that if one sees something on television it must be true,[11] something else adolescents confront. Seeing is believing but only within the narrative mode of thinking. In paradigmatic thinking, seeing an event or phenomenon hardly causes us to conclude what actually has transpired. Peering out the window of the airplane, I absolutely *know* the earth to be flat; I can *see* that it is.

Adolescents know well this seeing is believing business. Part of their everyday work is to present their own personal newscasts to the world. Every day they must integrate the products of their internal musings and reflections and decide what they will broadcast and how they will react to the critics' reviews of their efforts and the ratings that never cease. Not only that, they must present in narrative form one newscast to their families, another to their friends, another to their closest friends, and still others to their teachers and coaches, employers and ministers. They learn from this work that seeing is not always believing, for they know how to distract their audience and lead them away from their own personal truths and discoveries. Everyone knows, for example, that parents don't always hear the latest news or get the full story.[12]

A final point on this matter of modes of thought. When educators speak of teaching children to think critically, they do not necessarily mean that children should be taught to think strictly in the paradigmatic mode. Critical thinking, if it is to be employed for discerning truth from falsehood, logic from illogic, necessarily involves the use of both modes of thought as well as the ability to differentiate between the two modes and recognize the insufficiencies of each. It is said that Freud once remarked that when a decision is relatively insignificant, one should marshal all the relevant facts. When, however, the decision is momentous, it may be better to rely on instincts. In making an important decision, therefore, "going with one's gut," an expression every adolescent knows, may be a propitious course of action even though it requires strictly narrative thinking. Still, one wonders why thoughtfulness and reasoning ever have to take a back seat or be left out of the car altogether. As we have observed, distraction often results from an absence of thoughtfulness, careful reasoning, and an appeal to the laws of logic.[13]

The point is this: In the media's implicit advocacy of narrative thought and perpetuation of the notion that seeing is believing, adolescents are being taught not to reason logically or undertake disciplined self-reflection, although these disciplines are precisely what they require as they attempt to understand the nature of their being. For adolescents to feel they are constructing solid identities within their mind fields and then have the confidence to reveal the products of this work to selected others—all acts of narrative thinking—they must at times reflect on themselves in more paradigmatic terms. "Going with one's gut" or on a hunch is valuable but not under all conditions. In fact, personal hunches may seriously backfire when personal identity is at stake. Adolescents know this, that is why they tell each other to sleep on an idea, not act rashly, go home and think about it.

When adolescents announce they don't want to know the truth, all they care about is how it feels to them, they run the risk of eschewing the paradigmatic mode or any form of disciplined reasoning. In these moments, it seems that if they were to employ the paradigmatic mode, they would have to confront a truth they presently suspect. Why would they *not* want to know the truth of something, especially about themselves, and settle instead for their feelings about it? Why would they rest content hearing gossip about others when they themselves would bristle if similar untruths were spoken about them?

Perhaps the answer to these questions lies in the adolescent's desire to achieve perfection, precisely as Plato averred centuries ago. Perhaps narrative reasoning at times allows adolescents to perpetuate untruths in order to preserve their ideal or allusion of perfection as well as the belief in their own superiority. Paradigmatic investigations and reasoning would perhaps unearth the unthinkable, the unacceptable: that one is imperfect and incapable of achieving even acceptable levels of competence, much less excellence.[14]

In a distracted culture, albeit one with the most glorious instruments of technology, we cannot always differentiate truth from untruth, reality from unreality. Because they incessantly work their mind fields, adolescents probably do make these differentiations and probably do know when they are thinking and acting authentically and when they are not.[15] They probably do know when their broadcasts (like their personal identities) ring true and when they are airing little more than (personal) fiction and gossip.

If adolescents were to consistently pursue courses of (distracted) action, they would find themselves rationalizing untruths and psychologically adjusting to public as well as private falsehoods. It is perfectly understandable to hate one's father, but to live with the rationalization or justification that he abused you merely because it *feels* that way is hardly a valid representation of reality and a version that helps neither one's own development nor one's relationship with a father. In the narrative mode, these feelings *seem* valid, but then there is the matter of the actual behavior that ought to go into adolescents' considerations of what feelings they now might wish to hold in their minds about their fathers. Only the truth, the Bible states, sets one free, but, as adolescents discover, it doesn't necessarily bring happiness along with freedom.

Then again, collecting information about oneself and generating theories and hypotheses to explain oneself to oneself—the enterprise of the paradigmatic mode of thinking—may cause one to forfeit the contribution of narrative thinking to the content and nature of consciousness. Both modes of thought potentially prevent the forces of distraction from overtaking the adolescent's seemingly insatiable appetite for the rush of stimuli to the conscious mind. Both are required if adolescents are to reflect on themselves and their worlds, private and public, in authentic forms, free of misleading distraction. And all of this is part of that complex curriculum educators call "critical thinking," yet another activity of the adolescent mind fields.

In a manner of speaking, life experiences gradually emerge, or at least an adolescent is tempted to think of them emerging, as a complex charm bracelet. How the charms actually connect to one another is more difficult to articulate, but the point of the preceding pages is to suggest that the culture, and especially the visual media, has a powerful influence on the way adolescents think, particularly when they engage in the narrative mode. The nature of their mind fields, in other words, their most intimate resources, is hardly immune to the structures of the society. In fact, much of this book focuses on the relationship of experiences and perceptions, on the one hand, and the development of adolescent consciousness on the other. For these, in part, are the structures defining the mind fields, the structures defining the ways adolescents think and speak to themselves as well as to others. The charm bracelet of experiences may itself bespeak distraction if adolescents (are taught to) ignore the relationships between and among the various charms. This is what the novelist Saul Bellow referred to as the extraordinary state of distraction in which our lives are led.[16]

From the standpoint of the felt sense of conscious activities, when the items constituting consciousness are not integrated in some logical or meaningful pattern but rather jingle like charms on a bracelet, adolescents find themselves living in a state of conscious anarchy. Little makes sense to them; little has meaning; one event appears to have little or no effect on another; one second, seemingly, remains disconnected from the seconds immediately before and after it, and life itself loses its significance. These are the times we employ expressions like "everything is running together," or, "nothing is coming together." In part, this is what Erikson[17] meant when he suggested that the opposite of identity cohesion, ideally a fully integrated sense of self, is role confusion.[18] The disconnected charms on the bracelet represent a perfect image of the felt sense of this confusion.

As a result of the confusion, the individual charms cannot relate to one another, essentially becoming meaningless to the adolescent. Think in this context, of the commercial alleging the "finding" that women have more emotions than men and hence require a stronger deodorant; no one appears to be troubled by the premise of this pronouncement. Disregarding logic, we allow the words to pass. Or consider the words of an adolescent who when asked what she wants to be when she grows up, responds, "A star!" Few seem concerned that this statement may reveal a personal emptiness or a cultural pitfall. As stardom is the grand American objective, the young woman presumably is right on track. Who is about to question such ambition in a culture that teaches its young that image, status, and look represent the crowning glories of adolescence?

So what do adolescents do when feeling confused, disconnected from reality, or imagining that the pieces constituting their selves don't properly cohere to form a solid identity?[19] How do they begin to think about these matters? Enter the curriculum of American distraction: Adolescents drink or drug themselves primarily to alter their state of consciousness.[20] Or, they are offered classes on coping with stress; recommend shows, movies, music, and sporting events to one another, and do everything possible *but* what the state of their consciousness would have them do, in the form of reflective thinking in order to calm their state of distraction and liberate themselves.

By pursuing distraction, adolescents are taken away from the present moment, the here and now, so that they come to focus their thinking on everything in their line of vision *but* the here and now. This means that their thinking, too, feels to them as if it has become disconnected from the here and now, which only adds to their feeling anxious, conflicted, bored, and probably crazed as well, the very sensations of distraction. Yet notice the act of the self attempting to deceive itself: How can anyone *not* be thinking in the here and now? Reflecting, anticipating, recalling, all are mental acts of the here and now. As much as adolescents may wish otherwise, no brand of mental activity transports them into the future or vaults them back to the past.

For adolescents to imagine that the moment just passed or the moment about to arrive has nothing to do with the moment in which they are existing, a not uncommon belief, causes them to feel anxious, bored, conflicted, and crazed. If they pursue distraction to this extent, they learn, they might temporarily convince themselves they live in a time out of time, which while sounding poetic, is, of course, not possible, even for those young people who contend that their age alone allows them to dream along with Don Quixote of the impossible. Imagining that in pursuing distraction they have found ways to escape thinking, escape their own mind fields, or forfeit control of their consciousness, adolescents attempt to reach a state wherein they believe they have no consciousness, no awareness of that furious collision of molecules constituting their state of consciousness, no consciousness of self. Again, there is the result: the now-familiar boredom, agitation, anxiety, and, often too, a sense of impending madness.

Permit me to amend this last thought as I almost distracted myself: Adolescents don't *lose* control of their consciousness; they *forfeit* control of it by abandoning both narrative and paradigmatic modes of thought. By abjuring their right to decide who will be permitted inside the marketplace of their consciousness, they allow the street hawkers and merchandisers to prowl about their mind fields. Each of us knows this feeling as it is captured in that phrase of being overwhelmed by stimuli. We say something was "too much" for me to take it in all at once. We frequently observe adolescents and children becoming immobilized when too many stimuli are thrust upon them. Shower a hundred birthday gifts on a child, and he bawls; we say he "goes ballistic." It's too much for him (to think about), we say, hoping to excuse the child's inappropriate (and for us embarrassing) behavior, which now we recognize as quintessential distraction. Throw too many stimuli at the adolescent, and he or she is tempted to shop or drink.

The examples of distraction, what I have referred to as charms, as well their relationships one to another, our emerging charm bracelet, should begin to make sense. All representations of distraction, they are meant to reveal ways of thinking that reflect the state of an adolescent's consciousness or, more precisely, ways of thinking that structure the state of consciousness. The notion reminds me of the story of the father wheeling his baby who tells a friend, "If you think my daughter is cute, wait 'til you see the photographs." The authentic life, similarly, demands that consciousness be fed the genuine article. In distraction, adolescents supply it with counterfeit objects, ersatz brands, barely reasonable facsimiles, and every one of these objects and brands carries its own form of (distractive) thinking.

Recall the example of distraction having to do with victims of crime and a committee's proposal of a violence curriculum. The idea sounded reasonable, but remember the illogical aspects of the concept. A violence curriculum should aid students in dealing with their thoughts and feelings as well as introduce them to constructive ways of managing violent impulses and conflicts. Yet the greater problem of why America has the highest juvenile crime and murder rates in the world is not addressed.[21] If it is in our blood ("our" referring to American males) to kill or in our genetic structure to rape ("our" being, again, American males), as Randy Thornhill and Craig Palmer suggest in their book *A Natural History of Rape*,[22] then why is it that these substances are not found in the blood of men elsewhere on the planet? Violence curricula are worthwhile enterprises, but they may miss the mark of understanding why men, women, children, and especially cultures celebrate, tolerate, exonerate, and engage in violence. The violence committee's intentions are admirable, but even as the committee does its noble work, it may have settled unknowingly on a course of distraction, replete with ways to deliberate the problem that inevitably will be internalized by children and adolescents.

The statement "This facility permits smoking, and tobacco is known to the State of California to cause cancer" found a front-row seat in my consciousness as I paid my bill and found myself going meta. Perhaps I'm missing something, but is the state looking out for us or not? If tobacco causes cancer, why allow smoking in the restaurant? Shouldn't the "and" be changed to a "but?" The state of California *knows* tobacco causes cancer. Is this an unintentional case of anthropomorphizing, or has Big Brother suddenly turned into Big Sur?

We conclude this section by reiterating an earlier point about the connection between narrative and paradigmatic thinking and distraction.

Some adolescents employ distraction not only as a mode of thought but as a style of life as well. Various distractions ensure they never will know what urges them toward these distractions in the first place. Some might argue that the purpose of the entertainment business, which subsumes sports and politics as well, is to make certain that adolescents examine neither themselves nor the cultures in which they live. On the one hand, an adolescent may complain that the culture is so complex there's no sense even trying to think about it, much less understand it. Besides, understanding it wouldn't alter it. On the other hand, in thinking deeply about their lives, adolescents might come to understand that as a function of being distracted, they have concluded there is little they can do to change who they are, for that is determined by genetics or by that vague phenomenon known as "human nature."

A mystery that some adolescents begin to appreciate, particularly if they study at the feet of admirable teachers, is that the supposed nature of culture is itself partly a collection of the products, artifacts, ideologies, and social rituals that adolescents themselves perpetuate and create by dint of the ways they think about and construct these products and rituals—the state of their consciousness—as well as by the ways they define and react to them. To some degree, the culture is the resultant product of their collective consciousness, their collective constructs, their narratives about human experience, their accounts of their mind fields, their thinking. Like the child in the fable "The Emperor's New Clothes," any adolescent at any point in time can suddenly strip bare the contents of the society and seek to expose it to the world, which, in a sense, is precisely what followers of heavy metal music seek to do, sometimes experiencing severe consequences. All it takes is closing one's eyes and opening one's mind fields.

John Dewey and Reflective Thinking

We come now to what might be seen as an antidote to the adolescent's pursuit of distraction or distractive thinking. If distraction is one force affecting the adolescent's consciousness, then its polar opposite might be what John Dewey advanced as self-reflective thought, or simply, self-reflection.[23] Not always the easiest of enterprises, its troublesome nature was recognized by Dewey, who saw that it involves a "willingness to endure a condition of mental unrest and disturbance."[24] Self-reflection obliges the adolescent to concentrate not only on present action but on the antecedents and consequents of action. To be self-reflective is to explore the various external influences affecting consciousness, as for example, the culture's values, conventions, morality, and belief systems.[25]

As self-reflection is employed in the solving of problems and the appreciation of the contexts or frames of knowledge in which problems and experiences arise and come to be resolved and publicized, so, too, does it move adolescents away from (unthinking) routines and habit, while opening them to surprise and novelty, possibility, and growth.[26] According to Dewey, the self-reflective person eventually assesses his or her own action, although not immediately. There was, for Dewey, a period of time in which judgment must be suspended, during which a person renders his or her assessment of action or behavior, what Donald Schön has called "knowing in action."[27] In many respects, it is precisely this extended moment of suspending judgment that causes many adults to distrust or discredit the thinking and actions of the young.

To never judge action or thought or, conversely, to judge at the exact instant of action or thought in an almost reflexive or self-protective manner represent prime examples of non-self-reflective thinking—what we are calling distraction—and what many adolescents discover they often experience. Eventually, self-reflection, not distraction, becomes part and parcel of the act of questioning one's behavior and attitudes, one's self-speak, as well as the taking responsibility for one's thoughts and actions.[28] Active self-reflection allows the adolescent to assume the role of (public) actor and (private) critic alike. Conversely, passive distractive thought, essentially through the appeal of appetite, sense, caprice, and a focus purely on momentary circumstance, obliges the adolescent to remain in the role of audience member; he or she has found a way to evade the mind fields.

Granted, self-reflection takes time and practice. Carried to the extreme, as occasionally it is in the minds of adolescents, it may ignite the sensation, just as Dewey warned, that one is going mad. Self-reflection represents the contraposition of distractive thinking. Unlike the sense of joy adolescents imagine they will experience in distractive thinking, self-reflection, according to Dewey, puts people in a constant "state of perplexity, hesitation, doubt,"[29] sensations not uncommon among young people. Thoughtfulness, not caprice; reflection, not "gut response"; character, not personality; deliberation, not impulse; depth of thought, not mere reaction time are the words of the day. As Dewey put it, "Sometimes slowness and depth of response are intimately connected. Time is required in order to digest impressions and translate them into substantial ideas. 'Brightness' may be but a flash in the pan."[30]

The work of Arthur Beane is particularly helpful in examining the mind fields of the developing adolescent.[31] Beane points out that it is precisely in those aforementioned suspended moments of judgment that persons explore what events or values have shaped not only their actions but their assessments of these actions. He reminds us of what Dewey called "intellectual thoroughness," a process in which a person not only explores the details of action but attempts as well to understand the full meaning of his or her actions in the context of external pressures and so-called internal demands. There is a spatial aspect of adolescent self-reflection, therefore, represented by the worlds of external and internal influences as well as a temporal aspect, namely, the order of actions examined for the purpose of looking for causes and effects of action and thought. Again, according to Dewey,

. . . the most important factors in the training of good mental habits consist in acquiring the attitude of suspended conclusion, and in mastering the various methods of searching for new materials to corroborate or refute the first suggestions that occur. To maintain the state of doubt and to carry on systematic and protracted inquiry—these are the essentials of thinking.[32]

Self-reflection, Beane observes, is a process (of going meta) wherein one thinks through the meanings, purposes, and consequences of thought and action. Adolescents are bearing witness to their actions and thoughts and, hence, to themselves. It may be the first time in their life that they have undertaken such disciplined (and undisciplined) "study." They are watching themselves watching themselves, often using mirrors, in a process Ellen Langer called "mindful."[33] They seek proof of what they are doing, what they are, or at least justifiable rationales for their actions and being. All too often, they feel obliged to generate an answer to that frightful question: And what do you do to justify your existence? Adolescents hardly act or think because someone told them to, nor do they (wish to) constantly act in a particular manner merely because it has become (thoughtless) habit. At times able to recognize when they are engaging in distraction, they become mindful, thoughtful, careful, critical, self-examining, self-reflective. At least this is what happens when they have worked hard at cultivating their mind fields.

Without self-reflection, their actions, like their choices, remain unin-
formed. More importantly, self-reflection, if Dewey was correct, becomes
the basis of their (mind) growth and maturity. Rollo May similarly, noted
that "Man is the particular being who has to be aware of himself, be
responsible for himself, if he is to become himself."[34] We might suggest
that with the capability of being self-reflective, the adolescent stage of
development may be characterized by a person's emerging self-awareness
as well as responsibility to and for oneself, as well as the selves of others.
If there was for Dewey one antidote to distractive thinking, it was education:

> Education has accordingly not only to safeguard an individual against the beset-
> ting erroneous tendencies of his own mind—its rashness, presumption, and pref-
> erences of what chimes with self-interest to objective evidence—but also to under-
> mine and destroy the accumulated and self-perpetuating prejudices of long ages.[35]

George Herbert Mead,[36] too, examined self-reflection and wrote that
when a stimulus hits our consciousness, it is imperative that we analyze
not only the features of the stimulus but the features of our response to it.
In distractive thinking, conversely, we undertake neither activity; we accept the stimulus for what it is—as if its mere presence justifies its significance—and respond as unthinkingly, as we have always responded.[37] Is it
any wonder that a new movie, a new fashion, a new video game, or new
star in the Hollywood firmament would so captivate the mind fields of the
adolescent? The new stimulus is all important if for no other reason than
it stimulates the young person's insatiable appetite for new stimuli. This
seeming tautology is precisely what is captured in that phrase about people
being famous for being famous. Significantly, without these two facets of
analysis, examination of the stimulus as well as one's response to it, adolescents fail to construct knowledge for themselves, a failure that often
lies at the heart of distractive thinking. Dewey expressed it this way:

> Thinking is not like a sausage machine which reduces all materials indifferently to
> one marketable commodity, but is a power of following up and *linking together
> the specific suggestions that specific things arouse* (emphasis added).[38]

Truth be told, Dewey, like John Locke[39] before him, probably would
have argued that distraction, or more precisely distractive thinking, is thinking gone wrong. Locke had outlined at least three classes of so-called
"wrong-thinking" men: There was first the man who rarely reasoned anything at all but instead depended on others in whom he had faith to make
reasoned judgments for him. Second, was the man who eschewed reason, putting passion in its place. Reason for this man was to be tested
purely by feelings: If it felt good, it was good. Anything that "worked,"

presumably, could be considered true. More recently, Alan Ryan wrote of this very same dangerous offshoot of pragmatism that ". . . gave rise to endless misconceptions—such as the complaint that we are entitled to believe anything that makes us feel good, or that we need only to believe something firmly enough for it to be as good as true."[40]

Finally, Locke's third wrong-thinking man was the one who, while ostensibly following the dictates of reason, nonetheless was unable to determine what he needed to know in order to render his reasoning worthwhile. One might say that the process was willing, but the ingredients were omitted.[41]

Nondistractive thinking, in contrast, is thinking gone right. It results from the constant exercise of thoughtfulness, logic, careful reasoning, or the positive habits of the mind, which ideally are taught and nourished in schools. Not surprisingly, Dewey was well aware of the interconnections of external circumstances and internal deliberations when he identified what is required for thoughtful nondistractive thinking:

> The only way to achieve traits of carefulness, thoroughness, and continuity (traits that are, as we have seen, the elements of the "logical") is by exercising these traits from the beginning, and by seeing to it that conditions call for their exercise.[42]

In distraction, the culture and the individual together decide not to be careful about thinking habits, questioning neither the products of the culture meant to stimulate consciousness nor one's reactions to them just as Cooley alleged.

Which brings us to one last admonition regarding reflective thinking from Dewey that was published almost ninety years ago. I urge the reader to dwell on these words as they provide an insight into what distractive thinking is all about, for adolescents as well as their elders:

> If a man's actions are not guided by thoughtful conclusions, then they are guided by inconsiderate impulse, unbalanced appetite, caprice or the circumstances of the moment. To cultivate unhindered, unreflective external activity is to foster enslavement, for it leaves the person at the mercy of appetite, sense and circumstance.[43]

Dewey's admonitions regarding reflection should stay with us throughout our discussion of adolescence, for clearly the enslaved mind can do little else but accept through whim, impulse, sense, and appetite the stimuli hitting it from the marketplace of products and slogans. No one is more vulnerable than the young adolescent who is just beginning to appreciate the power of the mind to deal with or navigate through (go meta) external as well as internal stimuli. Recognizing this, Dewey makes the point again and again because it is essential for the liberation of the adolescent mind from the enslavement of habit, taste, and appetite of the sort he described. It is that matter of judgment to which Dewey referred, an element often omitted from discussions of reflective thinking, be it that of adolescents or adults.[44]

In the end, it may not be enough merely to reflect on something although it seems better than not to reflect at all. At some point, however, judgment is made or perhaps ought to be made. To buy this or that or nothing at all, to watch a television program or read, to act morally or not, faithfully or not, all imply that at some level judgments of potential actions are being rendered. And that they are implies that adolescents, too, are imputing value or worth to these activities of the mind. They are understanding distinctions, for example, between the good and the bad, the right and the wrong in terms of moral principles rather than memorized rules of behavior, what psychologists call respectively preconventional and postconventional reasoning.[45] As Piaget[46] observed, adolescents are balancing abstract notions, many of them inherently contradictory, and then reacting, as Cooley noted, to their ruminations and ultimate judgments. These are the activities, cognitive in nature, that distinguish the child from the adolescent. Stating this is a far cry from alleging that the onset of adolescence is determined purely by biological maturation and transformations.

Let us consider an example of the sort of judgment that leads an adolescent away from distractive thinking. Most all adolescents would report almost reflexively that they believe in the notion of tolerance. Coming to this position, of course, requires some thinking. In a reflective mode, the young student might say, "I have to think about what I think about that." Suppose a teacher asks, "Would you tolerate interfaith marriages?" Yes, say the students. "Would you tolerate interracial marriages?" Again the students answer, yes. The teacher raises the ante: "Would you tolerate homosexual marriages?" Yes, again, say the students, now perhaps falling into a somewhat distracted, unthinking mood. Teacher: "So you believe in tolerance even if you don't necessarily support any of the above notions?" Yes! Now, finally, her punchline: "Would you tolerate a Nazi party in this school advocating rape, theft, and the murder of students?" "Of course not!" the students reply. Though not yet reasoning the full measure of the questions, not yet engaging in what Dewey would call thoughtful self-reflection, a judgment nonetheless has been made.

Suddenly, through the probing of the teacher, the assessment of tolerance as some blanket ideal is transformed. Newer assessments and judgments of the sort presumably not called for in responding to the earlier questions have lead the students to a wholly different understanding of the concept of tolerance that at first had (unthinkingly) seemed so obviously pure and correct. In fact, it is just this sort of reasoning that leads philosophers to contend that tolerance ought not be advanced as a virtue. On further reflection and judgment, it is readily discovered there are activities that people find intolerable. Adolescents do place value and worth on objects, ideas, opinions; they do make assessments and judgments whether they admit to them or not, whether they are conscious of them or not, and whether or not they represent the product of whim, caprice, or serious study. The good teacher almost seems capable of entering the mind fields of her students, in which she churns up the soil, making possible the growth and harvest of new ideas. As Delattre suggests, one of the essential duties of adults is to educate young people rather than abandon them or "condemn them to their own untutored devices."[47] Karl Hostetler summarized the idea in this way:

> What distinguishes judgment from (mere) thinking and reflecting is that judgment is thought or reflection involving some evaluation of the objects of thought; it is a *discrimination* and *normative* form of thought or reflection. It is thought and reflection aimed at being judgmental (the emphases are in the original).[48]

One thing more on this matter of judgment: To make the assertion that it is the work of the mind fields rather than biological development of secondary sex characteristics that signals the commencement of the adolescent stage not only has the potential to shift the emphasis in research on adolescence, it affects the way we view adolescents generally. More precisely, it contributes to the manner in which the very concept of adolescence is defined,[49] which, in turn, means that it aids in the construction of adolescence, a construction that adolescents internalize as part of their identity. To repeat what we said at the outset, how adolescence is constructed by the culture contributes mightily to the individual self constructed during these years of the life cycle. What adolescents see as they peer inward is constructed in part from how the culture perceives the entire age group in terms of the most public and social criteria.

Having earlier explored some definitions of distraction, we conclude this chapter lingering on Dewey's three fundamental elements of distractive thinking: appetite, sense, and circumstance. Examples of these three roots of distraction are found everywhere in the world of adolescents. The entire advertising industry is predicated on creating appetite, actually encouraging adolescents to believe they need products rather than merely desire them. What is the adolescent to do in the face of an advertiser's claim that because a woman has more emotions than a man, she requires a stronger deodorant?

As for Dewey's notion of sense, two interpretations of what he had in mind are possible. On the one hand, adolescents often take as reasoned argument something they merely sense. On the other hand, and what Dewey did have in mind, adolescents employ their senses (ultimately perpetuating a thoughtless but sensation-driven culture) when, as we saw in the classroom discussion on tolerance, carefully exercised reasoning is required. For Sven Birkerts, the shift from a reading culture to a viewing culture has been as profound a transformation as the shift in physics from Newtonian to Einsteinian thinking.[50] Seeing is believing, adolescents tell themselves. They saw it on television; they heard it on the radio, and hence it must be true. Or, how about those slogans directed especially to adolescents: "Just do it!" and "Go with your gut." Once again, sense and sensation rather than thoughtfulness have the power to drive the (search) engines of the mind fields and thereby preclude cognitive acts of examination, discrimination, and judgment.

Finally, there is the matter of distractive thinking emerging as the result of a person's reactions to immediate circumstances. A presumably thoughtful author recently has written that the problem with the so-called baby boom generation is that they have never really experienced hardship or a profound setback. Apparently, from this one writer's perspective anyway, the hypothesis being advanced seems "reasonable." Yet if one looks beyond immediate circumstances, one might catch a glimpse of those men and women of the boomer generation who served in a war or who live in peril because of illness, unemployment, family pathology, or poverty.[51] One may sense the generation has never suffered, but even short-term study refutes the impression.

It is the fashion industry, one of the most influential industries in the lives of adolescents and those of the media reporting on it that best illustrates all three of Dewey's root causes of distraction.[52] Appetite, sense, and circumstance dominate the thinking of those men and women urging young people to wear the clothes of the season and convincing the young that they will be lost or left behind if they fail to comply with these most capricious dictates. Not ironically, one might also make the case that attention deficit hyperactivity disorder, anorexia and bulimia[53] also are grounded in appetite, sense, and circumstance. In response to the requirements of a male-dominated culture that has determined that thin people look better on television, in the movies, and on fashion runways, young girls are veritably instructed to curb if not obliterate their appetites altogether.

Everything about a sensation-oriented culture is rooted in how it looks, how it sounds, how it tastes, how it feels. Caprice, whim, impulse appear to reside within the distractive mind fields constantly generating the push for new appetites, new sensations, and the limited desire to peer beyond immediate circumstances much less question or judge the demands, styles, and rituals they proffer.

No one is more susceptible to all of this than young adolescents just beginning their first serious mind field harvesting. Whether the advertising and fashion industries have ever thought much about Dewey, Cooley, Piaget, and Birkerts, they know about the vulnerability of the young consumer, and they play on it. They know, too, as we will explore in some detail in the next chapter, they are not merely dressing adolescents nor urging them to purchase products; they are contributing to the mind fields and hence to the identities young people are seeking to establish, identities that ultimately cannot be assessed in terms of financial profit but rather in terms of a sense of an authentic self able to act responsibly and with genuine care.

If at times adolescents are to remain undistracted, they must not only learn to read and compute figures, they must learn the essence of character, which means, in part, learning to think and deliberate. Adolescents must be encouraged, therefore, to enter the fields of their minds and not follow the advice given to early Americans to go west but instead go meta.

Notes

1   See J. K. Flavell, "On Cognitive Development." *Child Development, 53,* 1882: 1–10; R. J. Sternberg and C. A. Berg (Editors), *Intellectual Development.* Cambridge: Cambridge University Press, 1992; and *Cognitive Development.* Englewood Cliffs, New Jersey: Prentice-Hall, 1982; Howard Gardner, *The Mind's New Science: A History of the Cognitive Revolution.* New York: Basic Books, 1987; *The Unschooled Mind: How Children Think and How Schools Should Teach.* New York: Basic Books, 1991; J. H. Flavell, "Metacognition and Cognitive Monitoring: A New Area of Psychological Inquiry." *American Psychologist, 34,* 1979: 906–911; and L. Baker and A. L. Brown, "Metacognitive Skills and Reading." In P. D. Pearson (Editor), *Handbook of Reading Research,* Part 2, New York: Longman, 1984.

2   See his *Actual Minds, Possible Worlds.* Cambridge, MA: Harvard University Press, 1986.

3   John Allen Paulos, *Once upon a Number: The Hidden Mathematical Logic of Stories.* New York: Basic Books, 1999.

4   See his *Philosophy and the Mirror of Nature.* Princeton, NJ: Princeton University Press, 1979.

5   See John P. Murray, "President's Message: Once upon a Time: Television, Children, and Social Policy—A New Fairy Tale." *The Child, Youth, and Family Services Quarterly,* American Psychological Association, Division 37, *13,* Summer 1990, page 10.

6   See Murray A. Strauss and Richard Gelles, *Behind Closed Doors.* Garden City, New York: Anchor, 1981.

7   One might begin with the significant threat to young people caused by alcohol and substance abuse. In surveys conducted by the National Council of Alcohol and Drug Dependence, 82 percent of high school seniors reported having used alcohol, in comparison with 65 percent who have smoked cigarettes, 50 percent who report having smoked marijuana, and 9 percent who admit to trying cocaine. In research published in *The Boston Globe,* 76 percent of high school students and 46 percent of middle school students reported that illegal drugs are kept, used or sold on school grounds. Not so incidentally, more than one third of the students surveyed claimed that drugs were the most pressing problem facing today's young people, and one can't be certain that these students classified alcohol as a drug. Despite numerous well-intentioned school programs, illegal drug use by adolescents is on the rise. In a 1996 survey conducted by the National Center on Addiction and Substance Abuse, 22 percent of teenagers reported the likeliness of their occasionally experimenting with an illegal drug. These data are reviewed in Samantha Stuart and Thomas J. Cottle, "Adolescents Still at Peril." Unpublished manuscript, Boston University, 2000.

8   Jerome Bruner, *Actual Minds, Possible Worlds,* op. cit., page 13.

9   Heinz Kohut, *Search for the Self,* Volume 2, Paul Ornstein (Editor). New York: International Universities Press, 1978.

10   See John Kotre, *White Gloves: How We Create Ourselves Though Memory.* New York: The Free Press, 1995; and Thomas J. Cottle, *Private Lives and Public Accounts.* Amherst, MA: University of Massachusetts Press, 1977.

11   Neil Postman, *Amusing Ourselves to Death: Public Discourse in the Age of Show Business.* New York: Penguin, 1986.

12   See Jean Hanff Korelitz, "How Well Can We Ever Know Our Kids?" *Newsweek,* March 6, 2000: 10–11.

13   See John Dewey, *How We Think.* Amherst, NY: Prometheus, 1991.

14   See R. Montemayor, G. Adams, and T. Gullotta (Editors), *From Childhood to Adolescence: A Transitional Period?* Newbury Park, CA: Sage Publications, 1990; K. A. Dodge and P. R. Murphy, "The Assessment of Social Competence in Adolescents." In P. Karoly and J. J. Steffans (Editors), *Adolescent Behavior Disorders: Foundations and Contemporary Concerns.* Lexington, MA: Lexington Books, 1983; Robert L. Selman, *The Growth of Interpersonal Understanding: Developmental and Clinical Analysis.* New York: Academic Press, 1980.

15   On a related point, see David Elkind, *Children and Adolescents: Interpretive Essays on Jean Piaget.* New York: Oxford University Press, 1974.

16   In a lecture at the Kennedy School of Government, Harvard University, 1989. See Saul Bellow, *It All Adds Up: From the Dim Past to the Uncertain Future.* New York: Viking, 1994.

17   Erik H. Erikson, *Childhood and Society.* New York: Norton, 1950.

18   S. L. Archer, "Identity and the Choice of Social Roles." In *Identity and Adolescence: Processes and Contents.* A. S. Waterman (Editor). San Francisco: Jossey-Bass, 1985.

19   See Erik H. Erikson, *Identity, Youth and Crisis,* NY: Norton, 1968; *Young Man Luther.* New York: Norton, 1962; T. Honess and K. Yardley (Editors), *Self and Identity: Perspectives Across the Lifespan.* London: Routledge & Kegan Paul, 1987; J. E. Marcia, "Identity and Self Development." In R. M. Lerner, A. C. Petersen, and J. Brooks-Gunn (Editors), *Encyclopedia of Adolescence* (Volume 1). New York: Garland, 1991; J. E. Marcia, "The Empirical Study of Ego Identity." In H. A. Bosma, T. L. G. Graafsma, H. D. Grotevant, and D. J. De Levita (Editors), *Identity and Development.* Newbury Park, CA: Sage Publications, 1994; A. S. Waterman, "Identity as an Aspect of Optimal Psychological Functioning." In G. R. Adams, T. P. Gullota, and R. Montemayor (Eds.) *Adolescent Identity Formation.* Newbury Park, CA: Sage, 1992.

20   See Joy G. Dryfoos, *Adolescents at Risk: Prevalence and Prevention.* New York: Oxford University Press, 1990; and Joy G. Dryfoos, *Safe Passage: Making It Through Adolescence in a Risky Society.* New York: Oxford University Press, 1998.

21   On a related point, see Derrick Z. Jackson, "No Wonder We're Afraid of Youths." *The Boston Globe*, September 10, 1997: A15.

22   Randy Thornhill and Craig T. Palmer, *A Natural History of Rape: Biological Bases of Sexual Coercion*. Cambridge, MA: MIT Press, 2000.

23   John Dewey, op. cit.

24   Ibid.

25   See William Damon, *Social Personality and Development*. New York: Norton, 1983.

26   Arthur Beane, "The Supervision of Student Teachers: An Emphasis on Self- Reflection." Unpublished manuscript, Boston University, School of Education, 1999.

27   See Donald A. Schön, *The Reflective Practitioner: How Professionals Think in Action*. New York: Basic Books, 1983.

28   See Thomas Lickona, *Educating for Character and Responsibility*. New York: Bantam, 1991.

29   John Dewey, op. cit., page 9.

30   Ibid., page 37.

31   Arthur Beane, op. cit.

32   John Dewey, *How We Think*, op. cit., page 13.

33   Ellen J. Langer, *The Power of Mindful Learning*. Reading, MA; Perseus, 1997.

34   Rollo May, *The Discovery of Being*. New York: Norton, 1983, page 98. Cited in Beane, op. cit., page 37.

35   Dewey, *How We Think*, op. cit., page 25.

36   George Herbert Mead, *Mind, Self and Society from the Standpoint of a Social Behaviorist*. Chicago: University of Chicago Press, 1934.

37   Ibid.

38   Dewey, op. cit., page 39.

39   John Locke, cited in Dewey, op. cit.

40   Alan Ryan, Book review of *The Revival of Pragmatism*, Edited by Morris Dickstein. *The New York Times Book Review*, April 4, 1999: 10.

41   Cited in John Dewey, op. cit., page 23.

42   Ibid., page 66.

43   Ibid., page 67.

44   Beane, op. cit.

45 Kohlberg, op. cit. See notes of chapter 1.

46 Piaget, op. cit. See notes of chapter 1.

47 Edwin J. Delattre, "The Idea of Normality." Unpublished document, Boston University, 1999, page 9.

48 Karl D. Hostetler, *Ethical Judgment in Teaching*. Boston: Allyn and Bacon, 1996, page 8.

49 See John Santrock, *Adolescence*, 7th Edition. New York: McGraw-Hill, 1998.

50 Birkerts, op. cit.

51 Thomas J. Cottle, *At Peril: Stories of Injustice.* Amherst, MA: University of Massachusetts Press, 2001.

52 For a discussion of this point, see Sherry L. Turner, Heather Hamilton, Meija Jacobs, Laurie M. Angood, and Deanne Hovde Dwyer, "The Influence of Fashion Magazines on the Body Image Satisfaction of College Women: An Exploratory Analysis." *Adolescence*, *32*, Fall, 1997: 603–605.

53 Patricia A. Neuman and Patricia A. Halvorson, *Anorexia Nervosa and Bulimia: A Handbook for Counselors*. New York: Van Nostrand Reinhold, 1983.

Chapter 6

Screen Speak, Screen Deep

The Role of Television

Throughout this book, television, its contents as well as the mode of learning and state of consciousness spawned by watching it, is seen to play a major role in the development of the contemporary adolescent.[1] It is not my intention to indict television yet again for all society's ills. It would be easy to blame all of America's problems on television, but if we do, we are only going to drown in a sea of distraction. Still, television must be examined—and probably watched as well—as it, along with the computer[2] is the most powerful technological instrument in our lives and has produced some of the most extraordinary transformations in the last century.[3]

If there is one point to make about television it is this: The experience of watching television restructures the mind fields of adolescents. It is not only that people are receiving information, albeit in hundreds of tiny servings, but their minds are changing; the way they think is changing; the way they tend to reason is changing, all as a function of experiencing television. The powerful impact is not necessarily the result of today's news or the pictures of refugees pouring into some foreign country. Unseen and unfelt, the impact is experienced as a transformation of consciousness caused merely by the constant act of watching television. Sven Birkerts expressed the notion in a slightly different way when he wrote that ". . . this is the first time, ever, that the perceptions of events and the transmission of the perceptions have become as important as the events themselves."[4] Once again we have an example of the messenger, technology in this case, being as or more important than the message or, more accurately, the millions of messages.

To appreciate this so-called restructuring of consciousness, we turn to the writings of Jean Piaget, who, to my knowledge, never commented on the advent of television in the development of the child's and adolescent's mind.

If the essential function of education for Piaget was to develop intelligence, then the essential function of intelligence was to understand and invent structures of the mind by the acts in which one structures reality.[5] To simplify this complicated notion, let us understand that Piaget believed that as adolescents "take in" reality, as for example, watch something on television or surf the Internet, their consciousness is transformed as a direct result of the act of watching as well as by the actual stimulus they are viewing. They are not simply copying behavior, attitudes, or opinions as much as they may cite the words of actors or play out familiar scenes in sit-coms. Rather, they are (cognitively) structuring reality because they are constantly organizing it in the ways they act in relation to it or merely think about it. These actions become the basis of their capacity to reason and judge.[6]

Although admittedly this seems complex, think of a fundamental action in which discerning some truth requires extraordinary cognitive sophistication.[7] A child sees a little doll. She smiles because she recognizes it, already an act of maturity. Then the doll is hidden and the child cries for she is unhappy that the doll has "gone away." In time, however, she will learn that the doll presently being hidden is "still there," somewhere in the world. She will learn, in other words, that disappearance does not mean permanent absence, for she is now able to hold the concept of the doll in her mind; thus the game of "Peek-a-boo" is born. This illustration indicates that reality is not predicated solely on what the child is able to directly sense or perceive. Cognitive maturity and the construction of what a culture defines as normality, in fact, depend on one's ability to hold competing abstract notions in mind. Without this capacity, there can be no mature form of reasoning. Notice again, it has nothing to do with what one is actually viewing or hearing.[8] The child knows the doll is gone, yet at the same time knows that it is not gone.

Generally speaking, reasoning requires profound transformations or what Piaget called *restructuring* of the mind.[9] Even small children go about generating hypotheses about the world as they attempt to make sense of it, but adolescents bring this capacity to a higher plateau. At each point in their thinking, children and adolescents reorganize their knowledge about the world. They are not merely accumulating information as much as they are restructuring the nature of their thinking apparatus. This means that with each experience, an adolescent not only absorbs information but, in the ensuing restructuring of the mind, makes it possible for still-newer information to be appreciated and understood, information to which the adolescent may react and adapt. Students of Piaget recognize these notions as assimilation and accommodation.[10]

Examples of restructuring abound. At one point in his life, a little boy learns that there is a big animal with four legs called a horse. Not surprisingly, he proceeds to call any large animal with four legs "horse." Zebras, tigers, lions, elephants all are large and have four legs, so only "logically" he would call them "horse." In time, however, the restructuring taking place (because of his own cognitive efforts and normal neurological maturity) becomes more sophisticated, which makes possible more refined perceptual discriminations. Now the boy laughs at someone calling an elephant or lion "horse." Note, however, that it is not rote memory that Piaget claims is at play here. Rather, the mind has become structured, literally "more intelligent." It is not that in a quantitative sense the child knows more; rather, the child thinks more thoughtfully, intelligently. Piaget envisioned childhood generally as involving the development of progressive syntheses of assimilation and accommodation.[11]

Quite possibly, the development of language in a child works much this same way. If we study the world of the autistic child, for example, we observe a phenomenon called echolalia,[12] in which the child copies or mimics what someone is saying. It is precisely the form of torture that siblings commonly perform on one another, repeating everything uttered word for word. In the case of echolalia, however, it becomes evident that the child, like a talking bird, is copying language but is not truly able to speak. Nothing is happening, in other words, *but* copying, which, in turn, suggests that copying alone does not establish an adequate foundation for language or speech. Some deeper (language) structure, as Noam Chomsky theorized,[13] must be in place in order for the child to learn to do more than utter words.

An analogy for what Piaget calls restructuring seems in order. On the first occasion of eating a very hot pepper, many of us feel we are on fire. We may even believe we should go to the nearest emergency room. By about the fourth or fifth time we eat this same species of pepper, however, we find our intestinal tract more adaptable and, hence, the pepper more agreeable; we even grow to like the taste of the pepper. In a sense, our digestive systems have been restructured by dint of the constant diet (assimilation) of peppers, and gradually we become prepared to take on (accommodation) even hotter peppers. By the mere action of eating the peppers, our insides have been transformed (restructured), thereby allowing us to transform our attitudes about and perceptions of the peppers.[14]

While we will have more to say about this matter later in this chapter, consider for the moment a fundamental premise of learning. If Piaget is right, if intelligence is truly something having to do with actions of the person *on* the environment and vice versa, affecting the structure of the mind, if choking on one pepper prepares us for reaching the point where we come to adore peppers, then knowledge is not something imposed on us by teachers or television broadcasters but rather something that is literally "called up" in us. (Recall the metaphor of the tolerance teacher churning up the earth in her students' mind fields.) Learning does not refer, in other words, to materials or information being piled on or shoved in as much as it is created, "brought up" or "brought forth" as if it were already there and "all" we have to do is fetch or recall it. What is already there, however, is a function of all our previous experiences, all our previous interactions with reality, all our previously consumed peppers (that is, assimiliations and accommodations). In turn, this suggests that every form of learning affects the structure of the mind as much as the actual "thing" being learned. More precisely, the mind is constantly being restructured by dint of the activities in which it is engaged, the most prominent in recent decades being ones of sensation and, in particular, the sensations instigated by scanning television and computer screens.

It is for this reason that we allege the act (or sensation) of watching television to be as profoundly influencing, if not more so, than what is being watched. Each act of watching, which means every second of sitting before the set, structures the mind, again, irrespective of the contents of the program. Not surprisingly, the continually changing visual image or interruptions generally, the effect of music, the appeal to senses, the creation of appetites, all become part of the television experience. It is for this reason and with Piaget's writings as encouragement that we argue that television seemingly produces a mind working in a manner some would be tempted to label as attention deficit disordered.

In Piaget's terms, experiencing television is merely a form of intelligence emerging.[15] Children in front of the tube are neither shutting down nor "dumbing down"; they are making mental leaps, imagining, literally conceiving mental images. They are experiencing a restructuring of the mind that on occasion dazzles (or depresses) us. We study the child watching a television show and say, "You really understand all this? You really know who all these people are?" No problem. In time, this same (sensation-based) cognitive structure will make, among other things, the child's encounters with computers and, especially, computer graphics that much easier as he or she will be able to "call up" ("remember") relevant modes of thinking if not actual information while encountering activities like reading a 300-page book without Cliff Notes that much more vexing.

To repeat, the mind assimilates not merely the information of television but the framework or paradigm, (defined as "mental models that we employ to put opportunities and problems in perspective"[16]) provided by the dynamic of television. Only naturally, the child turns (inside) to this same dynamic, this same framework when other realities, other circumstances present themselves. In this way, the framework acts almost as computer software or what cognitive psychologists call a neural net. By absorbing the substance of television, the child at the same time is mentally accommodating to television's framework. In facing newer circumstances, the child calls up older frameworks, older structures, and accommodates to these newer circumstances by reliving or reviving the older frameworks and structures.

One can envision this idea of framework or structure as computer software, word-processing programs, for example. What I write is one matter, but how the processing of these words takes place in fact is governed by the parameters and capacities of the word-processing software. It provides a structure, a framework that continues to exist irrespective of what substantively is being worked on.[17] A major difference, however, between the mind and actual software, is that the use of the mind's software may alter it. Yet because most of us do not work on television, we do not, alas, alter its structure.

If this sounds complicated, let us understand only that we cannot be surprised if television news, political campaigns, publicity events, and press conferences of all varieties are nothing but shows meant to affect our senses and hence restructure our minds. The people involved may not believe their purpose is to entertain or distract, but the framework they employ is predicated on earlier frameworks now lodged in their minds, the main frame, of course, being television. Television not only broadcasts the half-time show at the Superbowl or the lavish Oscar celebrations in Hollywood, it literally breeds a generation of people more than cognitively capable of producing such events. What one generation considers unthinkable, another generation finds perfectly rudimentary. (If parents presumably are "more intelligent" than their children, why is it that in most homes the younger generation is called on to reset the VCR clock, tape a television program, or solve some computer problem!)

Children glued, as we say, to the television set are actually performing a series of internal experiments although not too many that parents seem to treasure. They are making deductions and inferences and drawing conclusions on the basis not merely of program content but of the structure of the medium. As Marshall McCluhan[18] said, the medium is the message and, we now add, a root structure of the mind as well. Whereas once upon a time it might have been said that play represented the purest form of thinking for children because in play children assimilate reality into the self, now it might be alleged that television has supplanted play as the most common form of "thinking." This is the point: Children aren't merely watching television, they are absorbing, restructuring, *thinking!* And the adults sitting next to them? If Piaget is correct, they're doing the same thing.

One thing more about this matter of television's role in restructuring the human mind. For Piaget, what goes for thinking, intelligence, and reasoning also goes for morality.[19] What goes, in other words, for consciousness goes for conscience. The ways adolescents assimilate and accommodate to circumstances, knowledge, experiences, shape not only their thinking but the ways they conduct themselves with others as well. Television, therefore, becomes a significant influence on the structure of moral reasoning and moral behavior.[20]

Consider in this regard, two questions arising from the scandal caused by the former president of the United States and a young White House intern. Why did it seem not to bother everyone that Clinton lied to a grand jury as well as to the American people? Moreover, in the context of politics and morality, does it matter what a man does in the private domains of his life?

In great measure, responses to these questions were predicated as much on the television-generated portion of our cognitive framework as anything else. Lying on television, which some might think would be larger than life and utterly unforgivable, often turns out to be an insignificant event if only because television itself creates a framework of performances and sensations. People clearly do not lie all the time on television or in courtrooms, but adolescents know that much of what they see on television is fiction. In other words, adolescents are prepared daily for the illogical, the disconnected, the incoherent, the lie. It is part of the neural net, an inherent ingredient of the structure of their mind fields that has been formed in great measure by experiencing television; hence the lie is not deemed seriously immoral.[21] Damage-control artists, spin doctors, slick defense attorneys, the infamous talking heads, all become acceptable agents of possible untruth, because as the man said, "the play's the thing."[22]

As for the matter of what a man does in privacy, this question, too, is answered in great measure by the ways in which our thinking is structured by television. Reality, adolescents have been taught by television, is constituted of what they directly witness. Everything is in the looking, what the fashion industry calls "the look"; this is a fundamental component of television's framework. What goes on backstage, off screen, in the dressing room, or on rehearsal stages away from the camera doesn't count because it doesn't exist, because no one has seen it. The name of the framework is to bring us news, gossip, events about which we might otherwise not hear, although in common speech we say "see" rather than "hear." ("Did you see what the President said last night?")

The framework provided by television prepares adolescents, therefore, to assess circumstances in terms of what is directly there before them. That quintessential morality is unenforceable morality, that is, ultimate moral acts are those performed when no one is around to observe them or catch us performing them, seems irrelevant. Yet the irrelevance proves logical given the structure created in the adolescent's mind by experiencing television. A constant diet of disconnected events makes the generation of a unifying structure or logical framework difficult. Dewey's writings about reflection speak precisely to this matter:

> Reflection involves not simply a sequence of ideas, but a consequence—a consecutive ordering in such a way that each determines the next as its proper outcome, while each leans back on its predecessors.[23]

Some of Piaget's writings may be captured in the work of psychologist Ellen Langer. Instead of thinking of children or adolescents as being distracted (by television or some other stimulus), Langer suggested instead, that one think of them as being "otherwise attracted."[24]

Think in these contexts of local news programs, typically the most watched of all locally produced shows, and the source of news for vast numbers of citizens. These programs illustrate perfectly the points Dewey raised in his reference to the unself-reflective thinker's fascination with appetite, caprice, sense (or sensation), and immediate circumstance. Television news is summarized by the following passage from *The Boston Globe* describing the role of consultants in actual programming:

> Consultants have been the driving force behind some of the trends that have shaken up the once-staid world of local television journalism: the disappearance of one-hour newscasts; the proliferation of gory crime stories and the sky-is-

falling weather coverage; the information with easy-to-promote "news you can use" about health dangers and consumer rip-offs; the trend toward jazzy graphics; the ubiquitous "live shots" in which, for example, a reporter broadcasts from the lawn of the darkened State House hours after lawmakers have departed; the faster-paced, shorter news story; and the de-emphasis on foreign news and coverage in government and politics (even in Boston, this most political of cities).[25]

Given this apt description of fast-paced, quick story coverage of daily events, all of them, to some degree, restructuring our minds, it may surprise the reader to learn that the one piece of a news broadcast offering the most enduring and continuous coverage is the weather segment, not that all adolescents watch it on a regular basis. Furthermore, within the weather story, the bulk of the time is spent telling the viewer what presently is happening and what has happened today. In addition, much to the disgruntlement of knowledgeable meteorologists, television producers have instituted a five-day forecast that doesn't stand a very good chance of being accurate, not that the audience seems particularly perturbed by this fact.

The fascination with weather is revealed as well in the finding that audiences report the most compelling news story to be a natural disaster. Nothing causes us to run into our living (or TV) rooms quicker than a tornado, hurricane, or earthquake. We watch with awe, horror, and a certain degree of excitement as buildings and bridges are ripped apart, and the sea, with all its ferocity, smashes against shorelines and houses. Not unlike adolescents who are thrilled and terrified by horror movies, we are simultaneously thrilled and terrified by nature's wrath. We find ourselves simultaneously rooting for nature and the victims of its might. Before the 1989 Bay Area earthquake, television hadn't devoted as much continuous commercial free air time to any one story since the assassination of President John F. Kennedy.

There are still more connections between television viewing and the restructuring of the mind. Consider, for example, how rarely viewers react to the notion that forecasting actually "causes" weather to happen. "Well, Peter, you brought us a beautiful day today." Or, "So, George, I see that Mother Nature didn't behave as she was supposed to today, did she?" The mental gymnastics are subtle and often overlooked, but with our consciousness filled with (a belief in) technological certainty and the existing framework of television generally, we may well attribute a weather shift to a glitch in nature rather than to an inadequacy in forecasting.

A similar phenomenon occurs in the sports world where we learn not that the experts have been wrong but that one team "upset" another. We may be impressed that the underdog has won, shocked that the overdog has lost, but rarely does anyone question the essentially subjective methodology that determined the ranking of the teams in the first place.

Our preoccupation with television weather forecasting has a more insidious side. Ironic, isn't it, that while we cannot go to bed without hearing tomorrow's forecast, at the same time the culture has become increasingly alienated from nature and natural phenomena? We may watch more minutes of weather forecasting than any other story, but we nonetheless reveal a diminished respect for the environment and the planet generally. Fascinated by the power and destruction of earthquakes, how many of us actually study the causes of these events? Not only that, we tend not to be that interested in protecting our cities against future quakes or developing the technology that might aid us in the prediction of earthquakes.

Before our very eyes, weather, of all things, becomes the symbolic representation of consciousness and natural disasters the stages on which we play out our dread of destruction (aggression) and death (or more likely, the end of the world) and the fact that no one can predict the time or place of their occurence. The weather story perpetuates the illusion that we can predict and control nature. Only naturally, television will provide a larger-than-life coverage—some contend that it's television's purpose to scare us so that we will continue to watch—but it is *we*, through the restructuring of our mind fields, who have made weather and natural disasters larger than life perhaps because of our inability or reluctance to face real life head on in all of its authentic dimensions. Adolescents are not alone in sometimes choosing to face television's portrayal of real life despite the many inauthentic dimensions inherent in this popular activity. I've always wondered how people would react to a weatherman saying: "Truthfully, I don't have the faintest idea what tomorrow will bring." Would these words for some mark the end of the world?

Living in a state of distracted consciousness in which at some level we recognize that we are avoiding human and natural realities, we wait each night for the meteorologist to authoritatively announce that there will be weather tomorrow, which means that we too will be tomorrow. The sun will rise, and so will we. The sentiment is captured in these words of futurist Harris Sussman:

> ". . . I conclude that we are the future of the future. There's no magic to this. What we are becomes what we will be. That's the part that hasn't sunk in. . . . Despite the way that some techno-simpletons are trying to fool us, the future is not some electronic leap into nowhere. It grows directly out of us today.[26]

That we would sit transfixed before our television screens peering at famous anchormen in expensive safari jackets standing in front of workers on a broken Oakland highway searching for bodies says something about the molecular activity of our mind fields, the impact, really, of all those stimuli constituting our consciousness. It says something about the way adolescents learn about and make sense of nature and themselves as well as the ways they explain themselves and their world to themselves. It says something, too, about the way their consciousness works (and plays) to keep them from losing and, one hopes, someday finding their true selves.

We conclude this section on television and its effect on the structure of the mind by recalling one small part of the criminal trial of O. J. Simpson. Bowing to the seemingly irrefutable edict of the public's right to know, Judge Lance Ito allowed the proceedings to be televised. Thinking perhaps of democracy and freedom having to do with an informed citizenry, he permitted the placement of a television camera in his courtroom.

Fair enough, but notice again the influence of the medium on thinking and reasoning. During the intense camera debate, few people made the point that if the public maintains it has a right to know, it can always read the proceedings verbatim. When, after all, did knowing something become tantamount to viewing that something on television? Are we teaching generations of adolescents that information—"factoids" as they are now called—is tantamount to thoughtfulness and knowledge?

Ironically, the old adage seeing is believing has been destroyed by of all things, television. Surely we know by now that seeing and believing may have nothing to do with one another; neither may lead directly to knowing. Seeing predicts neither what people will believe nor what they will ultimately know. Consider in this regard another "television event": the beating of Rodney King, when seeing, perceiving, believing, and knowing yielded visions, dare I say, of all shapes and colors, and as always, truth lay in the eyes of the beholders.

Seeing, as we have noted, involves conception as well as perception and cognition. We might recall Immanuel Kant's notion that there is no percept without concept.[27] We perceive, in other words, as a function of that which we conceive, and television influences both actions in the mind fields of adolescents. Equally vexing, ideas, concepts, reasoning, imagination, morality exist but cannot be seen.[28] That a person or an idea appears credible or incredible—not so incidentally, one of the most oft-used words in the adolescent's vocabulary—says little about the fundamental substance of that person or idea. Equally significant, adolescents and adults alike often overlook the fact that television shapes even as it records. As it did in the Simpson trial, television remains an architect of cognition and behavior as much as a technological witness of it. It lives in the mind fields of the young as well as their elders.

Screen Speak, Screen Deep

In what he called the "Now this. . ." facet of American culture, sociologist Neil Postman put his finger on one of the troubling matters involving the impact of television on the restructuring of the mind.[29] Too regularly blamed for the country's ills, television has allowed us to feel comfortable digesting brief, discontinuous, and wholly disconnected messages. On average, Postman reports, we experience a change in visual imagery on the television screen every 3.5 seconds. Story themes and topics, similarly, shift every minute or so, perhaps less.

All of this suggests that in their need to be entertained, adolescents run the risk of becoming inured to the proposition that life's experiences are to be examined, reasoned out, and possibly lived as if indeed they were charms on a bracelet. Mere trinkets, the charms clink against one another, as we noted earlier, but possess little or no substance and certainly no connection to one another. That a train wreck story is sandwiched between a state house argument and a commercial for toothpaste hardly fazes the young mind. Adolescents appear to notice neither the intellectual nor the emotional seams, for they are not meant to; esthetically, they remain unruffled. Cognitively, they are prepared to reconcile, blend, mesh, juxtapose, accept, and, thereby, justify as truthful anything they see and hear and abjure any logical causal connections. This is what Postman meant when he wrote the announcement of a plane crash killing 250 people may be followed by the words, "Now this. . . ."

The epistemological point is hardly subtle: To be trained daily on a diet of sound bites, sight bites, and quick bursts of data prepares the unwitting adolescent to accept any order, shape, or form of charm on the bracelet. There is no cognitive reason (or reasoning) for suddenly claiming that a particular charm doesn't belong here or there. It belongs anywhere it wants to belong and, thereby, belongs everywhere and nowhere at the same time.

The idea puts me in mind of the words impact, access, and interface. In our culture, transforming nouns into verbs or verbs into nouns "proves" either one's linguistic creativity or that one is spending a great deal of time in front of television or computer screens. Because the experience of the stimulus is direct and immediate, it is only "natural" that one would ignore the ancillary words like prepositions and verbs and go right to the punch line, the actual stimulus. Click on Internet, bang! Click on connection, bang! Click, access, bang! Click, impact, bang!

If one wishes to bend the laws of grammar or break them entirely, one may pride oneself in having successfully mocked the use of what some still call those fancy three-syllable words. Nowadays, however, and due mainly to what we are calling "screen speak," Americans have begun to speak like Massachusetts motorists drive, seemingly obeying no laws whatsoever.[30] Everyone appears to believe that everything in verbal traffic is fair game. When, moreover, one breaks laws so regularly one tends to forget that laws exist at all. At that point, one calls oneself an artist and a rather creative one at that!

Conversely, a new order, a new set of experiences, a new cognition yields a new vocabulary or at least a new rendering of the old one. In the presence of computer or television screens, things become actions, one-dimensional icons, and prompts become actions; news stories and weather reports become actions, so it makes perfect sense that nouns would be transformed into verbs. In what might be called a world that is merely screen deep, it is only logical that conventional laws of grammar disappear and come to be replaced with language depicting or describing the felt sense, the immediate emotion, the sensation; it is also only logical that a host of social conventions disappears. Adolescents inhabit this new world, this new social order, these new mind fields.

Upon learning that her boyfriend was unable to attend a social function, a young woman attempts to communicate her mortification: "I was like, oh, my God." To be sure, she says it more succinctly, perhaps, than I did in establishing the premise. For whereas I have put down the story line, she merely threads another charm on the bracelet or utters a sound bite. I communicate more in prose derived from literature; she employs prose derived from media reportage, what we are calling screen speak, and what Brown University President Ruth Simmons calls "mall speak."

All of these contemporary linguistic patterns bespeak an emphasis on senses and sensations (and hence sensationalism). As reasoning skills decline, sensual talents become emphasized. The power of language shifts from logic and argument development to what T. S. Eliot called the "jingle of the words" and the expressions of sensations and feelings. The phrase "television impacts a culture" has a far more powerful, well, impact on us than does the word impact as a noun. "It was, like, oh, my God," on the one hand, says nothing at all. On the other hand, it is a clear-cut expression of the felt sense of an immediate sensation. More precisely, it represents or serves as the living embodiment of expression. "I was like, oh, my God" appears closer to communicating the actual sensation than had one employed words like stunned, mortified, shocked, paralyzed. In the mind, the words become the sensation (like the words "bam," "wham," "zap" found in comic books). This notion is generated directly from the impact of television on human cognition because vision without words is all and all. On no remote control unit does one find a visual analog to the mute button. What possibly does one say sitting in front of television or computer screens? What, for that matter, does one say in the face of viewing hundreds of thousands of refugees on television? "It's, like, oh, my God!"

President Simmons' depiction of "mall speak" also draws attention to the abundant use of the word, "like," in contemporary language. The verb "to feel" seemingly has been replaced by "like," just as "to say" has been replaced by "go" or "like." "Like" is strewn about in sentences almost as a tease to the listener that a simile is in the offing, but it rarely is. "Like" has become a shorthand signature for: "I can't think of the words to describe what I am trying to say about that which I am thinking and feeling." In other words, "I was surprised by his failure to turn up at the function and was made to feel profoundly hurt at the same time" is captured by the phrase "I was, like, oh my God." Appearing in crosswords under the clue, "common teenager filler," the abbreviation "like" practically stands as a verbal icon, again representing sensation to be utilized in a host of situations. When the menu offers words like ecstatic, rejected, mortified, anguished, elated, confused, irate, it's easier just to click on "I was like, oh my God."

Consider as well that the word, "like," while in one context emerging as vague expression, in another context bespeaks literal truth. Television and computer screens in fact are "like rendering" instruments. When adolescents see a baseball game on television, it is *like* they are actually at the game. Two seconds later when the camera pans a refugee camp, it is *like* they are there as well. When they go on the Internet and click on the Pushkin Museum, it is *like* they are there, just as it was a moment before when they clicked on the Library of Congress and felt *like* they were there as well. Screen deep and screen speak are nothing more than "like" experiences, for one is inevitably separated from the so-called "real event," "real site," "real source" by the medium. One could allege, therefore, that all of our screen experiences are similes. This is the essence of virtual reality, and the pass word is "like."

Another phrase heard repeatedly among adolescents is the infamous, "You know." It's a trifle more difficult to state precisely what "you know" signifies in everyday speech. Most of us would have to concede that when people utter, "You know," we, the listeners, in fact often don't know. Perhaps "you know," therefore, becomes "I don't know" or a (cognitive) stall in the hope that a reasonable idea just may come down the pike in time. In the end, "you know" appears to symbolize the space between the charms. For the present argument, however, when "you know" is uttered, it is rare that anyone ever interjects, "No, frankly, I don't know."

If it is not simply sloppiness in thinking and reasoning, then "you know" may symbolize for adolescents the "knowledge" held or assumed to be held by other people essentially because inhabitants of popular culture, many of them young, in fact represent the audience of television programming and now, increasingly, visitors to Internet sites. So, "you know," may be taken literally, because in all likelihood I do know what you know, and you know what I know.

Extending this argument, it is also probable that most of us know what others think and feel about significant events and experiences. Results of the omnipresent opinion polls on television suggest that everyone knows everyone's attitudes about a host of things. The essence of popular culture, and this is especially pertinent to adolescence, is that all young people do know things or more likely recognize things because they are so, well, popular. To not know popular culture icons, personalities, fashions, and trends becomes almost inconceivable to the adolescent. Television is the source of that phrase, "for those who have been living in a cave," a phrase implying an incredulity that popular culture personalities, events, and hot Web sites would not be known to the masses of people in the world. Everyone knows Madonna, Ali, Amazon.com, and hotmail. If you don't you must be living in a cave.

More complex is the notion that "knowing" things from television is probably not like "knowing" things from reading.[31] Describing thought is not like describing vision, sound, touch, sensation. Words don't come so easily to us; the picture, as they say, is worth a thousand words. "You know," therefore, may be the verbal icon for every one of those thousand words.

Quite possibly, memories stored and then activated by sight in the process of recalling them,[32] stimulate different regions of the brain than memories stored and activated by mere words, thoughts, or imagination.[33] Recent research on trauma victims indicates that the frequent inability to articulate one's traumatic experiences may be due to the fact that unlike pleasant or at least emotionally uncharged memories, traumatic memories activate (the occipital and amygdala) regions of the brain not directly associated with speech and organizing thought.[34] Recalling normal or uncharged memories, however, tends to stimulate the frontal lobes and speech center of the brain and hence results in more articulate verbal descriptions.[35] It is entirely possible, therefore, that visually acquired information, like the experience of traumatic events (and information gleaned from television and computer screens), may go to different parts of the brain where speech and language play a secondary role. This might account for the traumatized children psychologist Martha Straus describes in work she calls "no-talk therapy,"[36] who cannot speak about what has happened to them or how prior experiences might play out in present sensations and actions.[37] It might also account for this totally understandable utterance of a witness to the shootings at Columbine High School in Colorado:

> They were just, like, they thought it was funny. They were just, like, "Who's next? Who's ready to die?" They were just, like, "We've waited to do this our whole lives." And every time they'd shoot someone, they'd holler, like it was, like, exciting.[38]

If the words, "like," and "you know" cause consternation on the part of listeners, then consider the words, "I mean." Listen for them, they're everywhere. Sentences in the new millennium actually begin with, "I mean." Apparently, before an idea has even been put forth, the speaker has announced that he or she means something other than what is about to be uttered. Or is it that "I mean" suggests that what I think my brain is about to expel is not exactly what I mean for it to expel. Without even knowing for certain what I am going to say or want to say for that matter, I have some sense that it is not what I wish to say or should say, not that I am certain I know what I want to say or should say.

How to make sense of all this. One friend suggests that "I mean" is merely a speaker's plea to be taken seriously, a notion that might resonate with adolescents. Like "like," "you know," and "now this," "I mean" unites inchoate, unformulated, and inevitably discontinuous items of thought and language, the charms, in other words, on the cognitive bracelet. "I mean" appears to be the verbal equivalent of pushing the "pause" button on the VCR or the time spent waiting for the next Internet connection to be consummated. Or is it once again a byproduct of the tension between sensation and reason? The point becomes clearer by suggesting that one's very modes of thinking and speaking have become so incomplete, disconnected, interrupted (not unlike normal television broadcasting and Internet surfing), no continuous, linked, and logical line of reasoning can properly be established.

Television broadcasters know this fact well. During times of war and natural disasters, when anxiety among the population reaches high levels, all networks announce: "Stay with us for continuous coverage." Beside the obvious emotional power of the sights and sounds of the events we experience on TV, the intellectual value of *continuous* coverage should be noted. Continuous coverage grabs our focus and earns our complete and undivided attention. Inevitably, these presentations contain various distractions, but the structure of the viewer's learning becomes more continuous and closely knit than ever before with this one medium. In the same way, there will always be a significant difference between the animated (though discontinuous) classroom discussion, and the solitary work required to write a (continuous) long term paper.

It appears that the culture is instructing the young to click on brief, entertaining, sensational, immediate, arousing messages rather than well-examined, logical, coherent, or reasoned ones.[39] Screen work of all varieties ineluctably leads us to consider an eleventh commandment: "Thou shall not bore," and adolescents know how frightening is the prospect of boring oneself. The sights, sounds, and images must constantly change, we have decided, if the mind fields are to be properly nourished. What does it say about us that a poll conducted as I write these words reveals that the overwhelming reaction to a presidential candidate is that he is boring. Nothing is mentioned about his politics, ideology, intelligence, proposals, programs, morality. One is either good TV fare or one is not, so how is it surprising that adolescents would believe that national elections are little more than show business auditions. After all, young people see cars with bumper stickers that counsel, "If you see something boring, kill it!"

More serious is that screen-speak mentality causes adolescents to imagine that what they possess is knowledge, when frequently it is merely a collection of bits (or bytes) of information. In the manner of busy, hurried corporate or government officers, many young people feel overwhelmed by the information that ought to be installed in their minds. Briefed—an apt word—in the morning by television and quick newspaper reads, although adolescents tend not to pick up the daily paper, and during the day by radio (albeit call-in and music shows more than newscasts), they go about their business picking up daily tidbits and pieces of information.

No assimilation of facts ever resembles the work of the classroom or, even better, the dreaded long term paper.

Daily, adolescents play with computers—increasingly more often, the information transmitted to large television screens—where unwittingly, they advance the notion that data, bytes, and bookmarked Web sites constitute knowledge or the pathways to it. They admire quiz show contestants for their *incredible* range of knowledge, but it isn't knowledge, actually, that these contestants are asked to display; it's data, info, and bytes, usually about facets of popular culture. It is almost as if contestants and students alike are living in Web sites. Perhaps one should refer to their accumulation of information by the term television has created— factoids. One wonders why we need the suffix "oid"? Is it because "oid" lends a certain scientific aura to a screen-deep sliver of otherwise mundane information? I am troubled by this matter because it reminds me of a word connoting the transformation of something sacrosanct, the newspaper, into something despicable, the tabloid. (It's difficult to know, moreover, what to do with one definition of the word "tabloid": A drug in condensed form.)

Like human minicomputers, quiz show contestants and, alas, some students, are rewarded for their ability to collect and retain facts, but this has little to do, as Saul Bellow has pointed out, with knowledge.[40] It is wonderful that they know the author of *Jane Eyre*, or the celestial constellation with "bear" in its name, or the French word for sea. Yet although many of us swoon at a contestant's display of "knowledge," "ultimately *Eyre*, bear and "mer" constitute just another charm bracelet. Benjamin Barber enriches this point when he writes:

> In substituting data for purpose and in believing that facts are surrogates for values, informationalism and its anarchic products actually imperil our identities, corrupt our democratic institutions and destabilize the economic foundations of our tenets of social justice.[41]

In the hope of honoring many people, young and old, imagine a television quiz show called "Discourse," in which contestants are asked to speak on a chosen topic, absent any screens, for say, one hour. (Recall that in televised presidential debates, candidates are rarely allowed more than a minute or so to speak on any one topic.) Imagine further, that in order to reach this plateau of public presentation, contestants must write a 250-page monograph that will be independently judged by three people on its factual or scientific bases, the quality of its reasoning and logic as well as its contribution to the culture's understanding of that particular subject. In addition, the document will be assessed in terms of the argument's originality and use of language.

A television program of this description would die on the drawing board (or is it drawing "bored"?); it would be seen as garnering negative ratings points. Not only would one hear channels changing in all 50 states, one would hear television sets being smashed against living room walls. Yet that show, possibly titled "Discourse," describes the context in which doctors of philosophy and education compete. The theses generated by these women and men and the oral examination that traditionally follows the approval of the dissertation usually by a committee of three professors may seem wasteful or useless to some. Nonetheless, they do at least acquaint a person with the nature of the cognitive and intellectual efforts required to locate a certain truth or hard-earned and studied wisdom. Yet this is a generation raised on the principles of screen speak. So when there's a choice, a distracted culture tends to teach its young people to opt for ABC, NBC, and CBS over Ph.D, Ed.D, and L.H.D.

Notes

1   See G. A. Fine, J. T. Mortimer, and D. F. Roberts, "Leisure, Work, and the Mass Media." In. S. S. Feldman and G. R. Elliot (Editors), *At the Threshold: The Developing Adolescent.* Cambridge, MA: Harvard University Press, 1990; A. C. Huston, B. A. Watkins, and D. Kenkel, "Public Policy and Children's Television." *American Psychologist, 44,* 1989: 424–433; E. Wartella, K. Heintz, A. Aidman, and S. Mazzarella, "Television and Beyond: Children's Video Media in One Community." *Communications Research, 17,* 1992: 45–64; B. R. Clifford, B. Gunter, and J. L. McAleer, *Television and Children.* Hillsdale, New Jersey: Erlbaum, 1995; R. Larson, R. Kubey, and J. Colletti, "Changing Channels: Early Adolescent Media Choices and Shifting Investments." *Journal of Youth and Adolescence, 18,* 1989: 583–599; J. C. Condry, *The Psychology of Television.* Hillsdale, NJ: Erlbaum, 1989; F. Williams, R. LaRose, and F. Frost, *Children, Television, and Sex-Role Stereotyping.* New York: Praeger, 1981; K. Durkin, "Television and Sex-Role Acquisition 1: Content." *British Journal of Social Psychology, 24,* 1985: 101–113; N. Signorielli, "Television and Adolescents' Perception of Work." *Youth and Society, 24,* 1993: 314–341; and D. Buerkel-Rothfuss, and S. Mayes, "Soap Opera Viewing: The Cultivation Effect." *Journal of Communication, 31,* 1981: 108–115.

2   M. R. Lepper and J. Gurtner, "Children and Computers: Approaching the Twenty-First Century." *American Psychologist, 44,* 1989: 170–178.

3   See R. J. Sternberg, *Intelligence Applied.* San Diego: Harcourt, Brace Jovanovich, 1986; M. R. Lepper and J. Gurtner, op. cit.; M. R. Lepper, "Microcomputers in Education: Motivational and Social Issues." *American Psychologist, 40,* 1985: 1–18; A. Collins, "Teaching Reading and Writing with Personal Computers." In J. Oransanu (Editor), *A Decade of Reading Research: Implications for Practice.* Hillsdale, New Jersey: Erlbaum, 1986; D. F. Roberts, "Adolescents and the Mass Media: From 'Leave It to Beaver' to 'Beverly Hills 90210.'" In R. Takanishi (Editor), *Adolescence in the 1990s.* New York: Teachers College, 1993.

4   Cited in review of Sven Birkerts, *Readings,* by Melvin Jules Bukiet. *The Boston Globe,* February 21, 1999: C3.

5   Jean Piaget, *Six Psychological Studies.* New York: Random House, 1967; Jean Piaget, *The Growth of Logical Thinking from Childhood to Adolescence.* New York: Basic Books, 1958. See also, T. Revenson and D. Singer, *A Piaget Primer: How a Child Thinks.* New York: Plume, 1978; John J. Phillips, Jr., *The Origins of Intellect: Piaget's Theory.* San Francisco: Freeman, 1975; H. Beilin, "Piaget's Enduring Contribution to Developmental Psychology." *Developmental Psychology, 28,* 1992: 191–204; and R. Case, "Neo-Piagetian Theory: Retrospect and Prospect." *International Journal of Psychology, 22,* 1987: 773–791.

6   M. D. Berzonsky, "Formal Reasoning in Adolescence: An Alternative View." *Adolescence, 13,* 1978: 279–290.

7   J. R. Anderson, *Cognitive Psychology and Its Implications* (3rd Edition). New York: Freeman, 1990; S. Carey, "Are Children Fundamentally Different Kinds of Thinkers and Learners than Adults?" In K. Richardson and S. Sheldon (Editors), *Cognitive Development to Adolescence*. Hillsdale, NJ: Erlbaum, 1988; D. P. Keating, "Adolescent Thinking." In S.S. Feldman and G.R. Elliot (Editors), *At the Threshold: The Developing Adolescent*. Cambridge, MA: Harvard University Press, 1990; and J. R. Anderson, *Cognitive Psychology and Its Implications* (3rd Edition). New York: Freeman, 1990.

8   It is interesting to note that on various cognitive tests some autistic children appear not to understand "know" but do understand "see." In other words, they cannot figure out how another person might react to something. What they see is what they "know" to be true. Psychologists suggest that this is due to the fact that autistic children have no "theory of mind" which makes it difficult if not impossible for them to understand something by working it out in their heads. Similarly, autistic children, also on the basis of tests, can deal with hidden objects but not hidden knowledge. See Rita Wicks-Nelson and Allen C. Israel, *Behavior Disorders of Childhood* (3rd Edition).Upper Saddle River, NJ: Prentice-Hall, 1997, pages 299–321.

9   Jean Piaget, *The Growth of Logical Thinking from Childhood to Adolescence*. New York: Basic Books, 1958

10 Ibid; Robert Kegan, *The Evolving Self*. Cambridge, MA: Harvard University Press, 1982.

11 Jean Piaget, op. cit., see notes of Chapter 1; Jean Piaget, *The Language and Thought of the Child*. New York: Humanities Press, 1959.

12 See Luke Y. Tsai and Mohammed Ghaziuddin, "Autistic Disorder." In *Textbook of Child and Adolescent Psychiatry* (2nd Edition), Jerry M. Wiener (Editor). Washington, DC: American Psychiatric Press, 1997: 219–254.

13 Noam Chomsky, *Language and Thought*. Wakefield, RI: Moyer Bell, 1993; Massimo Piatelli-Palmarini, *Language and Learning: The Debate Between Jean Piaget and Noam Chomsky*. Cambridge, MA: Harvard University Press, 1980; Howard Gardner, *The Mind's New Science: A History of the Cognitive Revolution*. New York: Basic Books, 1987; and Stephen J. Pinker, *How the Mind Works*. New York: Norton, 1997.

14 I cannot resist at this juncture, reproducing the following advertisement: "Life is a rush into the unknown. You can duck down and hope nothing hits you, or stand up as tall as you can, show it your teeth and say, dish it up, baby, and don't be stingy with the jalapeños." In *Architectural Digest*, January 2000, pages 4 and 5.

15 Jean Piaget, *The Language and Thought of the Child,* op. cit.

16 This citation is taken from L. C. Burello and D. D. Sage, *Leadership and Change in Special Education*. Englewood Cliffs, NJ: Prentice-Hall, 1979, page 1. Cited in Dina A. Traniello, "Inclusion of Students with Disabilities in Three Elementary

Schools: Values, Policies, and Practices." Doctoral dissertation, Boston University, 1999, page 21. Thomas M. Skrtic defines a paradigm as "a set of implicit basic beliefs or presuppositions that unrandomize complexity and provide scientists with a general picture of the world and how it works." Cited in Traniello, op. cit., page 21.

17   See Stephen Pinker, *How the Mind Works*, op. cit.

18   Marshall McLuhan and Quentin Fiori, *The Medium Is the Message*. New York: Bantam, 1967; Marshall McLuhan and Eric McLuhan, *The New Science*. Toronto: University of Toronto Press, 1988; and *Understanding Media: The Extensions of Man*. New York: McGraw-Hill, 1964.

19   Jean Piaget, *Six Psychological Studies*. New York: Random House, 1967; Lawrence Kohlberg, *The Psychology of Moral Development: The Nature and Validity of Moral Stages*. San Francisco: Harper and Row, 1984; See also John Martin Rich and Joseph DeVitis, *Theories of Moral Development*. Springfield, IL: Thomas, 1985.

20   See A. C. Huston, B. A. Watkins, and D. Kunkel, "Public Policy and Children's Television." *American Psychologist*, 1989, *44*: 424–433; W. J. McQuire, "The Myth of Massive Media Impact: Savagings and Salvagings." In G. Comstock (Editor), *Public Communication and Behavior*. Orlando: Academic Press, 1986; J. C. Condry, *The Psychology of Television*. Hillsdale, NJ: Erlbaum, 1989; V. C. Strasburger, *Adolescents and the Media*. Newbury Park, CA: Sage Publications, 1995; R. M. Liebert and J. Sprafkin, *The Early Window*. New York: Pergamon, 1989; D. P. Phillips, "The Impact of Mass Media Violence on US Homicides." *American Sociological Review, 48*, August, 1983: 560–568; D. Zillman and J. Bryant (Editors), *Perspectives on Media Effects: Awareness in Theory and Practice*. Hillsdale, NJ: Erlbaum, 1994; and J. L. Salvaggio and J. Bryant (Editors), *Media Use in the Information Age: Emerging Patterns of Adoption and Consumer Use*. Hillsdale, NJ: Erlbaum, 1989.

21   On a related point, see George Noblit and Van Dempsey, *The Social Construction of Virtue: The Moral Life of Schools*. Albany: State University of New York Press, 1996.

22   On this same note, Michael Oreskes wrote "The real danger is not from the concentrated power of the state but from the diffusion of media voices so cacophonous and filled with trivia that they drown out everything more important for a civil society to function." See his review of *Monica's Story* by Andrew Morton, *The New York Times Book Review*, April 4, 1999: 6.

23   John Dewey, *How We Know*, Amherst, NY: Prometheus, 1991, page 3. Cited in Arthur Beane, "The Supervision of Student Teachers: An Emphasis on Self-Reflection." Unpublished manuscript, Boston University, 1999, page 15.

24   Ellen J. Langer, *The Power of Mindful Learning*. Reading, MA: Perseus, 1997.

25   *The Boston Globe*, April 30, 1999: A12.

26 Harris Sussman, "Americans Hurry into Future Without a Plan." *Sunday Camera,* Boulder, Colorado, January 20, 1991: 3B.

27 Immanuel Kant, *The Critique of Pure Reason*, translation by J. M. D. Meikeljohn. Boston: Tuttle Company, 1993.

28 W. M. Kurtines and J. Gewirtz (Editors), *Moral Behavior and Development.* Hillsdale, NJ: Erlbaum, 1991.

29 See Neil Postman, *Amusing Ourselves to Death: Public Discourse in the Age of Show Business.* New York: Penguin, 1986.

30 S. Scribner, "Modes of Thinking and Ways of Speaking: Culture and Logic Reconsidered." In P. N. Johnson-Laird and P. C. Wartson (Editors), *Thinking: Readings in Cognitive Science.* New York: Cambridge University Press, 1977.

31 L. B. Resnick, *Education and Learning to Think.* Washington, DC: National Academy Press, 1987; Howard Gardner, *Frames of Mind: The Theory of Multiple Intelligences.* New York: Basic Books, 1983; J. D. Bransford, R. Sherwood, N. Vye, and J. Reiser, "Teaching Thinking and Problem Solving: Suggestions from Research." *American Psychologist, 41,* 1986: 1078–1089.

32 John Kotre, *White Gloves: How We Create Ourselves Through Memory.* New York: The Free Press, 1995.

33 Martha Straus, *No-Talk Therapy for Children and Adolescents.* New York: Norton, 1999.

34 Bessel van der Kolk, Alexander C. McFarlane, and Lars Weisaeth (Editors), *Traumatic Stress: The Effects of Overwhelming Experience on Mind, Body and Society.* New York: Guilford, 1996; and van der Kolk, *Psychological Trauma.* Washington, DC: American Psychiatric, 1987.

35 John Ratey and Catherine Johnson, *Shadow Syndromes: The Mild Forms of Major Mental Disorders That Sabotage Us.* New York: Bantam, 1998.

36 Martha Straus, *No Talk Therapy for Children and Adolescents.*, op. cit.

37 D. K. Lapsley, "Continuity and Discontinuity in Adolescent Social Cognitive Development." In R. Montemayor, G. Adams, and T. Gulotta (Editors), *From Childhood to Adolescence: A Transitional Period?* Newbury Park, CA: Sage, 1990.

38 Crystal Woodman, cited in *The Boston Globe*, April 24, 1999: A19. See also Allan M. Hoffman (Editor), *Schools, Violence and Society.* Westport: Praeger, 1996.

39 J. P. Guilford, *The Structure of Intellect.* New York: McGraw-Hill, 1967.

40 In a lecture at the Kennedy School of Government, Harvard University, 1989.

41 Benjamin Barber, "Brave New World." Review of three volumes by Manuel Castells. *The Los Angeles Times*, May 23, 1999: A24.

PART IV

THE FIELDS OF THE INNER WORLD

Chapter 7

The Exploration of Self

The Modes of Being

A lovely child in a Nantucket home follows her mother around as the woman makes certain her guests' dinner plates are filled and their appetites satisfied. The child is bored, verging on irritability. Still, at age six, she finds the strength to show a happy face although she must wonder about the peculiar customs of tall people who stand for long periods of time just talking.

Suddenly, one of the guests goes to her, kneels down and says, "You know what I'd like?" She shakes her head, traces of fear appearing on her face. "I'd like to see your bedroom." Just like that, the child's expression is transformed. Grinning, she looks to her mother for permission, and before you know it the two new friends are bounding up the stairs to her second-floor room.

The child's lecture and tour of her belongings—what the French, who reserve such sojourns for castles and stately homes, call *son et lumière*—lasts 45 minutes. With the visitor sitting on the bed, the little girl speaks volumes about every object in her room. The stuffed animals and dolls come alive, and the descriptions of the wall murals her mother has painted are delivered with adoration and limitless enthusiasm. The child is revealing her inner world and in the process, hearing, recognizing, and probably discovering inner colors, inner voices. As for the adult, he merely shuts up and smiles.

Finally the man asks, "Do you like to draw?" "Oh yes," the girl answers, turning at once toward a painted cabinet under the window to fetch her little art supplies. Within seconds, party dress and party shoes and all, she is stationed on the carpeted floor bending over a pad of paper, her crayons in the wooden box beside her, hard at work. The adult knows he is witnessing hard work by the sounds of the little girl's deep breathing.

"What are you drawing?" comes the totally superfluous inquiry. "You'll see," comes the reply. One isn't certain whether she knows what she's drawing, but the less she knows, one hypothesizes, the more likely she is to tap the region of the inner voice. But this is a child at work. In the adolescent, the process works almost the same way but not quite. The main difference is that adolescents have become highly sensitive to and aware of the workings of their inner world, being thrilled as well as scared by its capacities and power. Borrowing the language of the day, exploration of the inner world, which is the basis of this chapter, reveals the true human internet and the adolescent as a most fascinated browser.

We commence our discussion of the adolescent search for the inner voice by reviewing a small portion of a theory advanced first by the philosopher Martin Heidegger[1] and later by the psychologist Rollo May.[2]

We live, according to Heidegger and May, in three distinct but overlapping aspects of the world or what has been called modes of being. There is first the *Umwelt*, "the world around us," which for the philosopher and psychologist alike means essentially our biological and genetic inheritance. In a sense, the *Umwelt* is the world without consciousness, the world of biological determinism. Like it or not, we have to sleep; we have to eat, and, something adolescents examine with a host of feelings, we have to die.

It may said that the *Umwelt* represents what neuroscientists call the genome.[3] Strange that we might be tempted to slight it in a discussion on searching for the inner voice inasmuch as so much of what we are, that which is called temperament or, more appropriately, our disposition, is what the genome establishes for us.[4] One's shyness, resilience, happiness, lingering sadness may all be part of the genome, for we know that moods or temperamental qualities of various sorts are determined in great measure by brain substances and the workings of neurotransmitters. Students of psychiatry and psychology recognize names like epinephrine, dopamine, cortisol, and serotonin. The rest of us, adolescents included, recognize the names of the drugs meant to manipulate the presence of these substances in the neurological bath. One suspects that the brand names Prozac, Zoloft, Paxil, and Ritalin are recognized by more than a few adolescents as are the names ecstasy, speed, acid, coke.

I simplify a colossal complexity when I suggest that the genome is a bit like the hardware that works one's computer. Or perhaps the reader prefers to envision it as the software that comes with the computer and makes possible all the functions that we ask of the computer after we pour in our own data, records, billing information, finances, addresses, the material that one might liken to experience, culture, and society, the so-called nurture side of the equation. From this analogy, we derive a sense of just how much the computer can do, how little of it we actually utilize or truly understand, how little of it we need to understand in order to perform our daily functions, and how, to a certain extent, it delimits the actions we take. When the computer breaks down—a process appropriately called "crashing"—we come to feel the same sickening sensations that stroke patients do who have lost some of their vital functions or seem unable to manage as they did before.[5] (Interesting that in computer work we speak of hardware and software, and in neurological assessments we speak in terms of hard signs and soft signs.)[6]

Our biological predisposition, the *Umwelt*, may bring forth yet another set of experiences for us. Consider our reactions to a newborn baby: She has her mother's eyes, we say, or her father's chin. Perhaps these resemblances actually exist, perhaps not, yet we hunt for them, nonetheless, usually imagining that we have found them. The eyes and the chin, therefore, become part of the world surrounding (and within) the baby, the attachments of a primitive order made to one's parents. What we are seeing, or more precisely insisting that we see, is a biological connection to parents and grandparents. We're hunting for or seeking to establish a line of familial alliances, a phylogeny, a biologically based sense of connection and mutuality that will forever link this baby to all of her ancestors, and even more, to all of the people with whom she will identify through racial, ethnic, possibly even religious affiliations. Think now, that at the moment of birth, even as we oooh and ahh over this precious miracle, we have begun the social portion of the *Umwelt* work: the establishment of phylogenetic attachments. As the child grows older, we will focus more on her ontogenetic features, her personal evolution, but the phylogenetic roots have already been laid. Surely we know the significance of rootedness, religious or secular, in a person's life and sense of well being.[7] At bottom, rootedness is the source of our being, the place where many of us imagine we are attached to all of those exactly like us. Rootedness, moreover, may show its face in our desire to carry on our "kind," our family name, our line. Rootedness may be a valuable concept for explaining why the most liberal defenders of the so-called rainbow coalition nonetheless fear racial, ethnic, or religious assimilation.

We all seek roots, we all seek pure, unadulterated origins. Competing for a special place in their parents' hearts, children and adolescents razz brothers and sisters about their being adopted almost as if they themselves need to occupy that one special phylogenetic position in the family's ancestry. Similarly, it has been argued, though not scientifically confirmed, that adopted children in some intuitive manner "know" that their parents are not their birth parents. In transracial adoptions, by a certain age, intuition is hardly required, but might it be possible that the adopted child knows or senses that her adoptive parents are not her birth parents?

If we, the baby's first visitors, hunt for some physical (phylogenetic) connections between baby and parents, then clearly young children and adolescents do the same thing. They, too, wish to know where they got their eyes or chin, and now for that matter, as they grow more sophisticated, their sense of humor and ability to do mathematics. Daily they are offered answers to some of their questions: "Believe me," their father tells them, "you didn't get your mathematical brains from me. Those you owe to your mother." Research indicates that disorders like substance abuse and depression also reveal connections between children and their birth parents. Twin and adoption studies suggest higher rates of disorders in children where one or both parents have the disorder.[8] Indeed, one of the prime issues adopted children offer for justifying their search for birth parents is the wish to obtain their medical history.[9] One suspects, however, they are hunting for something more profound, something to be discovered in the realm of the social world, what May called the *Mitwelt*, a mode of being we examine in a moment. One suspects, too, that residing in that realm as well, is the reason many people seem unwilling to adopt a child, fearing that no matter how much they loved him or her, the child ineluctably would not be "their own." Understanding these points regarding the biological connections to family, adolescents, too, debate the question of whether they might someday adopt a child.

There is more to this matter of the *Umwelt*. No one knows precisely how it works, whether it is science or mere metaphor, but one imagines that the phylogenetic connection of which we are speaking remains something more significant than mere philosophical musing. Perhaps it is the first grade assignment to create what used to be called a family tree, which, because of so many adoptions and blended families, teachers now speak of as a "family orchard." Perhaps it is the child hunting for photographs of Mom and Dad when they were her age. Perhaps it is the relatives who inevitably comment on her resemblance to her parents or grandparents or the moment when the infant looks in the mirror and recognizes that the face she beholds is her own. Perhaps it is the day when the child is told (incorrectly) that somewhere on the earth walks her *doppelgänger*, her *exact* likeness.[10] Whatever it is, part of the exploration of the inner (*Umwelt*) caves, the inner voices, is the hunt for a so-called pure affiliation with people who look and act and seem exactly like her.

What could be more relevant to the daily behavior of adolescents who also evaluate people according to how similar or different they seem. No, this is not precisely it: Adolescents crave more than what someone seems to be; they desire to know what he or she actually is. Evaluations and examinations of this sort are critical to adolescents as they develop associations and intimacies and ultimately prepare for their first sexual encounters. For the first time in their lives, adolescents confront the nature of their sexuality, surely a fundamental component of the *Umwelt*. Children have crushes on people, but adolescents take this feeling of a crush to the next step, acting on it perhaps, or at least confronting their sexual desires and preferences, all the while remaining discreetly conscious of the social definitions (and constructions) of proper and improper attraction and behavior. In these early moments of intimacy, adolescents are reacting as well as constructing the very nature of what they will experience as intimacy.[11]

For there to be relationships with others, the adolescent requires something the child never considered—some fundamental, almost biological connection. The most difficult connections of all perhaps are those with people who appear different from us. Under the skin, it is said, we are all alike, an invalid but nonetheless comforting sentiment. Yet many adolescents cannot get past the skin, the appearance, "the look," the solely physical. What they see tells them all they need to know: It is what might be called, after Heidegger, their "sight geist." When examining faces and skin, shapes and colors, adolescents are not only undertaking the work of perception and relating it to the development of felt senses at far more sophisticated levels than the young child does, they are hunting for something else: A connection to those with whom they choose to identify, those with whom they feel identical.[12] Hold in mind that identicality, as Erikson[13] pointed out, will play a major role in the development of their unique identities.

Philosophically sophisticated or not, parents observing the new brand of connections their children are developing with friends, remind their adolescents that blood is thicker than water, often urging them, perhaps, to stick with their own kind. (Interestingly, the words kin and kind derive from a similar root.) Whereas once, children were comforted by the knowledge that home and community were where one found people (exactly) like themselves, adolescents now seem conflicted by this knowledge.

Wishing to belong, they hunt for peer groups who relieve them from a sense of alienation, detachment, aloneness, and, ironically, individual uniqueness, the one feature they claim to treasure above all else. Still, there is that growing conflict among those young people who, while drawing security from the sameness of family, now find intolerable a parent's insistence that they "run with their own kind."

If inner city has become code for poor and black, then community may be the code word for people exactly like us, "our (kin and our) kind." Think of expressions like "giving back to the community," and "returning to the community." Think, too, of how in some communities there is a breakdown of neighborhoods into "turf," where occupants must look and act alike. The very notion of gang bespeaks identicality, social purity, and "collective uniqueness."

The culture may advertise its famous melting-pot slogan, but adolescents know the melting pot is the classroom in which every variety of integration of turf and differences has had to be worked out. The fundamental principle of America's democracy is embodied in the public school, in which religious integration, sex integration, racial integration, and now the inclusion of children with disabilities in regular classrooms continues to be enacted. Adolescents also recognize that many of their schools have witnessed very little melting, yet the process continues.

At every step of our social evolution, people have had to resolve a fundamental, biological felt sense of phylogenetic connection. Although people revel in what is called diversity or the rainbow coalition, we know that members of the coalition still feel a trifle more comfortable with their "own kind," which is perfectly normal and expected. Life in a school cafeteria is predicated on people hunting for and finding their brothers and sisters. Most of us prefer to break bread with our family.[14]

We also know that there are people experiencing the most horrendous revulsion of diversity and the rainbow coalition, people who want families pure, schools pure, communities pure, entire nations pure. Supremacist groups, ethnic cleansing, and nationalism taken to the extreme of jingoism reveal what happens when what we allege to be a perfectly natural biological process reaches abnormal proportions. Yet biology once again offers a template for this: It is called tumor formation. It is natural development gone mad, a process taken to destructive degrees, an evolution that cannot be properly controlled nor halted; we call it cancer. Sad to say, adolescents have had their encounters with this world as well. They have been victims, moreover, of this particular form of social pathology.

The second mode of being, the *Mitwelt*, or the "with world," is the world in which Heidegger and May postulated we live with others.[15] Meanings in this realm are determined in great measure by our relationships which must constantly be negotiated and to which we must adjust. In a word, the *Mitwelt* is a realm in which people are mutually affected by one another. It begins early in life even before children normally learn to manipulate people in order to shape relationships or at least draw some resource from others in an effort to be liked and cared for. It is also possible that in beginning to internalize another person, the child is beginning to feel that person's joy or even hopelessness living within them as part of themselves.[16]

Finally, there is the realm of what Heidegger and May call our "own world," the *Eigenwelt*. This is the context in which I relate to myself; it is the personal world turned on itself, and, hence, it is the world of self-exploration, self-knowing, experiencing, and most assuredly the world of personal attention to self and the formation of identity. It is also the world in which, borrowing from the dividends of the *Mitwelt*, the child is meant to learn the language of emotional states, how to soothe oneself and withstand occasions of emotional turmoil and flooding. Interestingly, May points out that the *Eigenwelt* is not merely the realm of subjective inner experience and emotional states although it does include these. More precisely, it is the basis on which we see the world in what we determine to be our "true perspective." It is here that we learn to understand what things genuinely mean to us, a concept all adolescents come to appreciate.

The *Eigenwelt* is also the world of identity and consciousness[17] that one probably begins to experience upon entering adolescence when one becomes conscious of one's identity and perhaps struggles with definitions of identity. (The ability to think about one's own thinking—"going meta"—assists the adolescent in the work of the *Eigenwelt*.) This onset of so-called *Eigenwelt* considerations likely marks the (philosophical) onset of adolescence. If the *Umwelt* teaches adolescents the meaning of fate and destiny, and the *Mitwelt*, the role of responsibility to others, then the *Eigenwelt* is the world (ideally) of nondistracted self-awareness.

If adolescents are deeply involved with self-awareness, identity seeking and personal explorations, all normal functions of the *Eigenwelt*, then their actions often are described as being little more than selfish indulgences and personal celebrations.[18] They are nothing more than narcissism writ large, and adolescents are seen as the leading characters in a dangerously narcissistic drama. Accordingly, it is believed that adolescents have to be distracted in order to slide them away from those inner caves in which the actions undertaken in the *Eigenwelt* take place, actions that ineluctably lead to manifestly narcissistic actions. In a word, the modern world seeks to suppress adolescents' experiences of themselves, their self-consciousness or perceived self-absorption, and the sense of that which is emerging as their identity and humanity.

Not surprisingly, May recognized that the modern world of technology and industry stood poised to oppose the "work" of the *Eigenwelt*, something to which Ann Weiser Cornell also subscribed:

> Inheritors of Western industrial culture, especially Americans, are very oriented toward doing, toward making something happen. So it can be a very powerful inner attitude to just be. This is a process of being with something without an agenda, spending time with it, keeping it company—and no more.[19]

Historically, cultural efforts to silence the adolescent's inner voice have resided mainly in schools, although to a certain extent in the home as well. Children, and particularly adolescents, it was believed, had to be taught to conform. They had to learn that individual expression could not always be condoned. Besides, what would make children feel more insecure than allowing them to search within themselves for those dreaded caves and the voices they safeguarded? To permit adolescents to express themselves, it was postulated, was to induce anxiety. In the same way, it was argued that to teach adolescents about sex was to encourage them to engage in sexuality. The less said, the sooner dangerous thoughts and trips to the inner caves would conclude.

May, predictably, took just the opposite approach in an argument that Fromm, too, engaged in *Escape from Freedom*.[20] Genuine repression, May argued, is not the stifling of purely unconscious drives and motives (of the *Umwelt*). More likely, it is the suppression of the human potential unique to every individual (in the *Eigenwelt*). It is a blocking (off) of awareness and the consciousness. It is a barricade against self-knowing, experiencing, and, hence, it is felt as anxiety, something most all adolescents know well.[21] Readers will recognize the familiar theme of Freudian repression of sexual and aggressive urges,[22] but it is important to point out that for May, repression referred not to the struggle between the surging id and a somewhat intimidated ego that derived its energy from the id,[23] but rather to the struggle of being against nonbeing. Not surprisingly, adolescents frequently engage (in) both of these matters not only intellectually but experientially as well. For it is not uncommon for adolescents to explore the outer limits of sexuality and being, both in their minds and in their public behavior.

Heidegger and May also differed from Freud in their theories of anxiety. For Freud, anxiety was spawned by the loss of objects or the unbearable tensions caused by imbalances (disequilibrium) of id and ego, the drives, and the emerging self constantly being obliged to manage tensions of the inner and outer worlds.[24] Although Freud wrote relatively little about the adolescent, believing the personality had formed well before the onset of adolescence or even the period of the life cycle that preceded it, the so-called latency period, what he did say seems relevant to the lives of adolescents:[25] Loss of significant objects, friends, parents, ideals, beliefs, dreams, often throws the adolescent into sadness or even serious depression.[26] In a developmental stage during which identity is being constructed and the inner caves explored, one becomes particularly sensitive to the absence or loss of traits, gifts, people, childhood. Or is it perhaps that adolescence is when young people discover what might be called their "anti-identity," that part of human capability and talent which they now recognize they may never possess? As the adolescent laments that he is now as tall as he will become, so might he lament the other cards with which he must now play out his entire life. These are the degrees of intelligences, as Gardner[27] has theorized, that will govern his public and private odysseys.

All of which leads us to May's definition of anxiety as the representation of a fear of one's power not only to know oneself but ultimately to take responsibility for (knowing) oneself. In many respects, this becomes the central dictate of the adolescent stage of development: the responsibility to fully learn about oneself and take responsibility for this self that is being constructed and examined. As Robert Coles wrote, "We also know way down within ourselves how eagerly most children look for moral clues from their parents, their teachers."[28] Without saying it, the moral component of identity lives within the notion of responsibility; to act responsibly is to act morally. The concept of responsibility assumes that one not only knows the right way but acts the right way. Indeed, the essence of ethical behavior as it is being learned by the adolescent is captured in this notion of responsibility.[29]

If pleasure and survival were the guiding principles for Freud,[30] the id demanding the former, the ego the latter, then it could also be said that the adolescent is now perceived as constantly desiring pleasure and his or her parents as often hoping for mere survival. One cannot overlook in this context the idea that pleasure-seeking drives of adolescents are associated in the minds of their elders with the pushing of life's outermost edges. Children die, most assuredly, but primarily as victims of crime, accident, and illness. Adolescents, in contrast, cause death to themselves and others. They not only flirt with the Devil, they challenge him but not because, as it is often alleged, they imagine they will live forever.[31] The challenge derives from the discovery that one can do more than reflect on the meaning of death; one can become the agent of death, the person solely responsible for terminating life. In a word, explorations of the mind fields lead adolescents to discover that they will die, and some young people, unfortunately, have no patience with fate or destiny.[32]

For May, self-knowledge was an essential principle underlying the concept of anxiety. Of course, a child made to feel insecure experienced anxiety. Yet anxiety could also be generated by not allowing children to stretch their wings, engage in personal curiosities, construct themselves, know themselves, and become filthy from climbing about those inner caves and go deaf listening to all those inner voices. The concern that "too much" self-discovery and self-revelation leads to depression, anxiety, and possibly, too, suicidal ideation[33] may just have to be turned on its head: If May is correct, granted the normal tensions, disruptions, and personal caving undertaken by the adolescent, the lack of self-knowledge, or more precisely the prevention of the adolescent from pursuing this knowledge, may ultimately create the most debilitating form of anxiety. This, in turn, becomes an essential ingredient of self-esteem, an overworked term in a distracted culture that chooses to interpret esteem primarily in terms of self-love.[34] At this point in the discussion, let us list self-knowledge as the first component of esteem,[35] a second component, what May called *agape*, or devotion to another, is discussed later on.

That adolescents don't always talk (to their parents and teachers) about these matters hardly means they are not struggling with them.[36] Lacking the vocabulary, as it were, of the *Eigenwelt*, some adolescents act out their struggles and conflicts; others turn them into artistic elaboration. Still others find no alternative but to turn their inner struggles into self-destructive behavior, possibly recognizing that this behavior mirrors their struggles or perhaps magically hoping to release them into the air. Perhaps this, too, should be seen as a form of personal distraction. Then again, as Martha Straus reminds us,[37] asking adolescents to speak about their inner worlds may also be a distractive endeavor inasmuch as not all young people, not all adults for that matter, possess the language for this sort of enterprise; they cannot always differentiate between *having* a problem and *being* a problem. Nor do they necessarily feel any therapeutic value in such conversations. As Straus[38] suggests, many adolescents reveal fragile emotional shields, which they use to protect their inner worlds from assaults from the outside. Truth be told, the same shields may protect the adolescent from internally motivated attacks as well.

Other young people prefer instead to listen to the inner turmoil, so their not speaking of the inner world suggests not very much at all. Preferring to listen to the sounds of the *Eigenwelt* hardly means that one is surrounded by a fragile shield. Again from Weiser Cornell:

> Most people are more used to talking to themselves ("Come on now, get it together!") than to listening to themselves. Even experienced focusers may find that patience is called for. Fortunately, if some inner aspect interferes with the attitude needed for this step, it itself can be treated as a felt sense to be focused on. ("Let me just be with this impatience I'm feeling.)[39]

When all is said and done, and we examine closely what adolescents are attempting in their work of the *Eigenwelt*, it turns out that we live in relationships precisely as Heidegger and May postulated. Relationships appear to form just as they inform. If the work of the *Mitwelt* is not successfully navigated, therefore, adolescents are at a disadvantage as they undertake the work of the *Eigenwelt*. One needs the security of relationships to go it alone in the world of self-examination, exploration, and the establishment of personal responsibility. As Heidegger brilliantly reasoned, one doesn't *have* relationships as much as one *is* relationships. The identity of adolescents, their confrontation with their own consciousness, their thinking about their thinking, and their reasoning about their reasoning, the stuff of the inner caves, are formed in great measure from the substance of relationships they carry in their heads as well as act out with others in the *Mitwelt*.

Although Erikson makes no direct reference to Heidegger in his theories of adolescent identity development, it is interesting that the dilemma of the adolescent stage was defined by him as one between identity cohesion and role confusion. Simply put, Erikson[40] contended that adolescents must work out the conflicts caused by the coalescence of genetic inheritance and social demands. Ideally, private and public worlds should coalesce to produce a stable, self-knowing, and responsible self. Failure of this stage results in role confusion, which essentially means that the adolescent has not been able to properly utilize the work of the *Mitwelt* in creating what Erikson called a healthy ego.[41]

You are there, the adolescent discovers; I am here, and my identity is constructed not within the place that lives between the two of us but more exactly from what the two of us create together in the world and in our own minds as well. This, in part, is the dilemma of Erikson's stage of adolescent development. What Erikson called maldevelopment in this stage, allegedly leads on the one hand (in the case of identity cohesion) to adolescent fanaticism, the extraordinary worshipfulness of icons, public figures, or even peers or, on the other hand (in the case of role confusion) to the utter repudiation of these figures, all figures, along with the greater society they represent.

One more point from Erikson makes especial sense in our examination of the relationship between the adolescent *Mitwelt* and *Eigenwelt*. Erikson contended that emerging from this momentous dilemma characterizing the adolescent period was the basic strength of fidelity. (Erikson postulated that love was the strength emerging out of a resolution of adolescent issues.) It seems true. Although the media may choose to run with stories of sex, drugs, crime, and rock 'n roll, a careful examination of adolescent culture reveals the intense degree to which fidelity in a variety of forms is played out. Whatever one thinks of gang behavior, fidelity and loyalty reside at the epicenter of the gang's social structure.

Now, however, one is faced with the dilemma that both May and Fromm discussed: Just how far out does one go in one's personal search, one's personal quest for responsibility and self-knowledge before possibly risking insecurity.[42] Like all relationships, personal examinations carry some degree of risk; there is always a chance that "things will be shaken up" and never quite put back in an order that seems right or settling. Always there is a chance that, in a state of inhibition, the adolescent hesitates in his or her approach to those caves, thereby losing, perhaps, a chance for (momentary) freedom. If one chooses to remain solely in the *Mitwelt*, one is obliged to construct one's identity almost exclusively from relationships. In May's words, one "disperses" oneself in relationships; one does this primarily out of the fear of being alone, solitary, on one's own. The adolescent hardly needs to be reminded of the supreme threat of rejection by others, what Kohut[43] meant when he wrote about the child or adolescent feeling unloved and hence unlovable. This may be the greatest of all adolescent fears: namely, a belief that one is alone because one is incapable of loving or even worse, unlovable. More generally, without others, the adolescent's self-definition is meaningless inasmuch as it conforms to nothing that the culture defines as having significant value, nothing the adolescent feels to be valuable.

We now understand May's logical assertion that every encounter opens the possibility for joy as well as anxiety. Every encounter allows the possibility of adolescents being "opened up," not only to other persons but to themselves. Yet opening up to another (*Mitwelt*) and to themselves (*Eigenwelt*) looms as risky business for adolescents, an exercise modern culture does not always underwrite, and hence adolescents are deluged with and obliged to attend to the culture's distractive forces. Here is where modern culture, just as Abraham Maslow[44] and others suggested, often gets in the way of adolescents creating authentic relationships with others and themselves.

One example of just such a distraction is found in the aforementioned concept of self-esteem.[45] To listen to popular culture pundits is to imagine that total mental health for adolescents will be found in the capacity to love oneself, accept oneself, believe in oneself. Freud's early criteria of health, namely the capacity for working and loving, appear to have vanished. Distractive culture, in contrast, focuses primarily on self-acceptance and ego gratification. Surely valuable human ingredients, these modern criteria cannot begin to approach the delicate and complex work of either the *Mitwelt* or *Eigenwelt*. Exploration, examination, consciousness, identity, and recognition, the cornerstones of the *Eigenwelt* that are made possible in part by maintaining and internalizing risky and joyous relationships, are not at all synonymous with self-esteem or any simplistic conception of it. In fact, May suggested that the concept of *agape*, self love for another or what some might call devotion and what Erikson labeled as the basic strength of fidelity, is more central to the personal exploration of self than self-esteem.

In other words, and Fromm,[46] too made this observation, the devotion to another is perhaps a higher form of love than self-love, although the former apparently requires the latter.[47] Distractive culture, however, often fails to teach the adolescent that self-love is the means to a greater and more transcendent end, namely, the acts of devotion and beneficence.[48] In a sense, self-esteem is little more than Eros turned inward: I love me, proclaims the adolescent, so the rest of you will have to deal with it.

On closer examination, self-esteem matters usually bespeak the symptoms of unsuccessful *Mitwelt* and *Eigenwelt* work. Of course, we want adolescents to feel good about themselves, but this notion is about as superficial as believing that a few good purchases at the mall make one feel healthy. Esteem, in other words, is the distractive objective, the distractive conception, not the genuine one. In fact, personal self-exploration and the genuine recognition of self that derives from it often are experienced as an assault on esteem. Some things adolescents discover about themselves and their world do not bring them joy. It is a reality of life that Freud explored in his work on the construct of repression;[49] apparently, there are certain things better left not only unsaid but unconscious. The genuine search for self leaves no stone unturned; sadness and joy lie just inside every cave. We recall Weisel's words about life being a collection of memories, many of them sad.

When Self-exploration and Distraction Collide

We begin this section with a question that initially may seem irrelevant: When can a person be said to enter adolescence? It is an intriguing question, especially because the very concept of adolescence is so new[50] and hence open to all sorts of definitions and as we saw earlier, perhaps nothing more than mere social construction at any point open to reinterpretation and redefinition.[51] Normally, the answer comes in *Umwelt* language: It is commonly argued that biology[52] dictates the commencement of adolescence; it is the descent of the testes in boys, the onset of menstruation in girls. Fair enough, but this is hardly sufficient given our focus on adolescent mind fields.

Perhaps psychologists felt a need to construct a section of the life cycle we now call adolescence because they recognized that young people were undertaking a sort of mind work, personal ruminations, that were to be distinguished from the mind work of children.[53] The very contemplation of identity, one's calling, the reasons for being alive, typical discussion topics in high school courses, are made possible by cognitive development[54] and signal that youngsters are beginning to find their way into the realm of the *Eigenwelt*. What do you want to be when you grow up is the rather cute and predictable question asked of all children. Who really am I? This is the question adolescents begin asking of themselves. Who really are we? That is the question they ask of their peers. (Here is yet another reason for the significant power of peer groups in shaping the lives of adolescents.) So another answer to what marks the onset of adolescence may be the point at which people begin to descend into the world of the *Eigenwelt*. Adolescence may commence when people first choose to explore their mind fields.

We recall that the descent into one's inner caves is not always the happiest of descents; it is replete with risk and often becomes a rather scary experience.[55] It may even be as scary as the child's *Mitwelt* or, conversely, scary in a way that the adolescent has never experienced. Either way, it brings a tremor to the adolescent that he or she responds to in a variety of forms. One can act out, even violently, or feel the fright, exhilaration, confusion, sadness, or anxiety associated with risk taking. As Rainer Maria Rilke wrote, "Killing is one of the forms of our wandering mourning."[56] (Similarly, Allan Young alleged that anger is pain remembered.[57]) One can attempt to deny these sensations that cause the adolescent to feel inauthentic or suppress them altogether, in which case alcohol and drugs seem useful paraphernalia. One message from the culture to the adolescent continues to be: When feeling uneasy, medicate yourself, or at least take your mind off whatever you are experiencing.[58]

A second message reads: When the going gets tough, the tough go shopping or seek some form of entertainment. Music after all, besides its obviously pleasurable qualities, can at times serve the purpose of driving out of the mind anything that may be lurking there in the form of unhappiness or anger. So the double message to youngsters, not to mention a gold mine for various industries, is pull yourself out of the *Eigenwelt* and work to feel good about yourself. Self-esteem, as we noted, becomes the order of the day, not self-knowledge; self-accumulation rules, not self-examination.

We describe this action as distraction since the culture is doing with the child exactly what Freud[59] postulated the ego is doing with the id: tricking it. Defense mechanisms like repression, sublimation, denial are little more than deceits, tricks played on the id or the pleasure-seeking, pain-avoiding impulses.[60] Luring the adolescent out of the *Eigenwelt* with fashion products and fatuous role models is no less a deceit. As someone once remarked—and it is especially apt for the world of the adolescent—there are three types of thinking: Inductive, deductive, and seductive. Nothing could be more seductive than the combination of consumerism acting to satisfy the needs of the *Eigenwelt* and good new-fashioned self-esteem.

Literally speaking, distraction means to tear apart, an action far more aggressive than the more benign concept of intellectual or psychological diversion. The notion of our attention being called away, as it were, or our focus, as Langer[61] suggests, being attracted to some other force or stimulus, has for adolescents the quality of their very ego being ripped apart. In common parlance, we speak of being of two minds; adolescents often describe their inner worlds as "schizophrenic," thereby communicating the sense of being internally pulled apart as if their minds were actually being shredded. The irony, of course, is that one distraction is all it takes for the shredding to proceed. The adolescent now imagines that the only remaining solution is new distraction for the prior distraction and still one more distraction until an endless pursuit of distractions becomes the inevitably fruitless solution to all dilemmas.

Still, there is a rational basis to this dialectic constituted by internal explorations and cultural demands and expectations. Recognizing the ennui, riskiness, eroticism, rebelliousness, and anger of adolescents, the culture in the form of schools and parents seeks to quiet the moods and cease the exploration of the inner caves by dragging the adolescent out of his or her private contemplation into the sunlight of public corporate America and a stable career. Simply put, the culture cannot tolerate these personal explorations of self and spirit in which adolescents indulge; they are precisely what make adolescence (and adolescents) so difficult for some people and seemingly so uncivilized. The adolescent has to be socialized. The name of the game is to get "rebellious" adolescents to be conforming adults and thus be done with this inglorious period of self-examination and self-indulgence, which some people continue to describe as mental masturbation. And why in part do adolescents do it? Why do they enter the *Eigenwelt*? Why might they conjoin *Mitwelt* work and *Eigenwelt* work in ways that would make Heidegger himself proud? Because they can. The sort of cognitive sophistication required in *Eigenwelt* work, as described best perhaps, by Piaget,[62] is exactly what adolescents discover they are capable of doing. Years before they learned how to ride a bike or swim under water. Now it is personal caving. And when an adolescent discovers a new muscle or a new talent, one can be certain he or she is going to exercise it, particularly when it can be done for free!

In this case, the muscle is the capacity to reason and reflect, which, in turn, assumes that adolescents are able to simultaneously hold several competing abstract notions in their mind and, not only that, work reasonably thoughtfully with all of them. Making it even more dramatic is the discovery that others of one's age are doing precisely the same thing: They're singing about it, rapping about it, writing poetry about it, or exhibiting moods that at least suggest they're on to it. Thus adolescents discover they are not alone in the *Eigenwelt* if only because they learn that others of their age (unless of course they discover Herman Hesse's *Siddhartha* and Jack Kerouac's *On the Road*) are undertaking the exact same ruminations and excavations in their own mind fields; much of their *Mitwelt* work with others confirms this. What, every parent has wondered, do adolescents find to speak about for hours on the telephone? Can you imagine if just once an adolescent responded: "Mother, I am engaging in *Mitwelt* work in preparation for some *Eigenwelt* work I'm hoping to get to this weekend!"

Normal, expected cognitive development[63] yields an adolescent celebration of self-knowing, and perhaps of self as well. The problem is that not all adults wish to attend the celebration, even if they know where the party is being held. For that matter, not that many adults are invited, but almost all adolescents will make it their business to learn of the celebration and think seriously of attending. And they'll party as long as they can until ultimately the culture will win them over to the ideas of security and conformity in great measure through distraction—again that idea of tricking the forces of the *Eigenwelt*—at which point the celebration will cease and never quite resume in the same way. This is what is meant when people describe adolescence as "the storm before the lull." In the end, as adolescence turns into young adulthood, the culture will ask not, "Was it good for you?" but instead, "Do you feel good about yourself?" If one's esteem is intact, one is taught, then one is healthy and officially over those paroxysms known as adolescent rebellion, indulgence, and mental masturbation. One is now officially an adult, which is precisely why so many people put off this transition as long as they can.

The caves remain, awaiting any and all explorers, like all the other fascinating and intriguing tourist sites on this earth. They are changing by the moment even when no visitors are in sight. They are changing because the work of the *Umwelt, Mitwelt,* and *Eigenwelt* goes on, the structure of the mind constantly accommodating to new possibilities;[64] people cannot escape the power of self-reflection, consciousness, mindfulness, identity formation, and personal recognition, their own and others. These are the genuine life forces for adolescents. The caves are there still because, in part, they are constituted of relationships, mutuality,[65] and nothing more than daily living. Someone is born; the caves are altered. Someone dies; they are altered again. Someone continues breathing, thinking, perceiving, remembering, anticipating, creating, wondering, and once again the caves undergo renovation and redecoration. The possibility of self-reflection never ends.[66] Like the rest of us, adolescents look at themselves in the mirror and all sorts of reflections, public and private, are launched.

The distracted world believes out of sight, out of mind (or is it out of mind, out of sight?). It advocates periodic home redecoration rather than architectural walking tours of the *Eigenwelt*. The distracted world misses the entire purpose of the esteem engine and its presence in the web of human connections and human spirit. Imagine then, parents or teachers who, able to empathize with the adolescent out of a capacity to genuinely perceive adolescents as well as remember their own childhood,[67] expose their reflections and imperfections to adolescents. Imagine them standing ready to offer what Straus[68] calls an "inner-centered warmth," and proposing to the adolescent the idea from both Alice Miller[69] and Robert Nozick[70] that the life lived without self-exploration is barren and essentially a life of nonbeing. Imagine these people instructing the adolescent that the descent to the caves is as inevitable as the reality that one must go it alone. The adults promise to make the journey as safe as possible for the adolescent by making their friendship with him or her a mutuality that the adolescent may forever carry as part of his or her makeup.[71] Empathy, Kohut reminds is, remains a major tool in working with the young.[72] This is essentially what *Mitwelt* work is all about. Elders will help connect the adolescent to others, to the social world and to the culture in as many ways as they can, fundamental acts, after all, of education (and counseling). This intellectual, social, and emotional mutuality ultimately will form the basis of the work of living in the world that *every* adolescent must undertake.

Mutuality (again the work of the *Mitwelt*) remains the quintessential ration that will sustain the adolescent during what Erikson called the "identity moratorium."[73] Once this life force of mutuality is established (and the reader may recall the enormous weight Freud placed on the transference relationship in psychoanalysis[74]), the adolescent will finally possess the tools to forage about in his or her inner caves. As Walt Whitman wrote, "It is time to explain myself—let us stand up."[75] So in the end, the work is never solitary; the dread of aloneness is counteracted by the mutualities, the literally living relationships which in good measure constitute the single soul. As Stephanie Dowrick observed,

> Being in good contact—with yourself in solitude and with others in intimacy—is not a matter of striving (as for slimmer hips) but comes out of increased knowledge and, with that, self-acceptance and self-encouragement.[76]

Here at last a fitting conclusion to this thought. One of the largest and most lucrative distractions of our era, the cinematic trilogy *Star Wars*, now replete with a prequel, should have taught the world's adolescents a monumental lesson. After a rather lengthy sojourn, Luke Skywalker finally got the message: No matter where he went in the universe (a space making our few personal caves pale in comparison), The Force, an instrument meant to encourage him in his exploration of his potential with the added capacity to create wonder, would be with him forever.

It is the same with adolescents. The genuine world acknowledges and encourages The Force; the distractive world seeks to wrest it away or transform it, leaving us with two questions: First, will the adolescent give in and relinquish The Force or cling, however clumsily, to it? Will the adolescent surrender to the distractions of conformity or remain, as Langer and the Zen master teaching the Sutra of mindfulness suggested,[77] literally mindful and otherwise attracted? Second, might it be that the instant of this momentous decision marks the conclusion of adolescence?

Notes

1 Martin Heidegger, *Being and Time*, translated by Joan Stambaugh. Albany: State University of New York Press, 1966.

2 See his *The Discovery of Being*. New York: Norton, 1983,

3 See C. K. Sigelman and D. R. Shaffer, *Life-Span Human Development*. Pacific Grove, CA: Brooks/Cole, 1991; L. Okagaki and R. J. Sternberg (Editors), *Directors of Development: Influences on the Development of Children's Thinking*. Hillsdale, NJ: Erlbaum, 1991; Jerome Kagan, *The Nature of the Child*. New York: Basic Books, 1984; A. Thomas and S. Chess, *Temperament and Development*. New York: Brunner/Mazel, 1977; Laura A. Berk, *Child Development* (4th Edition), Needham Heights, MA: Allyn and Bacon, 1997, chapter 3.

4 See A. Thomas and S. Chess, "Commentary." In H. H. Goldsmith, A. H. Buss, R. Plomin, M. K. Rothbart, A. Thomas, A. Chess, R. R. Hinde, and R. B. McCall. "Roundtable: What Is Temperament? Four Approaches." *Child Development*, *58*, 1987: 505–529; S. Chess and A. Thomas, "Temperamental Individuality from Childhood to Adolescence." *Journal of Child Psychiatry*, *16*, 1977: 218–226; S. Scarr and K. K. Kidd, "Developmental Behavior Genetics." In P. H. Mussen (Editor), *Handbook of Child Psychology* (Volume 2, 4th Edition). New York: Wiley, 1983; and S. Scarr and K. McCartney, "How People Make Their Own Environments: A Theory of Genotype-Environment Effects." *Child Development*, *54*, 1983: 424–435.

5 See Howard Gardner, *The Shattered Mind: The Person after Brain Damage*. New York: Knopf, 1974.

6 See B. Vitiello, D. Stoff, and M. Atkins, "Soft Neurological Signs and Impulsivity in Children." *Journal of Developmental and Behavioral Pediatrics*. *11*, 1990: 112–115; and D. Shaffer and L. L. Greenhill, "A Critical Note on the Predictive Validity of the Hyperactive Syndrome." *Journal of Child Psychology and Psychiatry*, *20*, 1979: 61–72.

7 Erich Fromm, *Escape from Freedom*. New York: Farrar and Rinehart, 1941.

8 Children of alcoholic parents are predisposed to become alcoholic themselves or marry an alcoholic. According to recent information, almost 30 million children have a parent or parents who are alcoholic. See Michael Houston and Jerry M. Wiener, "Substance-Related Disorders." In *Textbook of Child and Adolescent Psychiatry* (2nd Edition), Jerry M. Wiener (Editor). Washington, DC: American Psychiatric, 1997: 637–656.

9 See Joyce Maguire Pavao, *Family of Adoption*. Boston: Beacon, 1998; and Harriet E. Gross and Marvin B. Sussman (Editors), *Families and Adoption*. New York: Haworth, 1997.

10 In truth, given the manner of cell reproduction and the indescribable biological feat of cells identically reproducing themselves, it is highly unlikely that true *doppelgängers* exist.

11 See Andrew Garrod, Lisa Smuylan, Sally I. Powers, and Robert Kilkenny, *Adolescent Portraits: Identity, Relationships, and Challenges.* Boston: Allyn and Bacon, 1999.

12 See A. J. Horner, "The Unconscious and the Archeology of Human Relationships." In R. Stern (Editor), *Theories of the Unconscious and the Self.* New Jersey: Analytic, 1987.

13 Erik H. Erikson, *Identity, Youth and Crisis.* New York: Norton, 1968.

14 See Beverly Daniel Tatum, *Why Are All the Black Kids Sitting Together in the Cafeteria? And Other Conversations about Race.* New York: Basic, 1997.

15 See Martin Buber, *I and Thou,* translated by Ronald Gregor Smith. New York: Scribner, 1958.

16 On a similar point, see G. R. Adams and R. Montemayor (Editors), *Psychosocial Development During Adolescence.* Thousand Oaks, CA: Sage, 1996.

17 S. L. Archer, "Identity and the Choice of Social Roles." In *Identity and Adolescence: Processes and Contents,* A. S. Waterman (Editor). San Francisco: Jossey-Bass, 1985.

18 See B. P. O'Connor and J. Nikolic, "Identity Development and Formal Operations as Sources of Adolescent Egocentrism." *Journal of Youth and Adolescence, 19,* 1990: 149–158; and E. Fuller Torrey, "Oedipal Wrecks: Has a Century of Freud Bred a Country of Narcissists?" *Washington Monthly,* January-February, 1992: 32–41.

19 Ann Weiser Cornell, "The Focusing Technique: Confirmatory Knowing Thorough the Body." In Helen Palmer (Editor), *Inner Knowing.* New York: Jeremy Tarcher, 1998, page 162.

20 Erich Fromm, op. cit.

21 This point is taken from Viktor Frankl, *Man's Search for Meaning: An Introduction to Logotherapy,* translated by Ilse Lasch. Boston: Beacon, 1963.

22 Sigmund Freud, *The Ego and the Id.* Translated by James Strachey. London: Hogarth, 1949.

23 Ibid.

24 Sigmund Freud, *Inhibitions, Symptoms and Anxiety.* Translated by James Strachey. London: Hogarth, 1948.

25 Sigmund Freud, *A General Introduction to Psycho-Analysis.* New York: Liveright, 1935.

26 Fred Weinstein, *Freud, Psychoanalysis, Social Theory: The Unredeemed Promise.* Albany: State University of New York Press, forthcoming.

27   Howard Gardner, *Frames of Mind: The Theory of Multiple Intelligences*. New York: Basic, 1983.

28   Robert Coles, *The Moral Intelligence of Children*. New York: Random House, 1997, page 170. On a similar point, see Laura Berk, *Infants, Children and Adolescents* (2nd edition). Boston: Allyn and Bacon, 1996. On the notion of the development of the superego, see Sigmund Freud, *Civilization and Its Discontents*, translation by James Strachey. New York: Norton, 1961.

29   See N. P. Lyons, "Two Perspectives: On Self Relationships and Morality." *Harvard Educational Review*, *53*, 1983: 125–145. See also Darrell J. Fasching, "Beyond Values: Story, Character, and Public Policy in American Schools." In James L. Paul, Neal H. Berger, Pamela G. Osnes, and William C., Morse (Editors), *Ethics and Decision Making in Schools: Inclusion, Policy and Reform*. Baltimore: Brookes, 1997.

30   Freud, *The Ego and the Id*, op. cit.

31   On a related point, see Peter Giovacchini, *The Urge to Die*. New York: Macmillan, 1981.

32   Viktor Frankl, *Man's Search for Meaning*, op. cit.; See also Joseph C. Sabbath, "The Suicidal Adolescent: The Expendable Child." *Journal of the American Academy of Child Psychiatry*, *8*, 1969: 272–289; Jack Novick, "Attempted Suicide in Adolescence: The Suicide Sequence." In Howard Sudak, Amasa B. Ford, and Norman B. Rushfords (Editors), *Suicide in the Young*. Boston: Wright/PSG, 1984: 115–137; and Gregory Zilboorg, "Considerations on Suicide, With Particular Reference to That of the Young." *American Journal of Orthopsychiatry, 7*, 1937: 125–31.

33   R. F. Baumeister. *Masochism and the Self*. Hillsdale, NJ: Erlbaum 1989; L. Berman, Suicide Cases. Special Issue: "Assessment and Prediction of Suicide." *Suicide and Life-Threatening Behavior. 21*, 1991: 18–36; D. A. Brent, "Suicide and Suicidal Behavior in Children and Adolescents." *Pediatrics in Review, 10*, 1989: 269–275; and N. Bolger, G. Downey, E. Walker, and P. Steininger, "The Onset of Suicidal Ideation in Childhood and Adolescence." *Journal of Youth and Adolescence, 18*, 1989: 175–190.

34   See Maureen Stout, *The Feel Good Curriculum: The Dumbing Down of America's Kids in the Name of Self-Esteem*. Boston: Perseus, 1999; See also Seymour W. Itzkoff, *The Decline of Intelligence in America: A Strategy for National Renewal*. Westport: Praeger, 1994.

35   See R. C. Savi-Williams and D. H. Demo, "Conceiving or Mis-Conceiving the Self: Issues in Adolescent Self-Esteem." *Journal of Early Adolescence, 3*, 1983: 121–140.

36   See P. Noller and M. A. Fitzpatrick, *Communication in Family Relationships*. Englewood Cliffs, N.J.: Prentice-Hall, 1993.

37   Martha B. Straus, *No-Talk Therapy for Children and Adolescents*. New York: Norton, 1999. See also her *Abuse and Victimization Across the Life Span*. Baltimore: Johns Hopkins University Press, 1988.

38 Martha Straus, *No-Talk Therapy,* op. cit.

39 Ibid., page 162.

40 Erik H. Erikson, *Childhood and Society,* op., cit.

41 Erik H. Erikson, *Identity and the Life Cycle,* op. cit.

42 See, for example, Jane Ogden, "Psychosocial Theory and the Creation of the Risky Self." *Social Science and Medicine.* February 1995, 3, *40:* 409–415.

43 Heinz Kohut, *Search for the Self,* Volume 2, Paul Ornstein (Editor). New York: International Universities Press, 1978.

44 Abraham Maslow, *Toward a Psychology of Being.* Princeton, NJ: Van Nostrand, 1962. See also Rollo May, *Politics and Innocence: A Humanistic Debate.* New York; Norton, 1986.

45 S. Chess and A. Thomas, *Know Your Child.* New York: Basic Books, 1987; see also B. B. Brown and M. J. Lohr, "Peer-Group Affiliation and Adolescent Self-Esteem: An Integration of Ego-Identity and Symbolic Interaction Theories." *Journal of Personality and Social Psychology,* 52, 1987: 47–55; R. C. Savi-Williams and D. H. Demo, "Conceiving or Mis-Conceiving the Self: Issues in Adolescent Self-Esteem," op. cit.

46 Erich Fromm, *The Art of Loving.* New York: Harper, 1956.

47 Edwin J. Delattre, "The Test of Intimacy: Living up to Love and Duty." Unpublished manuscript, Boston University, 2000, Chapter 5.

48 Gerald S. Fain, "Special Education: Justice, Tolerance, and Beneficence as Duty." *Boston University Journal of Education.* 180, 1998: 41–56; and J. G. Miller, "A Cultural Perspective on the Morality of Beneficence and Interpersonal Responsibility." In S. Ting-Toomey and F. Korzenny (Editors), *International and Intercultural Communication Annual* (Volume 15). Newbury Park, CA: Sage, 1991.

49 See Sigmund Freud, *A General Introduction to Psychoanalysis,* op. cit.; See also Fred Weinstein, op. cit.

50 G. Stanley Hall, *Adolescence* (Volumes 1 and 2). Englewood Cliffs, NJ: Prentice-Hall, 1904; Kenneth Keniston, "Youth: A New Stage of Life." *American Scholar,* 39, 1970: 631–654.

51 On the construction of childhood, see David Elkind, "Children with Special Needs: A Postmodern Perspective." *Boston University Journal of Education,* Volume *180,* Number 2, 1998: 1–16.

52 See J. M. Tanner, *Growth and Adolescence.* Springfield, IL: Thomas, 1955; and J. M. Tanner and Bärbel Inhelder, *Discussions on Child Development: A Consideration of the Biological, Psychological, and Cultural Approaches to the Understanding of Human Development and Behavior.* New York: International Universities Press, 1971. See also B. B. Sommer, *Puberty and Adolescence.* New York: Oxford University Press, 1978; J. Brooks-Gunn and D. N. Ruble,

"The Development of Menstrual-Related Beliefs and Behavior during Early Adolescence." *Child Development, 53,* 1982: 1567–1577; and H. Stattin and D. Magnusson, *Pubertal Maturation in Female Development: Paths Through Life.* Hillsdale, NJ: Erlbaum, 1990.

53   Jean Piaget, *The Language and Thought of the Child.* New York: Humanities, 1959.

54   J. H. Flavell, "Cognitive Development: Past, Present, and Future." *Developmental Psychology, 28,* 1992: 998–1005; A. Bandura, "Social Cognitive Theory." In R. Vasta (Editor), *Six Theories of Child Development.* Greenwich, CT: JAI Press, 1989; A. Bandura, "Social Cognitive Theory of Moral Thought and Action." In W. M. Kurtines and J. L. Gewirtz (Editors), *Handbook of Moral Behavior and Development* (Volume 1). Hillsdale, NJ: Erlbaum, 1991; Jerome Bruner, Rose Olver, and Patricia M. Greenfield, *Studies in Cognitive Growth: Collaboration at the Center for Cognitive Studies.* New York: Wiley, 1967; and Howard Gardner, *The Mind's New Science: A History of the Cognitive Revolution.* New York: Basic Books, 1987.

55   See J. Taylor, C. Gilligan, and A. Sullivan, *Between Voice and Silence.* Cambridge, MA: Harvard University Press, 1995.

56   Cited in Rollo May, *The Discovery of Being.* New York: Norton, 1983, page 124.

57   Allan Young, "Suffering and the Origins of Traumatic Memory." *Daedalus.* Winter, *125,* No. 1, 1996: 245–260. See also his *The Harmony of Illusions: Inventing Post Traumatic Stress Disorder.* Princeton, NJ: Princeton University Press, 1995.

58   Brent B., Benda, Tracy Schroepfer, Carolyn Turturro, and Karen Ballard, "Heavy Use of Alcohol by Adolescents: A Conceptual Model of Use." *Alcoholism Treatment Quarterly, 3, 13,* 1995: 81–95; J. A. Halikas, J. Meller, C. Morse, and M. D. Lyttle, "Predicting Substance Abuse in Juvenile Offenders." *Child Psychiatry and Human Development, 21,* 1990: 49–55; J. Knop, T. W. Teasdale, F. Schulsinger, and D. W. Goodwin, "A Prospective Study of Young Men at High Risk for Alcoholism." *Journal of Studies on Alcohol, 46,* 1985: 273–278; R. E. Tarter, "Evaluation and Treatment of Adolescent Substance Abuse." *American Journal of Drug and Alcohol Abuse. 16,* 1990: 1–46; and B. U. Wilhelmsen, S. Laberg, and H. Aas, "Alcohol Outcome Expectancies in Adolescence." *Psychology and Health,* November, 6, *13,* 1998: 1037–1044.

59   Sigmund Freud, *Ego and the Id.* Translated by J. Strachey. New York: Norton, 1962.

60   On this point, the reader is advised to see Jerome Kagan, *Three Seductive Ideas.* Cambridge, MA: Harvard University Press, 1998. The pleasure principle is one of the seductive ideas.

61   Ellen J. Langer, *The Power of Mindful Learning.* Reading, MA: Perseus, 1997; Ellen J. Langer, *Mindfulness.* Reading, MA: Addison-Wesley, 1989; and Robert

Tremmel, "Zen and the Art of Reflective Practice in Teacher Education." *Harvard Educational Review*, 4, *63*, Winter, 1993: 434–458.

62   See Jean Piaget, *The Language and Thought of the Child*. New York: London: Routledge and Kegan Paul, 1932; H. E. Guber and J. J. Voneche, *The Essential Piaget*. New York: Basic Books, 1977; and Robert Kegan, *The Evolving Self*. Cambridge, MA: Harvard University Press, 1982, Chapter 2.

63   John Santrock, *Adolescence* (7th Edition). New York: McGraw-Hill, 1998.

64   See Jean Piaget, *The Language and Thought of the Child,* op. cit.

65   Jean Baker Miller and Irene Stiver, *The Healing Connection: How Women Form Relationships in Therapy and in Life*. Boston: Beacon, 1997; See also Max Sugar, *Female Adolescent Development*. New York: Brunner/Mazel, 1993.

66   Robert Tremmel, "Zen and the Art of Reflective Practice in Teacher Education," op. cit.

67   Sara Lawrence-Lightfoot, *Respect*. Reading, MA: Perseus, 1999. See also D. Scott-Jones, "Families as Educators in a Pluralistic Society." In N. F. Chavkin (Editor), *Families and Schools in a Pluralistic Society*. Albany: State University of New York Press, 1993.

68   Martha Straus, *No-Talk Therapy for Children and Adolescents,* op. cit.

69   Alice Miller, *The Drama of the Gifted Child*, translated by Ruth Ward. New York: Basic, 1981.

70   Robert Nozick, *The Examined Life: Philosophical Meditations*. New York: Simon and Schuster, 1989.

71   Miller and Stiver, op. cit.

72   Heinz Kohut, *The Chicago Institute Lectures*, Paul and Marian Tolpin (Editors). Hillside: Analytic Press, 1996. Cited in Donald S. Palladino, Jr. "Poets to Come: Walt Whitman, Self Psychology and the Readers of the Future." Unpublished manuscript, Boston, 1999.

73   Erik H. Erikson, *Identity and the Life Cycle*, op. cit. 1959; and Erik H. Erikson, *Identity, Youth, and Crisis*, op. cit.

74   Sigmund Freud, *A General Introduction to Psychoanalysis*, translated by G. Stanley Hall. New York: Liveright Publishing, 1935.

75   Walt Whitman, "Song of Myself." In *Leaves of Grass*. Garden City, NY: Doubleday, 1926, Sec. 44, page 61

76   Stephanie Dowrick, *Intimacy and Solitude: Balancing Closeness and Independence*. New York: Norton, 1991.

77   Langer, *The Power of Mindful Learning,* op. cit.; and Tremmel, op. cit.

Chapter 8

The Prize of Self-reflection

The "Inner Blossom Unfolding"

At some point most all adults ask most all children, "What do you want to be when you grow up?" Interestingly, we ask the question more often this way rather than, "What do you want to *do?*" Manifestly, we are asking children whether they have thought about the future. More to the point, we may be telling the child it is never too early to think about one's future and career. In effect, we are socializing the child by teaching him or her that although childhood is perfectly charming, it really is little more than a period one passes through in order to reach what truly matters: adulthood, that point in life, ironically, when one laments the passage of childhood and adolescence.[1]

Beneath the surface of the question, however, lies a more fascinating issue: What we wish to know in our interrogation is the degree to which children ponder what genuinely matters to them. The question holds out the possibility that we are socializing children to dream of the mysteries lurking inside them, the life path meant only for them, the voice belonging only to them: "Who do you want to be?" "Who do you want to become?"

The questions, ironically, tend to distract both adult and child from the appointed path to the inner voice. We cannot possibly know a child by asking these questions. They are some of many questions we ask that inadvertently assure us we will not learn about the child. In responding, children characteristically attempt to meet our expectation; they act for us, usually gracefully, or they demure, but our well-meaning inquiries do not assist them in delving into the realms of their inner voice. Perhaps we are more ambivalent about our concerns than we are willing to admit. Perhaps we do not want the child to undertake these sorts of personal reflections until we have executed them ourselves. Perhaps we are frightened of what children and adolescents tend to do on their own, in the absence of our controls and constructions. Come to think of it, all our best intentions notwithstanding, it may be that questions generally keep young people from encountering their inner voice although research shows that the who, what, when, where and why questions aid a child's thinking just as they help improve his or her acting skills.[2] The search for the inner voice, however, may require different sorts of interventions.

A better way, perhaps, to encourage adolescents to explore the sounds of their inner voice, is to not ask questions at all but instead discover modes wherein their inner voice may be naturally revealed, as Vivian Paley[3] does in her Chicago kindergarten class where she has her students writing, directing, and performing plays. Or perhaps we must merely sit quietly as the visitor to Nantucket did, as he watched a lovely child draw her pictures. Paley's work, not so incidentally, suggests that the search for the inner world may be a more natural process than we imagined and that adult interventions only inhibit the process. Yet inhibition may be the (unconscious) purpose of adult cultural distractions in the first place: Don't let children and adolescents play by themselves!

Various forms of intelligences[4] allow for all sorts of inroads to an inner world wherein ultimately one's own voice is found. Few people, actually, can describe their search for that voice or their discovery of it. Few can approach the experience of the "inner blossom unfolding" as D. H. Lawrence called it. Children and professional painters, a University of Chicago study indicated years ago, cannot fully articulate how they go about painting a still life from objects laid out on a table. Art history students and art critics, in contrast, prove to be highly articulate on the subject although their artistic products, not surprisingly, are judged by other critics to be inferior to the products of the artists and children.[5]

One group, apparently, gropes about in the mysterious (*Eigenwelt*) world of the unconscious and instinctual. Its performance, in this instance the act of painting, is almost a byproduct or afterthought of this grope. Or perhaps the painting is a representation of the grope, something we constantly find in the so-called internal dialogues of novels. The other group, no less intelligent, must wait for the first group to complete its groping. Its members find their own voice when analyzing, interpreting, or simply appreciating the product of the first group's personal explorations. Their work too, presumably, requires passage into mysterious realms. Both are valid enterprises, although painters and children take the greater risks not only because they dare hop aboard the trolley into the neighborhood of make-believe but in addition seek passage beyond to the neighborhoods of distraction and madness.

The genuine hunt for the inner voice takes place in those instants when one engages in the creative act, whatever it may be, artistic, mathematical, physical, interpersonal, and, significantly, intrapersonal.[6] As Robert Tremmel observed, when it comes to relationships people should be joint experimenters and artists.[7] These creative moments, as Gardner theorized,[8] are merely the various intelligences at work inasmuch as problems of all sorts are being solved and creative products manufactured by the individual. Once the product is revealed or the solution found, once the words are formed on the page or expressed to another, the dance movements seen, the equation developed, a judging ego takes over as one reassesses, edits, rethinks, reflects again on the personal exploration just completed. This looking back at what one has done, as Dewey observed,[9] becomes an essential ingredient of reflection and is characteristic of adolescent cognitive activity. And all of this action is quintessential *Eigenwelt* work.

Typically the hunt for the inner voice is accomplished in private, when acting is superfluous, unless of course, one is an actor, which allows one the rare opportunity to search for the inner voice in a public setting. It comes out of some strange, almost irrational sense of a person communing with himself or herself. Normally unseen by anyone, the activity feels as if an invisible hand carries one to the site where one's own words and ideas are (perpetually being) born; it is the center of a person's earth, a center one probably discovers for the first time during adolescence although very few would define adolescence in this way. Freud, actually, touched on these matters when he wondered about the nature and dynamic of creative writing:

> We laymen have always been intensely curious to know. . . from what sources that strange being, the creative writer, draws his material, and how he manages to make such an impression on us with it and to arouse in us emotions of which, perhaps, we had not even thought ourselves capable. Our interest is only heightened the more by the fact that, if we ask him, the writer himself gives us no explanation, or none that is satisfactory.[10]

The process of the adolescent's creative enterprise represents a momentous developmental position. Children of course are creative, producing all varieties of products, yet it is the capacity to reflect on their efforts that differentiates adolescents' creative processes from those of children.

It is a cornerstone of self-consciousness, itself a vital component of the *Eigenwelt*. One writes words not knowing for certain where they may lead, because the ideas are being formed as the writing takes place, writing being one way the mind's motion is captured in time and represented. One is not consciously aware of what the next words will be; one isn't even certain where one paragraph ends until the next paragraph seems (to want) to begin. Who can say whether it is an elementary school class on grammar years ago or mere hunch that ultimately determines the paragraph's conclusion? The music seems to pause, or one runs out of that peculiar energy, so one starts anew. When nothing comes, as adolescents always fear will happen, one doodles in the margins as if believing that by moving a hand a certain portion of one's brain once again will spin out fascinating ideas. The process always reminds me of the way that some artists before they commence a drawing, turn their hand about in the air as if their hand were an airplane circling the runway for a landing.

Like other creative enterprises, writing provides adolescents the extraordinary experience of imagining they are in control of their creative energies while at the same time feeling that the energies possess a power to compel them to action almost as if the writer were merely along for the ride. Riding the wave of this internal energy, a sort of psychological surfing, is what young people call "being in the zone" or what Mihaly Czikszentmihalyi[11] called, simply, "flow."

As all adolescents can attest, the search for the inner voice involves the matter of consciousness of consciousness, something that intrigues, mystifies, and compels adolescents. Although required for any creative enterprise, the judging self, derived from the cumulative power of internalized relationships (*Mitwelt*), nonetheless causes the adolescent a certain degree of consternation. Adolescents wish to get back to the caves, back into the zone or flow, and forsake the (*Eigenwelt*) matter of the consciousness of consciousness. Yet the judging ego is part and parcel of the reflective process, the looking back at what one has done, and been, so this too lies near the entrance to the inner caves and a long way from the external world of public distraction.

The search for the inner voice requires the adolescent to learn how to be conscious of the effort required to reach the inner caves (the unconscious) during the creative process. The trick to be mastered by adolescents for the first time in their lives is to suspend the work of the judging self so as to make possible the emergence of the inner voice. That is, adolescents learn that during the moments of creation, it is better not to be overly conscious of the work at hand. When the judging self appears, we know the angels of the unconscious have been called back to their invisible caves; the first creative moment has come and gone.

Judgment of work, and self, is essential in the intellectual and creative efforts of adolescents; in fact, judgment is inevitable. As Sartre proclaimed: "If we breathe, we judge." Without a judging self, a psychological component born in adolescence, we are left with a self celebrating all it does, moral and immoral. Yet there are moments when the judging self must step aside in order for the creative self, the inner voice, to have sufficient space in which to operate. The question then is whether a culture, family, school, or, more precisely, the agents of these institutions and most assuredly adolescents themselves allow for this space or instead rush to judgment and more likely cultural distraction, thereby silencing their inner voice. Granted, it is far more tempting to watch a television program than to do one's homework. Yet some adolescents retreat to cultural distractions because they require psychic relief from internal rumination and reflection. How ironic that adolescents themselves may be more troubled by their self-reflections—what others call their self-indulgence—than their elders are by this seemingly endless adolescent activity.

Consider in this regard what Piaget said in response to the normal explorations of adolescents:

> The adolescent, on the other hand, thanks to his budding personality, sees himself as equal to his elders, yet different from them, different because of the new life stirring within him. He wants to surpass and astound them by transforming the world. That is why the adolescent's systems or life plans are at the same time filled with generous sentiments and altruistic or mysteriously fervent projects and with disquieting megalomania and conscious ego-centricity.[12]

On second thought, it may not be weariness that falls upon the adolescent as he or she engages in the search for the inner voice as much as it is irritation or discomfort with one's own self-consciousness. Adolescents are capable of finding themselves tedious, even worse, boring. They may battle their own admonitions to themselves, learning to recognize that they can describe neither the search for the inner caverns nor the flight from distraction that leads them to find their voice. Even as they undertake their creative endeavors, they may feel themselves propelled away from the source of their own voice; it is as if their personal demons were expelling them from Oz. Adolescents come to imagine that in order to return to the world of normal human relationships (*Mitwelt*), and even to the world of cultural distractions, they must promise never to reveal the secrets they themselves safeguard of their inner voice.[13] The process is a bit like asking a centipede how he, or she, coordinates the actions of so many legs? Consumed by the question, one has to assume the centipede would fall flat on his or her face. There simply is a point when even adolescents cannot abide by the internal pressures to become conscious of their own consciousness.

Yet while all of this proceeds, adolescents are perfectly aware, as David Bowie intoned, of everything they are doing: ". . . And these children that you spit on as they try to change their worlds are immune to your consultations. They're quite aware of what they're going through."[14]

The adolescent writes a sentence, then a second sentence, but this one is suddenly crossed out, highlighted, and deleted. The judging ego has taken over. For a moment the path to the inner cave is closed, and the adolescent moves away from the inner path and hence away from the source of the inner voice. It is with this common experience in mind that he or she learns precisely what the adult culture wants for him or her to learn: By sticking exclusively to the performance (public) and often profane turf of distraction, one turns one's back on the sacred (inner) ground of personal exploration, the very activity constituting the essential psychological work of adolescence. Culture has once again taken hold; socialization is at work, and the adolescent knows it. He or she is being drawn away not only from childhood toward adulthood but from the inner world (*Eigenwelt*) to the cultural world. In the realm of public distraction, adolescents are left to hunt for the neatest ways, the best effects, and quickest impact, all the while knowing in their heart of hearts that none of these actions can possibly lead them to their inner voice. The sign above the inner caves reads "Serene Madness," which almost sounds like the name of a rock group, and more than a few adolescents crave entrance.

Most adolescents have a personal clue that signals when they have reached the boundary of the source of their inner voice. Some experience an exhilaration or lightness, as if magically they carried no weight whatsoever. Some feel as if at last they have encountered their own mind fields. Some feel as if they have been traveling far from the earth's surface or become larger than life (like the proverbial star), or conversely, they have become invisible, something most of us would dread as much as anything in the world save death. Or perhaps adolescents are soaring on a high they never thought possible (without the assistance of a drug). Perhaps they feel themselves, as Buddhists might proclaim, filled to the brim with immaculate emptiness. Or perhaps just for an instant, they imagine they have achieved perfection.

In some respects, the search for the inner voice constitutes a glorious meditation. Is it possible, then, that it is discovered when there is nothing at all there to be discovered! Perhaps adolescents have at last found, as Robert Tremmel suggests, a way to get out of the circle of their "own mind's making."[15] Is it possible that when adolescents move away from distraction, their inner voice or inner world simply reveals itself to them, returns to them as the Zen master might instruct or arises within them as if it were always there, just waiting for the "right" time and the "right" conditions, like knowledge itself.

If Piaget could argue that education ought be ruled by the "law of interest," that is, students only learn when they have genuine interest in the material, then it might also be alleged that learning is only possible when something creative, something of the inner voice is revealed to the learner. This notion is akin to Stephen Tigner's reminder to us of how knowledge is called up in us, remembered as it were, as if it were always there waiting for us to attend to it.[16]

For some philosophers, this "calling up" route to the inner voice is precisely what learning itself is all about. In writing about Plato's *Meno*, Tigner writes: "Learning is called *recollection* inasmuch as it involves *drawing upon* one's own resources in *raising up* knowledge from within" (emphases added).[17] Learning, Plato wrote, is really "recollection of what the soul has encountered in other worlds."[18] Mary Catherine Bateson captures this spirit in a description of her mother's (the anthropologist Margaret Mead) speaking style: "The paradoxical secret of her success was that often she was proposing ideas right at the threshold of what her listeners already knew, evoking an awareness ready to crystallize."[19]

Descartes, too, according to Tigner, speaks to the matter of this drawing up from within when he writes: ". . . it is not so much that I seem to learn anything new, but that I *recall* something I already knew. That is, I first *notice* things that were already in me, although I had not directed a mental gaze toward them" (emphasis added). Tigner points out that Plato essentially is "redirecting his mental gaze," 'turning the soul. . . to truth and reality.'"[20]

In a similar vein, Tigner supports his argument for the "calling up" rather than the "piling on" of knowledge and what this means for education generally, when he quotes Henry Rogers Seager. In describing the economist Carl Menger, with whom Seager had studied in Vienna in the late 1890s, Seager wrote: ". . . the student feels he is being led instead of driven, and when a conclusion is reached it comes into his mind not as something from without, but as the obvious consequences of his own mental processes."[21] ("Led instead of driven," something great religious leaders have always known, may not be a bad slogan for parenting as well as teaching.)

The critical point we take from Tigner's work is this: The process of learning, which is *recollecting* or the *lifting up* of knowledge "is one of *search* and *discovery*" (emphases added). This is what the child in Nantucket with her little art supplies was up to as well. This is what all adolescents are up to as they draw words and ideas out of themselves as if these words and ideas (and inner voices) had been there all along, waiting for the search and discovery team to rescue and release them. It goes without saying that without respect for or belief in oneself, this action of calling up knowledge is impossible. It also goes without saying that the adolescent must be taught this self-respect and self-acceptance in order for the search for the inner voice to occur. How are these delicate qualities taught? Presumably by agents like Vivian Paley[22] and Carl Menger who are able to call up the self-respect and acceptance that lie dormant in the mind fields alongside the words and ideas, gestures and computations. "The intellect is a cleaver," Thoreau wrote. "It discerns and rifts its way into the secret of things."[23] All we need, as Langer teaches, is to be mindful.[24]

Herein finally, the connection of the (internal) world of adolescents with the (external) world of distraction. For what the forces of distraction ask adolescents to do is look away and hence be drawn away from intellect and reason, from judgment and insight, from self-reflection and the realm of the mind fields, and instead call up nothing at all of value either to them or the culture. It is the essence of unintelligent action exactly as Gardner[25] defined it. In the heart of distractive activity lies not one single product, not one single solution the culture ultimately finds of lasting value. When, moreover, adolescents know that they produce no product of value and solve no problem of consequence, they must conclude that they are unintelligent. Adolescents recognize they may not know the shape and presence of the truth, as if any of us did, but they also learn that whatever it is it cannot be found in distraction. If ever adolescents observed a process of (mindless) stuff being piled on them, it is the process of distraction, and football fans know that piling on is cause for a major penalty.

The reader will recall our earlier discussion of how modern (popular) culture asks us to fill our consciousness with newer and still newer stimuli. With this constant meteor shower of intrusions, there is no possibility of adolescents turning what Descartes called a mental gaze on anything for more than a millisecond. Like meditation, mental gazing requires that one slow down all psychological processes. "Usually the mind is going in many directions," Dainin Katagiri writes, "instead of going out in all directions, let's go in."[26] Dewey[27] too, reminded us of this need for reflection. Conversely, accumulating stimuli requires that all mental processes be sped up so that little or nothing of the soul comes into play. In a sense, the mind is being tricked by the culture; the adolescent is being asked to respond to the exterior world only, not to the interior one. Thus search and discovery, the backbone of research and schooling and perhaps the greatest of all adolescent pursuits, are explicitly assaulted in distraction if not openly negated by it.

Some adolescents realize that in their creative efforts, efforts requiring a "friendship" among a combination of their intelligences, they are more in touch with themselves than ever before. (One is tempted to suggest that a certain variation of *Mitwelt* work goes on within the *Eigenwelt*.) Other people tend to imagine that when undertaken in psychotherapy, these same creative efforts come across—as much of the preceding discussion may have—"as irreal," a word Freud himself employed to describe psychoanalysis.[28]

It is a peculiar enterprise, this one of (nondistracted) self-exploration, search and discovery, what Schön calls "the awareness of the self acting in the world,"[29] particularly on those days when a person has entered the therapist's office feeling perfectly well but comes out trembling and exhausted. The person knows he or she has made a psychic effort of a sort one could never adequately describe to another person. One hopes that on these occasions, the person takes comfort in knowing that the therapist has borne witness to this effort and respected it lest he or she believe that madness is just around the corner. This is counseling's payoff, and it ought to be the same for adolescents in their classrooms: the trip away from pedestrian distraction toward the sacred high ground of learning, exploration of personal truth, noble character, and authenticity. Search and discovery, the mental gaze, meditations on the self, calling up knowledge from within, drawing upon one's resources, being led, not driven, recollection: how many of these terms are found in brochures aimed at adolescents advertising family, school, psychotherapy, or work environments?

The search for one's voice and genuine being is accomplished with the superhuman strength to which all adolescents have access, despite the interminable cultural forces and messages of distraction. The effort required is extraordinary, harder for some adolescents than speaking in public, despite the fact that many people still view artists as people on perpetual holiday, which in a sense they are, from real but not irreal life. Someone, after all, has to perpetuate the lies that tell the truths. Some may find it strange to learn that like dancers or athletes, students, too, rise from their desk sweating from the hard work just completed. Many muscles presumably continue to nap, but the psychic effort has been unimaginable. No one searches without getting a trifle weary. In this regard, the personal nondistracted search for self is not unlike playing football: There's a chance you may get hurt, and for sure you'll get dirty.

Many of us dread driving down unfamiliar streets or even taking a ride without a predetermined destination. Hunting for one's voice is much like this, with no one, not even parents, able to tell us what we'll find or where or when or how we'll find it. It is the very dilemma poor Meno encountered.[30] In their solitary searching, adolescents are going to have to force themselves as well as face themselves. Making this journey difficult, moreover, is the need to overcome barriers, defenses, protections, armor, distractions, that for years adolescents, with the help of the culture, unknowingly construct within themselves. Think of it: To get to you, I must not only overcome the barriers *you* have erected, even worse, I must overcome the barriers *I* have erected. Intimacy, therefore, becomes a trip through a (mind) field carefully mined by both of us (as well as unseen others), and neither of us wishes to acknowledge the mines we ourselves planted or conveniently had planted for us.[31]

Enter to Grow in Wisdom

Much of adolescent development is devoted to distracting people from themselves, keeping themselves, in other words, away from what is truly their own. We know how much that phrase "our very own" means to us when we see two children battling for possession of a toy. Each desperately wants the toy, but when, with all good intentions, parents instruct the children that life and death are hardly at stake, the children look at us with expressions that inform us that life and death are indeed at stake— the toy is essential to their very (unique) being. To tell children to share the toy is the logical and civil solution, the ideal fulcrum for negotiation, but it cannot be successful if, in these moments, the children are fighting for their right to possess their own caves, their unique being.

Much of childhood and adolescence finds the culture pushing young persons farther and farther away from their inner voice as if the culture has deemed it dangerous to oversee a population of people believing they are unique unto themselves. The word "oversee" provides a clue to why social institutions (parents and schools) struggle with adolescents to get them to behave and conform. (A school I recently visited writes the names of students as young as six on a publicly displayed honor roll, an award earned in part by the children's willingness to "do as they are told.") The culture fears it cannot oversee a population of genuine individuals, for to do this would countenance a war of all against all, instincts against instincts. To some degree this may be true. Perhaps the phrases "Don't chew gum!" "Remove that hat!" and "Don't run in the halls!" represent the underpinnings of modern civilization.

Cultures, in the form of behavioral standards, social conventions and the teaching of (or the failure to teach) morality, socialize adolescents, make them able to act civilly if not kindly toward one another. Unintentionally, these same standards and conventions also distract adolescents from the knowledge of their own and others' lives. The concept of resistance advanced by psychoanalysts reminds us that even people who choose to explore their own psychic contents four or five days a week with a person whose face they only infrequently observe fiercely battle their own stated desires and intentions. They find it painful to locate those roads, much less travel down them toward their genuine being. In part this is what psychologist Scott Peck had in mind when writing the perfectly titled book from the words of the poet Robert Frost: *The Road Less Traveled*.[32] They fear they will disappoint someone, be abandoned, or perhaps discover they weren't loved or wanted, or that they themselves did not or cannot love or be loved. They fear, as Kohut[33] reminds us, they are defective, and hence their inner caves corrupted or worse, empty.

The most common fear expressed by adolescents, all people actually, about to appear on television for the first time goes this way: "I'm afraid I'll sound dumb."[34] We are sympathetic to this fear; an appearance before a camera can be terrifying. Yet reflect for a moment on this fear. Rationally, how can anyone sound dumb when they are going to be speaking about their own experiences, an ordeal perhaps, or some momentous personal discovery? No one is about to test their knowledge of quarks or neurological synapses. Granted, it is normal to fear suddenly becoming inarticulate or incoherent, but perhaps another factor is at work.

In some people's minds, going on television or speaking in public as in classroom presentations is a bit like going through a personality x-ray machine or CAT scan of the soul. The camera, we imagine, reveals truth, at least the audience will be able to detect it. As Postman[35] suggested, the ultimate power of television is captured in the phrase, "seeing is believing"; without seeing, there is no believing.[36] Even worse, some adolescents fear that on television or in front of their class or entire school assembly, others will perceive things in them they themselves never knew were there. The adolescent won't be able to conceal those secret (even to them) parts of himself or herself; the capacity to resist themselves as well as distract others will be dissipated by the camera or the public appearance.

In the end, adolescents, like the rest of us, fear that others will see them naked and vulnerable as if the others could capture them on film or tape standing alone in front of their personal caves. In this highly public and publicized setting, the very setting some adolescents crave in their desire for stardom, they fear they will be obliged to confront themselves as they always prayed they never would, and they don't know how, or what will happen to them as a result of this self-encounter in a public environment. The camera or public eye (the socially framed judging self) becomes a psychological (search and discovery) spy satellite apparently able to detect the undetectable. A date on a talk show set would be marked on one's personal calendar as the real day of judgment. Manifestly, the adolescent fears he or she will sound stupid, but beneath the surface, in and among the caves where the demons reside, adolescents fear what analysands and artists fear: intense personal scrutiny combined with the hunt for the genuine voice will lead to madness; the distraction of the outer world will have taken hold within the inner world. It isn't unintelligent, therefore, that adolescents will sound, it is outright crazy. They will lose control before an audience, real or imagined, of millions and come completely apart. Then suddenly, in the midst of their imagined breakdown, they will recognize that death is their only escape, their only salvation. Suddenly they pray for a calamity to preempt their appearance or classroom presentation. If distraction breeds attention deficit disorders, then it may play a role in generating anxiety attacks as well.

Herein the ultimate irony of human distraction for adolescents: They tend to believe that the road leading to their unconscious, their inner voice, those private mind fields where they alone find the fire of life, will bring them closer to madness and death. Only naturally they come to believe they must stay away from those fields, especially in a public setting, and support instead the culture's directives meant to lead them to sanity, stability and long life, if not immortality. Stay distracted, the culture appears to be admonishing the young, and you'll never die. (In the end, distraction may just be a high-class word meaning "foggedaboutit.")

That's what institutions are meant to do, isn't it, ensure social order, civil action and hence personal sanity? That's why children cannot be allowed to run in the halls of their schools, chew gum in class, or play by (with?) themselves in their own bedrooms with the door closed, isn't it?[37] That's why it's so important that adolescents be obliged to tell everything they're doing and thinking, isn't it? Law and order must be preserved in the psyche as well as the society. And isn't it interesting that ruminations of the sort in which adolescents indulge have been called by some, mental masturbation, and don't some people claim that masturbation leads to mental illness?

Finding one's voice involves hunting for one's personal source of energy, instincts perhaps, creative mind fields, and then turning these mind fields into wondrous products merely by dint of knowing that in these moments one is leading a genuine life. Still, too many of us treat this task, allegedly one of normal adolescent development, in the same way we react to proposals for sex education in schools: Teach adolescents about drugs, and ineluctably these teachings will lead to experimentation. Teach adolescents about sex and they'll act out sexually. Adolescents suddenly are medical students, growing ill with each new disease they study. It is better, some conclude, to take the approach, out of sight, out of mind. The alternative is unthinkable: In sight (or is it insight?), out of your mind. All of this puts me in mind of John Dewey's provocative words: ". . . education must be conceived as a continuing reconstruction of experience; that the process and the goal of education are one and the same thing."[38]

When I have an insight, an idea, or understanding of something that heretofore has not existed in my mind, I have approached the source of my inner voice. I am elated, for I have encountered my mind, and "it" has offered me a sort of gift. Think of the ecstasy exhibited by children when suddenly they have understood or mastered something: They scream for their Mommies and Daddies so that they first may demonstrate the discovery and then gain recognition for their newly found competence or accomplishment. They are no longer the people they were moments before, and neither is the poet or dancer, athlete, mathematician, or student who has just pulled off a fabulous trick of the mind or body. In one form or another, all of these people have gained insight, a "sight" of the "in," and for long moments they fear nothing. Not only has their trip not been terrifying, it has made them feel capable of doing anything and, perhaps too, becoming immortal.

The same is true for adolescents undertaking their personal self-reflections, either alone or in the presence of others, although in a sense, as Heidegger observed,[39] we are always partly alone and partly with others. By discovering these self-truths, adolescents move farther away from the bevy of distractions constituting the world they and we, too, regularly call the "real" world (although one wonders why the inside world is any less real?) and closer to the world of make-believe in which anything is possible. For anything *is* possible within the adolescent's mind fields, exactly as Piaget's developmental theories proposed. All the adolescent has to do is conceive of it, call it up, and it will exist. Contrary to popular (culture) belief, it does not require the adolescent actually seeing it or buying it. Known to every child, the neighborhood of make-believe hardly disappears when one reaches adolescence.

Although these notions may sound naive, childish even, they should strike the adolescent as valid. Leading one closer to personal truths, the creative process is more appropriately called childlike. All creative efforts bring forth the child in us, the uncomplicated hunt for something missing, or for that voice that cries in us or, following Professor Tigner, calls to us. Unhampered by social conventions, fearless in the face of potentially humiliating circumstances, adolescents barrel ahead in their drawings, paintings, writings, self-explorations like willful children having tantrums in the supermarket. And is not the mind a sort of supermarket?

All that matters in these moments of search and discovery is the adolescent. Suddenly becoming blind to the needs of others, he or she cannot tolerate a simple interruption. Cannot people see that their very wills are being exerted to their limits? Can they not see that at last adolescents are engaged in genuine work? Selfish they are labeled, and they well may be, but selfishness in this context is healthy if it is in the service of the search and discovery of the authentic self.

To find it is to make it up or make it out. To do this, adolescents unconsciously regress to childlike forms and attitudes if only because this freedom to play make-believe was originally learned and abetted during childhood. Little wonder that creative artists, and adolescents, surround themselves not only with keepsakes and momentos of childhood but with toys as well. If adolescents seem selfish and childish, it is because they must rebel against cultural and societal boundaries demanding that in growing up, they move away first from being driven to being led, and then away from the imaginative powers and freedom of childhood make believe, the very powers and freedom required in the hunt for the authentic beings that once they knew (and were).[40]

The Rabbit in *The Velveteen Rabbit* by Margery Williams asks the Skin Horse, what is real and "does it happen all at once or bit by bit?" The Skin Horse replies: "It takes a long time. That's why it doesn't often happen to people who break easily, or have sharp edges, or have to be carefully kept. Generally, by the time you are Real, most of your hair has been loved off, and your eyes drop out and you get loose in the joints and very shabby. But these things don't matter at all, because once you are Real you can't be ugly, except to people who don't understand."[41]

Many of us remain afraid even to imagine possibilities, and hence we forfeit our capacity to conceive of the philosophical notion of human possibility. With all the forces of life driving us, our cultures, and our minds toward the future, we have determined that without the sense of possibility, there is no personal future. Unable to let ourselves regress into childlike imagination or adolescent personal discovery, we inadvertently deprive ourselves of reaching into the future in order to shape its content. We decide we will let the future come to us, an utter anathema for the adolescent, bringing whatever it chooses to bring, as if it were a gift-bearing relative visiting us from out of state. Strangely, we continue to utter that expression about how time is running out, when everyone knows that time, presumably, will remain and that it is *we* who are running out of it.

What could be more alienating than this? Do we honestly believe that all that lies out there before us is but empty time? Would an adolescent allow himself or herself to believe this? Why would any of us be afraid of emptiness? The future will come, and somehow we will be in it, but it all appears vacuous. Is this why some of us look to psychics and astrologers to tell us what our futures will provide? Do we believe that the future is totally unknown and that we have forfeited any control over its contents? Would an adolescent be content with this sentiment? Would adolescents be comfortable with the notion that someone else can delineate their destinies for them, and they themselves possess no such power? Is the adolescent but a part of the audience for the future's show? Why wouldn't the adolescent believe that the future is to the present as, say, a pregnant woman's belly is to her body? Is she not part of this protruding package? Can the present not be pregnant with the future? Henri Bergson suggested this very proposition decades ago. Erikson, too, pointed out that the creation of the future, notably in terms of careers, ideologies, and relationships, is a fundamental task of the adolescent, one that is seriously compromised by the belief that life is predetermined. For adolescents, to know their future is to destroy their will, purpose, reason for living, perhaps. To know the future, although a fantasy of some young people,[42] denies adolescents a basic right to discover their potential and turn it into reality. Prescience devastates the essential task of the adolescent stage of development; it negates the self.

A friend tells me that when he feels sad, he imagines his life as a moving sidewalk in an airport. Standing still, the wide conveyor belt transports him from one position to the next. Alongside him people walk, expending effort but eventually reaching the same end. Surveying the sights of the airport, he feels nothing other than the satisfaction that he has saved energy. The final destination for him, that which was the future when he stepped upon the conveyor belt, now has been reached. There is nothing exciting about getting here, no sense of accomplishment or joy, neither search nor discovery, in part because no effort was made; a mechanical force guided him. Most depressing, the future looks to be the same as the past, which was the present when he commenced his journey. Past, present, and future remain indistinguishable; TWA looks like Delta, a word ironically meaning change. The time is empty, the journey dull, the only question for the astrologer: When, ultimately, does the moving sidewalk stop? In some respects, this image describes all too well the lives of those adolescents who find nothing of consequence in their schools, families, or communities.

Without a future, especially one they can construct from their intellect and imagination, there is no voice, no self, and there may never be one. These adolescents fear perhaps that they literally are dumb, not in the sense of being unintelligent but rather unable to speak. Is this what they fear waiting to address their class or school assembly or the world? Do they imagine they will become voiceless? Might adolescents fear they will have nothing to say when asked to describe personal experiences, attitudes, and outlooks?[43] If that is what they fear—and we cannot be surprised by this reaction—then the powers of distraction are even more insidious and pervasive than ever we imagined. Such a fear suggests that the ultimate purpose of culture would be to socialize (or distract) adolescents to the point where they forfeit all rights to their inner voice, which we now understand represents their genuine identity.

Adolescents who find their voice cannot possibly be (or feel) dumb, and good parents and teachers know this, so they help young people discern the means by which that voice may be heard.[44] With the proper education, adolescents learn that their voice will always be there. ("Mother wit," I often whisper before a lecture, "don't leave me now." I always wonder if I need the wit part.) Be it a computation, a story, a part in a play, and yes, rebellion and resistance, repudiation and rejection, voices must be heard, voices that assure adolescents they are the people they were meant to be. Most all adolescents respond positively to the voice's sound even if no one else does. It surely feels good when there's someone to watch you open your presents—even the ones you give to yourself.

It isn't difficult recognizing when drawing children are nearing the boundaries of their inner voice. One hears those characteristic deep breathing sounds I heard in that Nantucket bedroom. I have learned from experience when I, too, am getting closer to hearing (or approaching) my voice. In psychotherapy the clue was that I grew slightly depressed (and to think I had to pay for this). Other than that, it occurs when I am alone writing and discover that my tongue has been pushing hard against my lower teeth; it is the only time I ever do this. I imagine that all adolescents can identify their own idiosyncratic clues, at least those adolescents who are permitted to speak about such matters.

If one of the challenges of human life that in many respects defines adolescent individuality and uniqueness is that of finding one's voice, then determining precisely what finding one's voice means is an equally daunting challenge. If, moreover, the search for truth involves a search for (and a calling up of) genuine knowledge about something and not merely a collection of (piled on) facts, then it also must involve the ongoing use of Thoreau's intellectual cleaver, fixing one's mental gaze, and ultimately discovering and protecting one's own personal truths, one's genuine being.

To live in any society, any community, family, or school, one must act.[45] One acts the role of son, daughter or student.[46] One acts even when one doesn't care to act, like the obedient student who would prefer to be on the ballfield instead of in the classroom reciting multiplication tables. For one J. D. Salinger character, acting was akin to being a phony, which led to this remark: "How would you know you weren't being a phony? The trouble is, you wouldn't."[47] Some adolescents act without needing to, as if they were beginning their social routines before the cameras were even set up. And if anyone believes that adolescents, or the rest of us for that matter, only act when others are around, conjure up your own daily bathroom ablutions often carried out as if one were on stage at the Grammy Awards.

Somewhere along the line, however, amidst all their public (and private) acting, amidst their being in the world, adolescents discover what constitutes their being, their personality, their art, their authentic roles, so they imagine, as opposed to their required life roles. People embarked on Peck's road less traveled proclaim they have found what they were meant to do, which puts them on the road to this grand discovery. Some people make the discovery early in childhood, though more likely during adolescence. Others don't find it (or themselves) even when they have fallen right into the middle of it, and still others die never knowing for certain where that precious voice resided, although one suspects they knew that much of their life was ingenuine. They sensed, in other words, they hadn't lead the lives they were meant to lead, a terrifying thought that strikes the adolescent as well, and that there was more to life than what they had externally and internally experienced. Probably too, they would have announced all this to others had anyone ever asked them. (And still others might choose to go along with Asleigh Brilliant, who wrote *I Have Abandoned Any Search for the Truth and Am Now Looking for a Good Fantasy*.)

Solutions to distraction during adolescence, such as they are, may be found in any activity of the mind that leads to disciplined self-reflection and the truths of experience, no matter how much it hurts to undertake that self-reflection. Breaking through the denials that disingenuously imprison us, individually and collectively, means looking inward to our own life-sized beings rather than outward to the larger-than-life-sized worlds of "superstars" and false role models, a distracting emphasis on self-esteem, and a life built on materialism. It is found in allowing oneself to dream along with actors and playwrights in darkened theaters rather than escape from these same quintessential human dreams via products that block one's passage to one's interior world. It all begins with paying attention.

There is a sign etched in stone on one of the gates leading into the Yard at Harvard University. For some reason its wording has always stayed with me: "Enter to grow in wisdom." Above the sign is the Harvard crest containing the Latin word *veritas* (truth). Perhaps this entry into an esteemed university provides us a valuable guide post. Genuine wisdom does seem a reasonable antidote to distraction, for, by definition, its acquisition becomes a life-long endeavor involving exquisite investigation, examination, and discovery. Quite possibly, adolescents' attraction to their grandparents bespeaks this sense of safety and certainty found among reputedly wiser citizens.

Equally significant, those words "truth" and "enter" provide clues to something adolescents know: When truth and morality are avoided, when we lie to one another and ourselves, or cheat (on) one another, and ourselves, when we are not responsible to ourselves[48] or for one another, faithful to one another or ultimately respectful of one another, and when we fail to be sufficiently self-reflective, we only stoke the fires of distraction that burn away the fabric of the culture and the individual soul. It happens this way in national scandals in business, politics, the law, and sports or in the covert operations and hostile takeovers occurring in families, some-thing all too many adolescents are obliged to witness. The fires are stoked as well when adolescents lie to themselves, escape from themselves, or generally turn away from the signs and indications entreating them to enter into the inner world of the intellect and the emotions where their inner voice resides.

Americans have taken literally and built industries from the words, "In the pursuit of happiness." Yet no one to my knowledge guaranteed that the pursuit itself would be a happy experience, something I am certain adolescents quickly discover. The pursuit ought to be a truthful one, and the result, though not necessarily the goal, may well be personal bliss to borrow Joseph Campbell's[49] word. If adolescence teaches anything it is that the journey often evokes sadness and pain, particularly at those moments when, through personal examinations and detailed self-reflec-tion as Dewey[50] defined it, cultural distractions are stripped away, one's consciousness is no longer diverted, and nothing lies before young men and young women but the essence of their own being and its finitude, that is, *their* finitude.

The Prize of Self-reflection

Having read through these pages about distraction and reflection and considered Dewey's thoughts on the enslaved mind and the discipline required to become reflective and properly judgmental, the reader may imagine that reflection is one of the most private, individualistic, and esoteric enterprises a human being could ever undertake. In point of fact, this is not the case. Self-reflection, the antidote to distraction for adolescents as well as adults, is neither purely personal nor limited merely to thinking. As it turns out, reflection looms as a powerful political action.

Hold in mind that thinking and action go hand and hand.[51] Thinking is shaped in great measure by the world in which adolescents reside. If the people around them continually communicate disappointment in them, eventually adolescents are going to think of themselves in negative and discouraging tones. Moreover, because thoughts and action go hand and hand, the adolescent's opinion of himself or herself, learned originally in a variety of social contexts, will lead to behavior that others will not only witness but assess.

Stephen Kemmis[52] makes these same points when he states, some-what surprisingly, that reflection is not purely an internal process but a social one and that a culture's ideology ultimately shapes the adolescent's (seemingly personal) reflections in the same way that an adolescent's reflections shape ideology, even though one rarely contemplates this side of the equation. Reflection, Kemmis notes, isn't something that goes on only in one's head. In reflection, the adolescent surely looks inward, as Dewey too, suggested, but he or she looks outward as well, for it is the social order that ultimately determines the products of reflection and, hence, the action taken by the adolescent as a result of (ostensibly personal) reflection.

Adolescents think about thinking; much of adolescence we suggested is about the process of going meta, preparing young people for reflection, as Tremmel notes,[53] and ideally making judgments about one's thinking prior to acting. The training for this action was begun in childhood, in what Piaget termed preconventional reasoning.[54] That is, the child does something to avoid punishment or simply because a powerful authority figure has directed his or her actions. In contrast, adolescents reflect and reason, often in the most complex forms of which human beings are capable. A young man decides he needs a new shirt, so he plans to go shopping. Then he looks back at his thoughts and actions and makes further judgments not only upon these thoughts but upon the actions and effects they may have on others. This is quintessential self-reflection of a sort rarely undertaken by people before the commencement of adolescence. Upon purchasing the shirt, the young man fears he may have spent too much money, or he concludes that the store is overpriced and that he must never again shop there, or perhaps he believes he has insulted the salesperson. Whatever the considerations, they only spring forth when one is acting in a self-reflective manner. Most likely, none of this occurs to adolescents when they are distracted.

Kemmis further notes that as the individual undertakes purposeful self-reflection in both thought and action, all three of Aristotle's fundamental modes of reasoning reveal themselves.[55] Every thought and action, for example, must contain what Aristotle called the technical or instrumental form of reasoning. There are always means and ends, and both must be considered and judged. In order to get an A in the course, the students will have to write additional research papers. Do they want to do this writing? Do they crave an outstanding grade that much? The purpose of what the adolescent is thinking and doing and what might emerge as the practical result or product of this thinking remain fundamental concerns in instrumental reasoning. Technical reasoning is also the foundation of a person's need to control natural powers, the way one imagines one is doing by endlessly listening to weather forecasts, yet another form of distraction.

Second, there is what Aristotle called the practical aspect of thinking and acting. Adolescents must consider how they will judge thinking and acting. Will they, for example, act rightly or wrongly given the nature of historical events or existing social circumstances? Will they reflect on the moral way to conduct themselves? Without practical deliberation, there will never be anything resembling a conscience.

Finally, there is theoretical reasoning or what Aristotle called speculation and the pursuit of truth for its own sake. And here we must pause for we have come to a critical juncture in our discussion of adolescent consciousness in a culture of distraction.

In reflecting on theoretical reasoning or speculation, we ask these questions: Why should adolescents even be concerned about distraction? Why should they occupy themselves with the notion of self-reflection? And in these final pages of our discussion, why even bring up issues of theory and speculation and the pursuit of truth for its own sake? We do so because in Kemmis's words, we hope to understand how the adolescent may "achieve emancipation from irrationality, injustice and social fragmentation."[56] We contemplate these notions, in other words, to create a template for adolescents that might allow them to free their minds from enslavement precisely as Dewey[57] advised, and equally important, free themselves from the societal powers that push them toward unjust values, immorality, and irrational if not openly self-deceptive behavior,[58] which, in turn, causes them to feel isolated, fragmented, alienated, lonely, painfully dissatisfied, and, alas, distracted. Given the nature of our global culture, we already notice, as Benjamin Barber writes, that "identities are compromised and lost and our sense of concrete temporality and fixed place, hence our essential security—social, familial and personal—is put permanently at risk."[59] At no other time in the developmental cycle is the notion of self-reflection more relevant than during adolescence.

If this were not sufficiently convincing, consider that undistracted or self-reflective adolescents, as Kemmis points out, are aware of how history has affected them and how they, in turn, affect history. There is nothing radical about this notion; Aristotle observed it centuries ago, and one imagines that adolescents understand it as well, for adolescence is inherently a period for reflecting on the nature of the self in society. We recall Erikson's rather remarkable terminology for the adolescent stage on the (psychosocial) life cycle: Identity cohesion (the self) versus role confusion (the society and culture).[60]

Adolescents appreciate, in other words, their culture's history as well as their own personal history. They seek to understand or at least make sense of what appears to them as cultural misunderstanding, prejudice, or outright injustice. Adolescents, after all, have a keen sense for what is fair and unfair.[61] Adolescents become self-reflective when they recognize they make a difference, they matter, and in so doing discover the power of identity along with a genuine sense of purpose and possibility. Not only do they matter to themselves, but moment by moment through their self-reflective thought and action they are, at all moments, part of the creation of the world.

No longer mere consumers, members of some giant audience or classroom, nor passive observers awaiting their destinies, adolescents become participants, shapers, creators, artists, free. They question decisions, decision making, and decision makers, precisely as they are told to do in most every graduation ceremony speech, just as they question communication, communications, and communicators. In a self-reflective mode, they study well the message as well as the messenger.

They do this in part by recognizing that a culture—its values and belief systems and, ultimately, its history and ideologies—has no more power to shape their thoughts and actions than they themselves through (self-reflective) thought and action have the power to shape these very same values and ideologies, this very same history. They may wish to be a member of the club or clique, the gang or team, but they will never allow themselves to be owned by the team; free will and disciplined self-reflection ought to preclude this. As Paulo Friere observed, inasmuch as reality is a construction, each of us has the capacity to transform it.[62] This, in turn, suggests, as Kemmis asserted, that reflection is a form of ideology. For all we know, the very concept of adolescence may be just another ideological construction.

If the world constructs adolescents' thoughts and actions, their language and communication, their ideas and the ways they perceive and comprehend things, then they, in turn, maintain the power to shape and reconstitute the world. Each exercise in self-reflection, as Kemmis observed (each moment when one is not distracted), makes possible a reconstituting of oneself as well as one's social world. This means that adolescents can invent and reinvent themselves; they can live freely in a sphere beyond the actual (sadly, some now imagine this is made possible only through the use of drugs), the sphere, as Marcuse noted, of the possible.[63] This is the crowning achievement of Erikson's adolescent stage of development.

The possible, however, is there for the taking only if adolescents shed distractive thinking and action in favor of self-reflective thinking and action. In distraction, adolescents merely consume what has been fed to them by the culture in homes and schools, in political realms, in the malls, magazines, theaters, restaurants, and local hangouts, because the culture's agents recognize that adolescents continue to consume these (distracting) products and ideologies. Through self-reflection, adolescents come to recognize that others often see them as nothing but members of some team, group, or gang. Yet all adolescents at times seek individual recognition; they do not wish to be known merely as "adolescents." So, for them to consume the products and ideologies of the culture is surely to know periodic sensations of self-fulfillment (Dewey's appetite, sensation, and appeal to momentary circumstance), but it is never to know the emancipated experience of genuine fulfillment, satisfaction, and liberty.

By transforming one's identity, decision making, thinking and actions, what popular culture itself calls reinventing oneself—a far cry from the notion of "marketing" oneself—the adolescent may actually change the culture's products and ideologies. This action is more significant than merely banding together as an enormous consumer group and choosing not to buy certain products. It transforms these products and their attending ideologies by nature of the most private of thought (*Eigenwelt*) leading ultimately to the most public of action (*Mitwelt*). According to Kemmis,

> The emancipatory interest is aimed at emancipating people from the dictates of taken-for-granted assumptions, habits, tradition, custom, domination and coercion, and self deception.[64]

As Friere might have asserted, adolescents are freer than ever they might have believed, or more accurately, than the culture wishes them to believe. Self-reflection reinforces this belief, but distraction prevents its birth within the mind fields of the adolescent in the first place. In the mode of distractive thinking, adolescents honestly believe that many things about life remain forever immutable and, alas, must be taken for granted. Similarly, distractive thinking often causes adolescents to believe they have power to control outcomes when in truth they remain totally powerless, something adolescents oppose with fantasies of the sort they learned in childhood. (Need we mention that infamous phrase "Computers don't lie?")

In the mode of self-reflective thought, adolescents learn that although all sorts of pressures are exerted on them to purchase products, even worship certain icons, they themselves are neither icons nor mere products of history and contemporary society. They discover their actions need not be merely the result of habits of the mind nor of the heart for that matter nor unthinking repetitive social action of the sort adolescents claim to abhor. (To a certain extent, this is precisely what much of psychotherapy is about.[65]) They learn they are more than passive consumers or audience members; they have the power to become active thinkers and agents who recast the fundamental visions and forms of the culture in which they live and not merely exist.

They learn, moreover, that they are inalterably determined neither by genetic force nor instinct (nor by the unseen hand of destiny) to the point that their entire being is formed by the third year of life, or the fifth year, or even the fiftieth year. All of their being cannot be formed by the nature of their intelligences, a disability, a disorder, all terms which, in a self-reflective world, would go through constant redefinitions. Adolescents possess the power to create a fragmented, atomized world of alienated people, many of them acting uncivilly toward one another as one observes in certain schools, or skimming the surface of television and computer screens as Birkerts wrote,[66] imagining that material culture will eventually yield genuine happiness.

In contrast, adolescents also possess the power to formulate and then construct the social forms of solidarity that each of them knows they require in order to feel nurtured, secure, and comfortable in intimate contexts.[67] (This too, ought to be the work of psychotherapy.) What can one young man or one young woman do? Nothing more than change his or her own fate and the fate of an entire world if he or she retreats from a distracted stance, employs self-reflection as a means of simultaneously turning inward and outward, and so chooses. As Stephen Kemmis remarked:

> . . . reflection is a power we choose to exercise in the analysis and transformation of the situations in which we find ourselves when we pause to reflect. It expresses our agency as the makers of history as well as our awareness that we have been made by it.[68]

As Freud spoke of a life force (Eros) and a death force (Thanatos), so did Erich Fromm speak of a death-oriented (necrophilus) culture, and the love-oriented (biophilus) culture. Fromm would have looked two seconds at America as it raced past the twenty-first century starting point and claimed it was necrophilus to the nth degree. All one has to do is watch the stories dominating the nightly news to see what would have struck

Fromm's eye.[69] Incidentally, part of the necrophilus orientation, Fromm alleged, is an obsession with law and order, which means insisting that punishment, prisons, and guns stop crime and that nature's forces can be predicted and harnessed.

Adolescents are not alone in their struggle with the idea of life's brevity and human finitude. Adolescents are not alone in wishing to believe that they might matter just a bit or make a tad of difference to someone somewhere over time. Perhaps they feel they will leave their mark by continuing the family name or leaving behind some product or, as Thoreau suggested, making even meager improvement in the social conditions and the land they inherited. They want to imagine that their conscious worlds are dominated by life and not death forces, a desire that is momentarily shattered when murder and suicide take hold of their families and schools. They wish to believe they are worthy, useful, loving, lovable, that they know the good and do the good. Perhaps they just wish to believe.

My own father claimed there was little sense working on anything unless life or death hung in the balance. Easy for him to say, he was a physician dealing with life and death on a daily basis. The rest of us just imagine our own efforts warrant life and death status. Most writers, I am certain, imagine that the unfinished book lives in them and causes the same joy and nausea as the unborn baby does for the pregnant woman. Readers must forgive a writer's self-absorption and periodic self-importance, for to undertake any project leading to a book gradually comes to be felt as a life or death affair; it almost can't be helped.

I'm no different; I believe that distraction is a significant part of the death force Fromm, Marcuse, Freud, Dewey, Friere, and others observed and that self-reflection, disciplined, moral, properly judged thinking and action represent fundamental ingredients of a genuine life force.[70] I honestly believe each of us can change ourselves *and* the world, making it more just, more rational, even more loving by dint of transformations of which we are uniquely capable in reasoning and action. Granted, luck plays a role in all of our lives as does that mysterious conglomerate of proteins known as genetic structure.

Then there's the matter of the human will and the choices, even the seemingly insignificant ones, each of us undertakes *every* moment of our life unless, of course, we are distracted. With this choice, as Kemmis reminds us, comes the possibility of a just, rational and moral life filled with satisfaction—unless, of course, we are distracted.

Think in this context of theories of human development. Life begins, and our brains and habits form. We are told by some scientists that our brains have fully formed by age three, or is it fifteen or is it now thirty? (Does not everyone feel maddening frustration when scientists and physicians change their minds!) In our teens, it is alleged, we are allowed a bit of rebellion, but by the time we reach our twenties we are meant to settle into careers.[71] By our thirties, if we are leading a so-called "normal life," we have chosen a life partner. Then, following the (culturally constructed) parameters of the life cycle, all of this is developed and elaborated in our forties and fifties so that by the time we reach sixty, we can commence the psychological work required to accept our demise, reconcile the lives we have led, and not punish ourselves too severely for roads taken or not taken, friends and deals made or not made.

Developmental theories are often taken to be blueprints of the way life necessarily evolves. This piece of life business *is meant* to be accomplished by this date; that piece of life business is the ultimate act of elderly wisdom. Yet much of this is pure construction, the result of theorizing, thinking, and acting or what Kemmis has called the construction of ideology. For something amazing always takes place to alter our thinking and acting. A child executes something extraordinary, and we realize we do not have a secure grasp of what development or adolescence mean. We hear about thousands of people well into their forties, fifties, and sixties attending college for the first time,[72] or a fifty-year-old woman deciding that the moment is perfect for her to attend medical school. We learn of a prominent lawyer at age fifty-nine deciding he is going to give up a lucrative practice and open an inn in Vermont or a seventy-five-year-old woman who has decided she will fulfill a life-long dream and climb mountains in Tibet.

What is it with these people? Why don't they act their age? Don't they know about the (theories of the) human life cycle and its inherent (that is, theorized) constraints? Or we mutter, is it just another deviant case or mid-life crisis? A little counseling will shock them back to their senses.

All that is happening here (and it happens every moment in the world of adolescents) is that people are thinking and acting and, hence, shaping and constructing the history of other individuals and collective history and knowledge as well. They are constructing what too regularly we call facts (or factoids), thus, they are reconstructing their own identities and, with them, social reality. With courage and daring and out of a sense of reasoned freedom, these people are solving complicated mathematical problems at age thirteen or trekking in the Himalayas at age eighty. They are thinking about the dynamics of something called a mid-life crisis (something that could only have been invented in America[73]), or they are recalling the writings of Ortega y Gasset,[74] who spoke of changes in mid-life as *rebirth,* and of Lawrence Durrell who wrote that man (and we must add woman) is not born to lead but one life. It is all in the thinking and acting, all in the reflection or the distraction, the new construction or the (un-thinking) settling for old structures. Do I go on as before, every adoles-cent asks himself or herself, or do I transform myself and take you with me? It is not all in the genes nor in human nature; it is not all in the hands of the fates or the luck of the draw.

So it is not precisely how old I am or how I feel about how old I am, it is how I think and act about how old I am, that eventually carries the day for adolescents. I am not only the way fifteen looks or eighty looks; I am changing the way I look and hence think about fifteen or eighty. Like all other parts of reality, including the construct of intelligence, age itself is but a social construct, another product of our self-reflective mind fields. We already think this way; what we have to do now is think about the way we think. We all know that in the eyes of children, people in their fifties and sixties seem really, really old, except of course for their grandparents, who even in their seventies and eighties, children choose not to consider old.

Granted, some of the ingredients of destiny (like tomorrow's weather) lie just out of our reach, but the best part, as all adolescents discover, lies right inside each one of us, in the form of a three-pound world of mystery and possibility known as the brain. It is the first thing we inquire about when a baby is born, but then we seem to forget that it, like the heart, requires regular, disciplined exercise, and that to a certain extent, when it comes to consciousness, thinking and reasoning, which neuroscience only recently has begun to comprehend, we are in control. In our minds, we always have the possibility of being free—it's the one ball that never leaves our court—even immortal, if we so choose. Is this not part of our theo-logical reflections? Children lead their lives as if everything were possible; adolescents are left to ruminate on the remains of childhood, the expec-tations of adulthood, and, hence, the possibility of possibility.

This is why I tend to think of self-reflection and distraction, respec-tively, as life and death forces, especially in the lives of adolescents. Most of us share with the young the need for diversion, entertainment for the senses, gratification of certain esthetic and sensate appetites. Who doesn't like a good movie and a modicum of creature comforts? Yet as we have argued, distraction misleads us, causes us to feel isolated, alienated, and hungry for something we can no longer describe although many of us sense this missing fragment goes by the name of the spiritual. Working out of habit and a belief that, alas, this is what life is about and we're just going to have to accept it, a rather common admonition offered to adolescents, we look to the same stimuli and products to satisfy our needs and whims. Then we say, it's painful to think that after a rather young age, our cells begin to self-destruct; time is running out, and we are dying.

By now we recognize this as distractive thinking. We don't really know that our cells are self-destructing. We don't really know that this is what life is all about. We don't really know that at a certain point we are dying rather than living. And if, in the strictest biological terms, we are beginning to die the moment we are born, then it is up to us to determine what this dying business means. For could we not also allege that at the moment of birth the death cycle commences? So then by the time we learn to walk, death is well underway. What we know is what we think and how we act, what we create for ourselves and others, and what they create for us, and upon what of all of this we choose to reflect. Having encountered the depression and despair associated with the self being blocked and aspirations being temporarily thwarted and recognizing the need not only for ego integrity but moral integrity as well, the adolescent period ideally concludes with strength; the self experiencing the joy of fulfillment forever remains a possibility.[75]

The choices now present themselves, for there are always more moments of joy and despair, more potential prizes derived from self-examination and reflection. There is also that endless line of distractions filled with glittering sights, tantalizing sounds, and wondrous tastes. All one need do is look up from these pages and they will be there, or at least the instruments of these sensations will be there in the form of computers, television sets, DVD players and VCRs, Walkmans and boom boxes, tape recorders, cell phones, and a host of catalogues and Web sites advertising products for the home, products for the bath, products for the skin and hair, products for the body, products for the gym, products for the day, products for the night. The instruments of sensation are also there in the form of other people and in the form of ourselves, each one (of us) manufacturing products for the world of consciousness. Look up from these pages only if you dare.

Yet in and among these products lives the sound of a human voice. Because of my advancing age, I choose to imagine it is the voice of an elderly person, a grandparent perhaps. Think about what you just said, the voice whispers. Think about what you just did; think about what you might think or do next, make a reasoned judgment, and then take a deep breath, reveal yourself to the world and experience the prize of reflection. In Walt Whitman's words, "It's time to explain myself—let us stand up."[76] It's either that or we could stay in and rent a movie.

Notes

1   Neil Postman, *The Disappearance of Childhood*. New York: Vintage, 1982.

2   See Laura E. Berk, *Child Development* (4th edition). Boston: Allyn and Bacon, 1997.

3   See Vivian G. Paley, *The Boy Who Would Be a Helicopter*. Cambridge, MA: Harvard University Press, 1990; and *The Kindness of Children*. Cambridge, MA: Harvard University Press, 1999.

4   Howard Gardner, *Frames of Mind: The Theory of Multiple Intelligences*. New York: Basic, 1983.

5   See Jacob Getzels and Mihaly Csikszentmihalyi, *The Creative Vision: A Longitudinal Study of Problem Finding in Art*. New York: Wiley, 1976. See also Jacob Getzels and Philip Jackson, *Creativity and Intelligence: Explorations with Gifted Students*. New York Wiley: 1962.

6   B. A. Hennessey and T. M. Amabile, "The Conditions of Creativity." In R. J. Sternberg (Editor), *The Nature of Creativity*. New York: Cambridge University Press, 1988.

7   Robert Tremmel, "Zen and the Art of Reflective Practice in Teacher Education." *Harvard Educational Review*, 63, 4, Winter 1993: 434–458. I am grateful to Arthur Beane for this citation.

8   See J. Baer, *Creativity and Divergent Thinking*. Hillsdale, NJ: Erlbaum, 1993; D. P. Perkins and H. Gardner (Editors), *Art, Mind, and Education*. Urbana: University of Illinois Press, 1989; and J. P. Guilford, *The Structure of Intellect*. New York: McGraw-Hill, 1967.

9   *How We Think*, Amherst, NY: Prometheus, 1991.

10   Ethel Specter Person (Editor), *On Freud's "Creative Writers and Day-Dreaming."* New Haven, CT: Yale University Press, 1995, page 3.

11   Milhaly Csikszentmihalyi, *Flow: The Psychology of Optimal Experience*. New York: HarperCollins, 1990; and Milhaly Csikszentmihalyi, *Creativity: Flow and the Psychology of Discovery and Invention*. New York: Harper, 1996.

12   Jean Piaget, *Six Psychological Studies*. New York: Random House, 1967, page 66.

13   See Thomas J. Cottle, *Children's Secrets*. Reading, MA: Addison-Wesley, 1990.

14   David Bowie, "Changes." New York: EMI Music Publishing.

15   Robert Tremmel, "Zen and the Art of Reflective Practice in Teacher Education." *Harvard Educational Review*, op. cit., page 441.

16   Stephen Tigner, "Homer, Teacher of Teachers." *Journal of Education, 175,* 3, 1993: 43–64; and Stephen Tigner, "A New Bond: Humanities and Teacher Education." *Liberal Education, 80,* 1, Winter, 1994.

17   The citation within the citation is attributed to Plato, in *The Republic.* Introduction by Charles M. Bakewell. New York: Scribners, 1928. Cited in Tigner, "A New Bond: Humanities and Teacher Education," op. cit.

18   Cited in Stephen Tigner, "Plato's Meno. Intellectual History of Education." Unpublished manuscript, Boston University, 1998, page 2.

19   Mary Catherine Bateson, *Full Circles, Overlapping Lives.* New York: Random House, 2000. Citation taken from Mary Loeffelholz, "An Anthropological Hand on a New Kind of Genre." *The Boston Globe,* March 12, 2000, page C2.

20   Cited in Stephen Tigner, "Plato's Meno," op. cit, page 2.

21   Henry Rogers Seager, "Economics at Berlin and Vienna," in Charles A. Gluck, Jr. (Editor), *Labor and Other Economic Essays.* New York: Harper and Row, 1951. Cited in Tigner, "Plato's Meno," op. cit., page 2.

22   Vivian Paley, *The Boy Who Would Be a Helicopter,* op. cit.

23   Cited in Donald Palladino, "Poets to Come: Walt Whitman, Self Psychology and the Readers of the Future." Unpublished Manuscript, 2000.

24   Ellen Langer, *The Power of Mindful Learning.* Reading, MA: Perseus, 1997.

25   Howard Gardner, *Frames of Mind: The Theory of Multiple Intelligences.* New York: Basic, 1983.

26   Dainin Katagiri, cited in Tremmel, op. cit., page 30.

27   Dewey, *How We Think,* op. cit.

28   Sigmund Freud, *New Introductory Lectures on Psychoanalysis.* Translated by J. Strachey. New York: Norton, 1965.

29   D. A. Schön, *Educating the Reflective Practitioner: Toward a New Design for Teaching and Learning in the Professions.* San Francisco: Jossey-Bass, 1987.

30   Plato, *The Meno.* In E. Hamilton and H. Cairns (Editors), *The Collected Dialogues of Plato.* Princeton, NJ: Princeton University Press, 1961: 353–584.

31   See Erich Fromm, *The Art of Loving.* New York: Harper, 1956.

32   M. Scott Peck, *The Road Less Traveled: A New Psychology of Love, Traditional Values, and Spiritual Growth.* New York: Simon and Schuster, 1978.

33   Heinz Kohut, *Search for the Self,* Volume 2, Paul Ornstein (Editor). New York: International Universities Press, 1978.

34   R. J. Sternberg, B. E. Conway, J. L. Ketron, and M. Bernstein, "People's Conception of Intelligence." *Journal of Personality and Social Psychology, 41,* 1981: 37–55.

35   Neil Postman, *Amusing Ourselves to Death: Public Discourse in the Age of Show Business*. New York: Penguin, 1986.

36   Neil Postman, *Amusing Ourselves to Death,* ibid.

37   Fromm alleged that law and order is the preoccupation of cultures orienting life around matters of dying, destruction, and death. He offered the term "necrophilus" to describe this preoccupation. Those cultures orienting life around living and preserving the spirit appear to be preoccupied with loving. Fromm labeled this orientation "biophilus."

38   John Dewey, "My Pedagogic Creed." In Kevin Ryan and J. M. Cooper (Editors), *Kaleidoscope: Readings in Education* (8th Edition). Boston: Houghton Mifflin, 1998, page 283.

39   Martin Heidegger, *Being and Time,* translation by Joan Stambaugh. Albany, NY: State University of New York Press, 1966.

40   See Stephanie Coontz, *The Way We Never Were: American Families and the Nostalgia Trap*. New York: Basic, 1992.

41   Margery Williams, *The Velveteen Rabbit: How Toys Become Real*. New York: Doubleday, 1991. Cited in Dianna Townsend, "Distractions from Real." Unpublished manuscript, Boston University, December 20, 1999, page 10.

42   See Thomas J. Cottle, *Perceiving Time: A Psychological Investigation with Men and Women*. New York: Wiley, 1976, chapter 5.

43   Martha Straus, *No-Talk Therapy for Children and Adolescents,* New York: Norton, 1999.

44   Vivian Paley, *The Boy Who Would Be a Helicopter,* op. cit.; and *The Kindness of Children*, op. cit.; see also S. A. Beebe and J. T. Masterson, *Family Talk*. New York: Random House, 1986; and F. Earls and M. Carlson, "Towards Sustainable Development for American Families." *Daedalus*, Winter 1993, 1, *122*: 93–122.

45   See Erving Goffman, *The Presentation of Self In Everyday Life*. Garden City, NY: Anchor, 1959; and George Herbert Mead, *The Philosophy of the Act*, edited with an introduction by Charles W. Morris. Chicago, IL: The University of Chicago Press, 1938.

46   M. A. Fitzpatrick and A. L. Vangelisti, *Explaining Family Interactions*. Thousand Oaks, CA: Sage Publications, 1995.

47   J. D. Salinger, *The Catcher in the Rye*. New York: Bantam 1951, page 172.

48   On a related point, see A. Bandura, *Self-Efficacy: The Exercise of Control*. New York: Freeman, 1997.

49   Joseph Campbell, *The Hero with a Thousand Faces*. Princeton, NJ: Princeton University Press, 1972.

50   Dewey, *How We Think*, op. cit.

51   D. P. Keating, "Adolescent Thinking." In S. S. Feldman and G. R. Elliot (Editors), *At The Threshold: The Developing Adolescent*. Cambridge, MA: Harvard University Press, 1990.

52   See his "Action Research and the Politics of Reflection." In D. Boyd, R. Keogh, D. Walker (Editors), *Reflection: Turning Experience into Learning*. London: Kogan Page, 1985: 139–164. I am grateful to Arthur Beane for calling my attention to this volume.

53   Robert Tremmel, op. cit.

54   See T. Revenson and D. Singer, *A Piaget Primer: How a Child Thinks*. New York, Plume, 1978; A. Blasi and E. C. Hoeffel, "Adolescence and Formal Operations." *Human Development*, *17*, 1974: 344–363; and L. Walker, "The Sequentiality of Kohlberg's Stages of Moral Development." *Child Development*, *53*, 1982: 1330–1336.

55   Aristotle. *Rhetorica* , Translated by W. R. Roberts. In R. McKeon (Editor), *The Basic Works of Aristotle*. New York: Random House, 1941. Cited in Kemmis, op. cit.

56   Kemmis, op. cit., page 142.

57   Dewey, *How We Think,* op. cit.

58   Thomas J. Cottle, *At Peril: Stories of Injustice*. Amherst, MA: University of Massachusetts Press, 2001.

59   Benjamin Barber, "Brave New World." Review of three volumes by Manuel Castells. *The Los Angeles Times*, May 23, 1999, page A23.

60   Erik H. Erikson, *Identity, Youth and Crisis*. New York: Norton, 1968.

61   See William Damon, *The Moral Child*. New York: Free Press, 1988; and W. Damon and D. Hart, *Self-Understanding in Childhood and Adolescence*. New York: Cambridge University Press, 1988.

62   See his *Cultural Action for Freedom*. Cambridge, MA: Center for Study of Development and Social Change, 1970.

63   Herbert Marcuse, *One Dimensional Man: Studies in the Ideology of Advanced Industrial Society*. Boston: Beacon, 1964.

64   Kemmis, op. cit., page 145.

65   See Carl Rogers, *Counseling and Psychotherapy*. Cambridge, MA: Riverside, 1942.

66   Sven Birkerts, *Readings*. New York: Graywolf, 1999.

67   Note again, Felton Earls and Mary Carlson, "Towards Sustainable Development of American Families," op. cit.

68   Kemmis, op. cit., page 149.

69   Erich Fromm, *Escape from Freedom*. New York: Farrar and Rinehart, 1941.

70   See H. Markus and P. Nurius. "Possible Selves." *American Psychologist, 41*, 1986: 954–969; A. Blasi, "Identity and the Development of the Self." In D. Lapsley and F. C. Power (Editors), *Self, Ego, and Identity: Integrative Approaches*. New York: Springer-Verlag, 1988.

71   See Daniel J. Levinson, *The Seasons of a Man's Life*. New York: Knopf, 1978; and Daniel J. Levinson and Judy D. Levinson, *The Seasons of a Woman's Life*. New York: Knopf, 1996.

72   On this point, see Scott Horton, "Transformation: Risk-Taking and Meaning-Making in the Mid-Life Adult." Unpublished manuscript, Boston University, 1999. See also M. Gerzon, *Listening to Mid-Life: Turning Your Crisis into a Quest*. Boston: Shambhala, 1996; J. Mezirow, *Transformative Dimensions of Adult Learning*. San Francisco: Jossey-Bass, 1991; and M. Stein, *Transformation: Emergence of the Self*. College Station, TX: Texas A&M University Press, 1998.

73   See Gail Sheehy, *Passages: Predictable Crises of Adult Life*. New York: Dutton, 1976; and Gail Sheehy, *New Passages: Mapping Your Life Across Time*. New York: Random House, 1995.

74   Ortega y Gasset, *The Revolt of the Masses*. New York: Norton, 1932.

75   Heinz Kohut, *Search for the Self*, Volume 3, Paul Ornstein (Editor). New York: International Universities Press, 1990, page 214; and *Search for the Self*, Volume 2. Cited in Donald Palladino, Jr. "Poets to Come: Walt Whitman, Self Psychology and the Readers of the Future." Unpublished Manuscript, 2000.

76   Walt Whitman, "Song of Myself," From *Leaves of Grass*. Garden City, NY: Doubleday, 1926, section 44, page 61.

References

Adams, G. R., Gulotta, T. P. & Montemayor, R. (Editors) 1992. *Adolescent Identity Formation*. Newbury Park, CA: Sage.

Adams, G. R. & Montemayor, R. (Editors), 1996. *Psychosocial Development During Adolescence*. Thousand Oaks, CA: Sage.

Adler, T. 1991. Put Primates in Groups, a Scientist Recommends, *The APA Monitor,* February, *22,* 2: 10.

Allen, J. P., Hauser, S. T., Bell, K. L. & O'Connor, T. G. 1994. Longitudinal Assessment of Autonomy and Relatedness in Adolescent-Family Interactions as Predictors of Adolescent Ego Development and Self Esteem. *Child Development, 65:* 179–194.

Allison, K. W. & Lerner, R. M. 1993. Adolescents and the Family. In R. M. Lerner (Editor), *Early Adolescence*. Hillsdale, NJ: Erlbaum.

Anderson, J. R. 1990. *Cognitive Psychology and Its Implications* (3rd Edition). New York: W. H. Freeman.

Archambault, R. (Editor). 1964. *John Dewey on Education: Selected Writings*. New York: Random House.

Archer, S. L. 1985. Identity and the Choice of Social Roles. *In Identity and Adolescence: Processes and Contents*. A. S. Waterman, Editor. San Francisco: Jossey-Bass.

Aristotle. 1941. *Rhetorica* , translation by W. R. Roberts. In R. McKeon (Editor), *The Basic Works of Aristotle*. New York: Random House.

Armsden, G. & Greenberg, M. T. 1987. The Inventory of Parents and Peer Attachment: Individual Differences and Their Relationship to

Psychological Well Being in Adolescence. *Journal of Youth and Adolescence, 16*: 427–454.

Ausubel, D.P. 1958. *Theory and Problems of Child Development.* New York: Grune and Stratton.

Bachman, J. G., O'Malley, P. M. & Johnston, J. 1987. *Adolescence to Adulthood: Change and Stability in the Lives of Young Men.* Ann Arbor, MI: Institute for Social Research, University of Michigan.

Baer, J. 1993. *Creativity and Divergent Thinking.* Hillsdale, NJ: Erlbaum, 1993.

Baker, L. & Brown, A. L. 1984. Metacognitive Skills and Reading. In P. D. Pearson (Editor), *Handbook of Reading Research*, Part 2, New York: Longman.

Bandura, A. 1989. Social Cognitive Theory. In R. Vasta (Editor), *Six Theories of Child Development.* Greenwich, CT: JAI.

Bandura, A. 1991. Social Cognitive Theory of Moral Thought and Action. In W. M. Kurtines and J. L. Gewirtz (Editors), *Handbook of Moral Behavior and Development* (Volume 1). Hillsdale, NJ: Erlbaum.

Bandura, A. 1997. *Self-Efficacy: The Exercise of Control.* New York: W. H. Freeman.

Banks, J. A. 1996. *Multicultural Education, Transformative Knowledge, and Action: Historical and Contemporary Perspectives.* New York: Teachers College.

Banks, J. A. 2000. The Social Construction of Difference and the Quest for Educational Equality. In *Education in a New Era: ASCD Yearbook 2000.* Ronald S. Brandt (Editor). Alexandria, VA: Association for Supervision and Curriculum Development.

Barber, B. 1999. Brave New World. Review of three volumes by Manuel Castells. *The Los Angeles Times*, May 23: 6–7.

Barkley, R. A. 1990. *Attention Deficit Hyperactivity Disorder: A Handbook for Diagnosis and Treatment.* New York: Guilford.

Bateson, M. C. 2000. *Full Circles, Overlapping Lives: Culture and Generation in Transition.* New York: Random House.

Baumeister, R. F. 1989. *Masochism and the Self*. Hillsdale, NJ: Erlbaum.

Beam, A. 1999. If You're Dull You'll Be Dull on the Web Too. *The Boston Globe*, May 5: F1.

Beane, A. 1999. The Supervison of Student Teachers: An Emphasis on Self-Reflection. Unpublished manuscript, Boston University, School of Education.

Becker, E. 1973. *Denial of Death*. New York: Free Press.

Beebe, S. A. & Masterson, J. T. 1986. *Family Talk*. New York: Random House.

Beilin, H. 1992. Piaget's Enduring Contribution to Developmental Psychology. *Developmental Psychology, 28*: 191–204.

Bell, R. M. 1985. *Holy Anorexia*. Chicago: University of Chicago Press, 1985.

Bellow, S. 1994. *It All Adds Up: From the Dim Past to the Uncertain Future*. New York: Viking.

Benda, B. B., Schroepfer, T., Turturro, C. & Ballard, K. 1995. Heavy Use of Alcohol by Adolescents: A Conceptual Model of Use. *Alcoholism Treatment Quarterly* (3), 13: 81–95.

Bender, W. 1998. *Learning Disabilities: Characteristics, Identification, and Teaching Strategies*. Boston: Allyn and Bacon.

Bennett, K. & LeCompte, M. D. 1990. *The Way Schools Work: A Sociological Analysis of Education*. White Plains, NY: Longman.

Berger, P. L. & Luckman, T. 1966. *The Social Construction of Reality: A Treatise in the Sociology of Knowledge*. New York: Anchor.

Berk, L. A. 1996. *Infants, Children and Adolescents* (2nd edition). Boston: Allyn and Bacon.

Berk, L. A. 1997. *Child Development* (4th Edition). Needham Heights, MA: Allyn and Bacon.

Berman, L. 1991. Suicide Cases. Special Issue: Assessment and Prediction of Suicide. *Suicide and Life-Threatening Behavior, 21*: 18–36.

Bernard, H. S. 1981. Identity Formation in Late Adolescence: A Review of Some Empirical Findings. *Adolescence, 16*: 349–358.

Berscheid, E. M., Snyder, M. & Omoto, A. M. 1989. Issues in Studying Close Relationships. In C. Hendrick (Editor), *Close Relationships.* Newbury Park, CA: Sage.

Berzonsky, M. D. 1978. Formal Reasoning in Adolescence: An Alternative View. *Adolescence, 13*: 279–290.

Birkerts, S. 1999. *Readings.* New York: St. Paul: Graywolf Press.

Blain, M. D., Thompson, J. M. & Whiffen, V. E. 1993. Attachment and Perceived Social Support in Late Adolescence. *Journal of Adolescent Research, 8*: 226–241.

Blasi, A. 1988. Identity and the Development of the Self. In D. Lapsley and F. C. Power (Editors), *Self, Ego, and Identity: Integrative Approaches.* New York: Springer Verlag.

Blasi, A. and E. C. Hoeffel, E. C. 1974. Adolescence and Formal Operations. *Human Development, 17*: 344–363.

Bloch, H. 1958. *The Gang: A Study in Adolescent Behavior:* New York: Philosophical Library.

Blos, P. 1962. *On Adolescence: A Psychoanalytic Interpretation.* New York: Free Press.

Blos, P. 1979. *The Adolescent Passage.* New York: International Universities.

Bolger, N., Downey, G., Walker, E. & Steininger, P. 1989. The Onset of Suicidal Ideation in Childhood and Adolescence. *Journal of Youth and Adolescence, 18*: 175–190.

Bornstein, M. H. (Editor). 1995. *Children and Parenting* (Volume 3). Hillsdale, NJ: Erlbaum.

Bowie, D. "Changes." New York: EMI Music Publishing.

Bowlby, J. 1980. *Attachment and Loss, Vol. 3: Loss, Sadness and Depression.* New York: Basic Books.

Brandt, R. S. (Editor), 2000. Alexandria, VA: Association for Supervision and Curriculum Development.

Bransford, J. D., Sherwood, R., Vye, N. & Reiser, J. 1986. Teaching Thinking and Problem Solving: Suggestions from Research. *American Psychologist, 41*: 1078–1089.

Brent, D. A. 1989. Suicide and Suicidal Behavior in Children and Adolescents. *Pediatrics in Review, 10*: 269–275.

Brilliant, A. 1980. *I Have Abandoned Any Search for the Truth and Am Now Looking for a Good Fantasy: More Brilliant Thoughts.* Santa Barbara, CA: Woodbridge.

Brooks-Gunn, J. & Ruble, D. N. 1982. The Development of Menstrual-Related Beliefs and Behavior during Early Adolescence. *Child Development, 53*: 1567–1577.

Broughton, J. 1983. The Cognitive Developmental Theory of Adolescent Self and Identity. In B. Lee and G. Noam (Editors), *Developmental Approaches to Self.* New York: Plenum.

Brown, B. 1990. Peer Groups and Peer Cultures. In S. S. Feldman and G. R. Elliot (Editors), *At the Threshold: The Developing Adolescent.* Cambridge, MA: Harvard University Press.

Brown, B. M., Lohr, M. & McClenahan, E. 1986. Early Adolescents' Perceptions of Peer Pressure. *Journal of Early Adolescence, 6*, 147: 139–154.

Brown, B. B. & Lohr, M. J. 1987. Peer-Group Affiliation and Adolescent Self-Esteem: An Integration of Ego-Identity and Symbolic Interaction Theories. *Journal of Personality and Social Psychology, 52*: 47–55.

Bruch, H. 1978. *The Golden Cage: The Enigma of Anorexia Nervosa.* Cambridge, MA: Harvard University Press.

Brumberg, J. J., 1988. *Fasting Girls: The Emergence of Anorexia Nervosa as a Modern Disease.* Cambridge: Harvard University Press.

Bruner, J. 1986. *Actual Minds, Possible Worlds.* Cambridge: Harvard University Press.

Bruner, J., Olver, R. & Greenfield, P. M. 1967. *Studies in Cognitive Growth: Collaboration at the Center for Cognitive Studies.* New York: Wiley.

Buber, M. 1958. *I and Thou*, translated by Ronald Gregor Smith. New York: Scribner.

Buerkel-Rothfuss, D. & Mayes, S. 1981. Soap Opera Viewing: The Cultivation Effect. *Journal of Communication, 31*: 108–115.

Buhrmester, D. & Furman, W. 1987. The Development of Companionship and Intimacy. *Child Development, 58*: 1101–1113.

Bukiet, M. J. 1999. Book Review of *Readings* by Sven Birkerts. *The Boston Globe*, February 21: C3.

Burello, L. C. & Sage, D. D. 1979. *Leadership and Change in Special Education.* Englewood Cliffs, NJ: Prentice-Hall.

Burnes, D. 1985. *Intimate Connections.* New York: William Morrow.

Callaghan, K. A. (Editor). 1994. *Ideals of Feminine Beauty.* Westport, CT: Greenwood.

Campbell, J. 1972. *The Hero with a Thousand Faces.* Princeton, NJ: Princeton University Press.

Caplan, G. & Lebovici, S. (Editors). 1969. *Adolescence: Psychosocial Perspectives.* New York: Basic Books.

Caputo, P. 1991. War Torn. *The New York Times,* February 24: 34ff.

Carey, S. 1988. Are Children Fundamentally Different Kinds of Thinkers and Learners than Adults? In K. Richardson and S. Sheldon (Editors), *Cognitive Development to Adolescence.* Hillsdale, NJ: Erlbaum.

Carroll, J. 1999. That Knot of Longing That Strikes in Early June. *The Boston Globe*, June 15: A27.

Case, R. 1987. Neo-Piagetian Theory: Retrospect and Prospect. *International Journal of Psychology, 22*: 773–791.

Chess, S. & Thomas, A. 1977. Temperamental Individuality from Childhood to Adolescence. *Journal of Child Psychiatry, 16*, pages 218–226.

Chess, S. & Thomas, A. 1987. *Know Your Child.* New York: Basic Books.

Chomsky, N. 1993. *Language and Thought.* Wakefield, RI: Moyer Bell.

Christiansen, B. A., Goldman, M. S. & Inn, A. 1982. Development of Alcohol-Related Expectancies in Adolescents. *Journal of Consulting and Clinical Psychology, 50*: 336–344.

Chubb, H. 1990. Looking at Systems as Process. *Family Process, 29*: 109–175.

Clifford, B. R., Gunter, B. & McAleer, J. L. 1995. *Television and Children.* Hillsdale, NJ: Erlbaum.

Coleman, J. C. (Editor). 1992. *The School Years: Current Issues in the Socialization of Young People.* London: Routledge.

Coleman, J. & Hendry, L. 1990. *The Nature of Adolescence.* New York: Routledge.

Coles, R. 1997. *The Moral Intelligence of Children.* New York: Random House.

Collins, A. 1986. Teaching Reading and Writing with Personal Computers. In J. Oransanu (Editor), *A Decade of Reading Research: Implications for Practice.* Hillsdale, NJ: Erlbaum.

Colton, M. E. &. Gore, S. 1991. (Editors), *Adolescent Stress.* New York: De Gruyter.

Condry, C. 1989. *The Psychology of Television.* Hillsdale, NJ: Erlbaum.

Conger, J. J. and Galambos, N. L. 1997. *Adolescence and Youth: Psychological Development in a Changing World.* New York: Longman.

Conger, J. J. 1988. Hostages to the Future: Youth, Values, and the Public Interest. *American Psychologist, 43*: 291–300.

Coontz, S. 1992. *The Way We Never Were: American Families and the Nostalgia Trap.* New York: Basic.

Cornell, A. W. 1998. The Focusing Technique: Confirmatory Knowing Through the Body. In Helen Palmer (Editor), *Inner Knowing.* New York: Tarcher.

Cose, E. 1993. Review of *Volunteer Slavery: My Authentic Negro Experience* by Jill Nelson. *Newsweek,* June 28: 54.

Cote, J. & Allahar, A. 1994. *Generation on Hold.* New York: New York University Press.

Cottle, T. J. 1976. *Perceiving Time: A Psychological Investigation with Men and Women.* New York: Wiley.

Cottle, T. J. 1977. *Private Lives and Public Accounts*. Amherst, MA: University of Massachusetts Press.

Cottle, T. J. 1990. *Children's Secrets*. Reading, MA: Addison-Wesley.

Cottle, T. J. 2001. *At Peril: Stories of Injustice*. Amherst, MA: University of Massachusetts Press.

Cromwell, E. S. 1994. *Quality Child Care*. Boston: Allyn and Bacon.

Cummings, E. M. & Davies, P. 1994. *Children and Marital Conflict: The Impact of Family Dispute and Resolution*. New York: Guilford.

Csikszentmihalyi, M. & Larson, R. 1984. *Being Adolescent: Conflict and Growth in the Teenage Years*. New York: Basic Books.

Csikszentmihalyi, M. 1990. *Flow: The Psychology of Optimal Experience*. New York: HarperCollins.

Csikszentmihalyi, M. 1996. *Creativity: Flow and the Psychology of Discovery and Invention*. New York: Harper.

Damon W. 1988. *The Moral Child*. New York: Free Press.

Damon, W. & Hart, D. 1988. *Self-Understanding in Childhood and Adolescence*. New York: Cambridge University Press.

Damon, W. 1983. *Social Personality and Development*. New York: Norton.

Davis, S. & Mares, M. L. 1998. Effects of Talk Show Viewing on Adolescents. *Journal of Communication*, Summer, *48*: 69–86.

De Jong-Gierveld, J. 1987. Developing and Testing a Model of Loneliness. *Journal of Personality and Social Psychology, 53*: 119–128.

de Tocqueville, A. 1966. *Democracy in America,* two volumes. New Rochelle, NY: Arlington.

Delattre, E. J. 1999. Civility and the Limits to the Tolerable. Unpublished manuscript, Boston University.

Delattre, E. J. 1999. The Idea of Normality. Unpublished manuscript, Boston University, School of Education.

Delattre, E. J. 2000. The Test of Intimacy: Living up to Love and Duty. Unpublished manuscript, Boston University, School of Education.

Descartes, R. 1980. *Discourse on Method and Meditations on First Philosophy*, translated by Donald A. Cress. Indianapolis, IN: Hackett.

Dewey, J. 1933. *How We Think: A Restatement of the Relation of Reflective Thinking to the Educative Process.* Lexington, MA: Heath.

Dewey, J. 1998. My Pedagogic Creed. In Kevin Ryan and J. M. Cooper (Editors), *Kaleidoscope: Readings in Education* (8th Edition). Boston: Houghton Mifflin.

Dewey, J. 1929. *The Sources of a Science of Education.* New York: Liveright.

Dewey, J. 1991. *How We Know.* Amherst, NY: Prometheus.

Diller, L. H. 1996. The Run on Ritalin, Attention Deficit Disorder and Stimulant Treatment in the 1990's. Hastings Center Report, March-April 12–18.

Dodge, K. A. & Murphy, P. R. 1983. The Assessment of Social Competence in Adolescents. In P. Karoly and J. J. Steffans (Editors), *Adolescent Behavior Disorders: Foundations and Contemporary Concerns.* Lexington, MA: Lexington.

Dowrick, S. 1991. *Intimacy and Solitude: Balancing Closeness and Independence.* New York: Norton.

Dragastin, S. E. & Elder, Jr., G. H. (Editors), 1975. *Adolescence in the Life Cycle: Psychological Change and Social Context.* New York: Halsted.

Dreyfus, E. A. 1972. *Youth: A Search for Meaning.* Columbus: Charles E. Merrill.

Dryfoos, J. G. 1990. *Adolescents at Risk: Prevalence and Prevention.* New York: Oxford University Press.

Dryfoos, J. G. 1998. *Safe Passage: Making It Through Adolescence in a Risky Society.* New York: Oxford University Press.

Durkin, K. 1985. Television and Sex-Role Acquisition 1: Content. *British Journal of Social Psychology, 24*: 101–113.

Earls, F. & Carlson, M. 1993. Towards Sustainable Development for American Families. *Daedalus*, Winter, 1, *122*: 93–122.

Elder, Jr., G. H. 1980. Adolescence in Historical Perspective. In J. Adelson (Editor). *Handbook of Adolescent Psychology*. New York: Wiley.

Elkind, D. 1974. *Children and Adolescents: Interpretive Essays on Jean Piaget*. New York: Oxford University Press.

Elkind, D. 1981. *The Hurried Child*. Reading, MA: Addison-Wesley.

Elkind, D. 1984. *All Grown up and No Place to Go*. Reading, MA: Addison-Wesley.

Elkind, D. 1998. Children with Special Needs: A Postmodern Perspective. *Boston University Journal of Education, 2, 180*: 1–16.

Ellmann, M. 1993. *The Hunger Artists: Starving, Writing, and Imprisonment*. Cambridge, MA: Harvard University Press.

Engel, S. 1995. *The Stories Children Tell*. New York: Freeman, 1995.

Engelhardt, T. 1999. Book review of *The Norton Book of American Biography*, edited by Jay Parini. *Los Angeles Times Book Review*, April 4: 9.

Ennis, R. H. 1991. Critical Thinking: Literature Review and Needed Research. In L. Idol and B. F. Jones (Editors), *Educational Values and Cognitive Instruction*. Hillsdale, NJ: Erlbaum.

Enright, R. D., Levy, V. M., Harris, D. & Lapsley, D. K. 1987. Do Economic Conditions Influence How Theorists View Adolescents? *Journal of Youth and Adolescence, 16*: 541–559.

Erdelyi, M. H. 1985. *Psychoanalysis: Freud's Cognitive Psychology*. New York: Freeman.

Erikson, E. H. 1950. *Childhood and Society*. New York: Norton.

Erikson, E. H. 1959. Identity and the Life Cycle. *Psychological Issues Monograph 1*. New York: International Universities Press.

Erikson, E. H. 1962. *Young Man Luther*. New York: Norton.

Erikson, E. H. 1968. *Identity, Youth and Crisis*. New York: Norton.

Esman, E. 1990. *Adolescence and Culture*. New York: Columbia University Press.

Fain, G. S. 1998. Special Education: Justice, Tolerance, and Beneficence as Duty. *Boston University Journal of Education, 180*: 41–56.

Fasching, D. J. 1997. Beyond Values: Story, Character, and Public Policy in American Schools. In James L. Paul, Neal H. Berger, Pamela G. Osnes and William C. Morse, (Editors), Ethics and Decision Making in Schools: Inclusion, Policy and Reform. Baltimore: Brookes.

Field, T. & Robertson, E. (Editors). 1981. Teenage Parents and Their Offspring. New York: Grune and Stratton.

Fine, G. A., Mortimer, J. T. & Roberts, D. F. 1990. Leisure, Work, and the Mass Media. In. S. S. Feldman and G. R. Elliot (Editors), At the Threshold: The Developing Adolescent. Cambridge, MA: Harvard University Press.

Fitzpatrick, M. A. & Vangelisti, A. L. 1995. Explaining Family Interactions. Thousand Oaks, CA.: Sage.

Flavell, J. H. 1977. Cognitive Development. Englewood Cliffs, NJ: Prentice-Hall.

Flavell, J. H. 1979. Metacognition and Cognitive Monitoring: A New Area of Psychological Inquiry. American Psychologist, 34: 906–911.

Flavell, J. H. 1982. On Cognitive Development. Child Development, 53: 1–10.

Flavell, J. H. 1992. Cognitive Development: Past, Present, and Future. Developmental Psychology, 28: 998–1005.

Frankl, V. 1963. Man's Search for Meaning: An Introduction to Logotherapy, translated by Ilse Lasch. Boston: Beacon.

Freud, S. 1935. A General Introduction to Psychoanalysis, translated by G. Stanley Hall. New York: Liveright.

Freud, S. 1938. The Basic Writings of Sigmund Freud, translated and edited by A. A. Brill. New York: Modern Library.

Freud, S. 1948. Inhibitions, Symptoms and Anxiety, translated by James Strachey. London: Hogarth.

Freud, S. 1961. Civilization and Its Discontents, translated by James Strachey. New York: Norton.

Freud, S. 1962. Ego and the Id, translated by James Strachey. New York: Norton.

Freud, S. 1965. *New Introductory Lectures on Psychoanalysis*, translated by James Strachey. New York: Norton.

Freud, S. 1966. *The Complete Introductory Lectures on Psychoanalysis*, translated by James Strachey New York: Norton.

Friere, P. 1970. *Cultural Action for Freedom*. Cambridge, MA: Center for Study of Development and Social Change.

Frith, S. 1981. *Sound Effects: Youth, Leisure, and the Politics of Rock 'n Roll*. New York: Pantheon.

Fromm, E. 1941. *Escape from Freedom*. New York: Farrar and Rinehart.

Fromm, E. 1956. *The Art of Loving*. New York: Harper.

Gabler, N. 1998. *Life The Movie: How Entertainment Conquered Reality*. New York: Knopf.

Gallatin, J. E. 1974. *Adolescence and Individuality: A Conceptual Approach to Adolescent Psychology*. New York: Harper & Row.

Gans, H. J. 1999. *Popular Culture and High Culture*. New York: Basic.

Gardner, H. 1974. *The Shattered Mind: The Person after Brain Damage*. New York: Knopf.

Gardner, H. 1983. *Frames of Mind: The Theory of Multiple Intelligences*. New York: Basic Books.

Gardner, H. 1987. *The Mind's New Science: A History of the Cognitive Revolution*. New York: Basic Books.

Gardner, H. 1991. *The Unschooled Mind: How Children Think and How Schools Should Teach*. New York: Basic Books.

Garfinkle, H. 1967. *Studies in Ethnomethodology*. Englewood Cliffs, NJ: Prentice-Hall.

Garrod, A. Smulyan, L. Powers, S. & Kilkenny, R. 1999. *Adolescent Portraits: Identity, Relationships, and Challenges*. Boston: Allyn and Bacon.

Gasset, O. Y. 1932. *Revolt of the Masses*. New York: Norton.

Gemelli, R. 1996. *Normal Child and Adolescent Development*. Washington, DC: American Psychiatric.

Gerzon, M. 1996. *Listening to Mid-life: Turning Your Crisis into a Quest.* Boston: Shambhala.

Getzels, J. & Csikszentmihalyi, M. 1976. *The Creative Vision: A Longitudinal Study of Problem Finding in Art.* New York: Wiley.

Getzels, J. & Jackson, P. 1962. *Creativity and Intelligence: Explorations with Gifted Students.* New York Wiley.

Gilligan, C. 1982. *In a Different Voice: Psychological Theory and Women's Development.* Cambridge, MA: Harvard University Press.

Gilligan, C., Lyons, N. P. and Hanmer, T. J. (Editors), 1990. *Making Connections.* Cambridge, MA: Harvard University Press.

Giovacchini, P. 1981. *The Urge to Die.* New York: Macmillan.

Goffman, E. 1959. *The Presentation of Self in Everyday Life.* Garden City, NY: Anchor Books.

Goldscheider, F. K. & Waite, L. 1991. The Future of the Home in the Twenty First Century. In *New Families, No Families? The Transformation of the American Home.* Berkeley: University of California Press, pages 193–209.

Goldstein, S. 1990. *Managing Attention Deficit Disorder in Children.* New York: John Wiley.

Goldstein, T. 1993. It's Not up to You. Review of *Queer in America* by Michelangelo Signorile. *The New York Times Book Review,* June 27: 15–16.

Goodman, E. 1993. Here They Come, There They Go. *The Boston Globe,* June 9: 15.

Greenfield, P. M., Bruzzone, L., Koyamatsu, K., Satuloff, W., Nixon, K., Brodie, M. & Klingsdale, D. 1987. What Is Rock Music Doing to the Minds of Our Youth? A First Experimental Look at the Effects of Rock Music Lyrics and Music Videos. *Journal of Early Adolescence, 7:* 315–329.

Gross, H. E. &. Sussman, M. B. (Editors). 1997. *Families and Adoption.* New York: Haworth.

Grotevant, H. D. & Cooper, C. R. 1985. Patterns of Interaction in Family Relationships and the Development of Identity Exploration. *Child Development, 56:* 415–428.

Guber, H. E. & Voneche, J. J. 1977. *The Essential Piaget*. New York: Basic Books.

Guilford, J. P. 1967. *The Structure of Intellect*. New York: McGraw-Hill.

Halikas, J. A., Meller, J., Morse, C. & Lyttle, M. D. 1990. Predicting Substance Abuse in Juvenile Offenders. *Child Psychiatry and Human Development, 21*: 49–55.

Hall, G. S. 1904. *Adolescence* (Volumes 1 and 2). Englewood Cliffs, NJ: Prentice-Hall.

Hallowell, E. & Ratey, J. 1994. *Driven to Distraction*. New York: Pantheon.

Hanff Korelitz, J. 2000. How Well Can We Ever Know Our Kids? *Newsweek*, March 6: 10–11.

Hartup, W. W. 1991. Friendships. In R. M. Lerner, A. C. Petersen, and J. Brooks-Gunn (Editors), *Encyclopedia of Adolescence*, Volume 1. New York: Garland.

Hartup, W. W. & Zubin, R. 1986. *Relationships and Development*. Hillsdale, NJ: Erlbaum.

Hechtman, L. 1993. Editor, *Attention Deficit Hyperactivity Disorder*. New York: Guilford.

Heidegger, M. 1966. *Being and Time*, translated by Joan Stambaugh. Albany: State University of New York Press.

Hendin, H. 1975. *The Age of Sensation*. New York: Norton.

Hennessey, B. A. & Amabile, T. M. 1988. The Conditions of Creativity. In R. J. Sternberg (Editor), *The Nature of Creativity*. New York: Cambridge University Press.

Hetherington, E. M., Anderson, E. R. & Hagan, M. S. 1991. Divorce: Effects on Adolescents. In R. M. Lerner, A. C. Petersen, and J. Brooks-Gunn (Editors), *Encyclopedia of Adolescence,* Volume 1. New York: Garland.

Hetherington, E. M. & Arasteh, J. (Editors). 1988. *Impact of Divorce, Single Parenting, and Stepparenting on Children*. Hillsdale, NJ: Erlbaum.

Hill, J. P. & Holmbeck, G. N. 1986. Attachment and Autonomy During Adolescence. *Annals of Child Development, 3:* 145–189.

Hine, T. 1999. *The Rise and Fall of the American Teenager.* New York: Bard/Avon.

Hoffman, A. M. (Editor), 1996. *Schools, Violence and Society.* Westport, CT: Praeger.

Honess, T. & Yardley, K. (Editors). 1987. *Self and Identity: Perspectives Across the Lifespan.* London: Routledge & Kegan Paul.

Horner, A. J. 1987. The Unconscious and the Archeology of Human Relationships. In R. Stern (Editor), *Theories of the Unconscious and the Self.* Hillsdale, NJ: Analytic.

Horton, S. 1999. Transformation: Risk-Taking and Meaning-Making in the Mid-Life Adult. Unpublished manuscript, Boston University.

Hostetler, K. D. 1996. *Ethical Judgment in Teaching.* Boston: Allyn and Bacon.

Houston, M. & Wiener, J. M. 1997. Substance-Related Disorders. In Jerry M. Wiener (Editor), *Textbook of Child and Adolescent Psychiatry* (2nd Edition). Washington, DC: American Psychiatric, pages 637–656.

Hughes, R. 1993. *Culture of Complaint: The Fraying of America.* New York: Oxford University Press.

Hunt, J. D. 1994. The Family and the War. In A. Skolnick and J. Skolnick (Editors), (8th Edition). New York: HarperCollins, pages 537–547.

Huston, A. C., Watkins, B. A. & and Kenkel, D. 1989. Public Policy and Children's Television. *American Psychologist, 44:* 424–433.

Inhelder, B. & Piaget, J. 1958. *The Growth of Logical Thinking from Childhood to Adolescence.* New York: Basic Books.

Inkeles, A. 1983. *Exploring Individual Modernity,* with contributions by David H. Smith. New York: Columbia University Press.

Inkeles, A. 1997. *National Character: A Psychosocial Perspective,* with contributions by Daniel J. Levinson. New Brunswick, NJ: Transaction.

Inkeles, A. 1998. One World Emerging? *Convergence and Divergence in Industrial Societies.* Boulder, CO: Westview.

Itzkoff, S. W. 1994. *The Decline of Intelligence in America: A Strategy for National Renewal.* Westport, CT: Praeger.

Jackson, D. A. 1997. No Wonder We're Afraid of Youths. *The Boston Globe,* September 10: A15.

Jersild, A. 1957. *The Psychology of Adolescence.* New York: Macmillan.

Josselson, R. 1994. Identity and Relatedness in the Life Cycle. In H. A. Bosma, T. L. G. Graafsma, H. D. Grotevant, and D. J. De Levita (Editors), *Identity and Development.* Newbury Park, CA: Sage.

Josselson, R. 1992. *The Space Between Us: Exploring the Dimensions of Human Relationships.* San Francisco: Jossey-Bass.

Kagan, J. 1978. *The Growth of the Child: Reflections on Human Development.* New York: Norton.

Kagan, J. 1981. *The First Two Years.* Cambridge, MA: Harvard University Press.

Kagan, J. 1984. *The Nature of the Child.* New York: Basic Books.

Kagan, J. 1998. *Three Seductive Ideas.* Cambridge, MA: Harvard University Press.

Kalter, N. 1990. *Growing up with Divorce.* New York: Free Press.

Kandel, D. B. 1983. Socialization and Adolescent Drinking, in O. Jeanneret (Editor), *Child Health and Development: Volume 2, Alcohol and Youth.* Basel: Karger, pages 66–75.

Kant, I. 1993. *The Critique of Pure Reason,* translated by J. M. D. Meikeljohn. Boston: Tuttle.

Kaplan, L. J. 1984. *Adolescence, The Farewell to Childhood.* New York: Simon and Schuster.

Kassin, S. 1998. *Psychology.* Englewood Cliffs, NJ: Prentice Hall.

Katagiri, D. 1988. *Returning to Silence: Zen Practice in Daily Life.* Boston: Shambhala.

Kazdin, A. E. 1993. Adolescent Mental Health: Prevention and Treatment Programs. *American Psychologist, 2, 48*: 127–141.

Keating, D. P. 1990. Adolescent Thinking. In S. S. Feldman and G. R. Elliot (Editors), *At the Threshold: The Developing Adolescent.* Cambridge, MA: Harvard University Press.

Kegan, R. 1982. *The Evolving Self.* Cambridge, MA: Harvard University Press.

Kelly, J. G. Editor. 1979. *Adolescent Boys in High School: A Psychological Study of Coping and Adaptation.* Hillsdale, NJ: Erlbaum.

Kelly, M. 1999. Class of '99, Listen up. *The Boston Globe*, June 3: A23.

Kemmis, S. 1985. Action Research and the Politics of Reflection. In David Boud, Rosemary Keough and David Walker (Editors), *Reflection: Turning Experience into Learning.* London: Kogan Page, pages 139–163.

Kemper, K. 1996. Constructing a True Story: The Moral Autobiography of a Survivor. *Thresholds-in-Education, 22, 3*: 23–26.

Keniston, K. 1970. Youth: A New Stage of Life. *American Scholar, 39*: 631–654.

Kiell, N. 1969. *The Universal Experience of Adolescence.* London: University of London Press.

Kierkegaard, S. 1954. *Fear and Trembling*, translation by Walter Lowrie. New York: Doubleday.

Kindlon, D. & Thompson, M. 2000. *Raising Cain: Protecting the Emotional Live of Boys.* New York Ballantine.

King, M. L. 1994. *Letter from the Birmingham Jail.* New York: HarperCollins.

Knop, J., Teasdale, T. W., Schulsinger, F. & Goodwin, D. W. 1985. A Prospective Study of Young Men at High Risk for Alcoholism. *Journal of Studies on Alcohol, 46*: 273–278.

Koback, R. R. & Sceery, A. 1988. Attachment in Late Adolescence: Working Models, Affect Regulation, and Representations of Self and Others. *Child Development, 59*: 135–146.

Kohlberg, L. 1981. *Essays on Moral Development*. San Francisco: Harper and Row.

Kohlberg, L. 1984. *The Psychology of Moral Development: The Nature and Validity of Moral Stages*. San Francisco: Harper and Row.

Kohlberg, L. 1987. *Child Psychology and Childhood Education: A Cognitive-Developmental View*. New York: Longman.

Kohut, H. 1977. *The Restoration of the Self*. New York: International Universities.

Kohut, H. 1978. *Search for the Self,* Volume 2, Paul Ornstein (Editor). New York: International Universities.

Kohut, H. 1990. *Search for the Self,* Volume 3, Paul Ornstein (Editor). New York: International Universities.

Kohut, H. 1996. *The Chicago Institute Lectures,* Paul and Marian Tolpin (Editors). Hillside: Analytic.

Kotre, J. 1995. *White Gloves: How We Create Ourselves Through Memory*. New York: The Free Press.

Kroger, J. 1989. *Identity in Adolescence: The Balance Between Self and Other*. New York: Routledge.

Kurtines, W. M. & Gewirtz, J. (Editors). 1991. *Moral Behavior and Development*. Hillsdale, NJ: Erlbaum.

Laing, R. D. 1967. *The Politics of Experience*. New York: Pantheon.

Langer, E. J. 1989. *Mindfulness*. Reading, MA: Addison-Wesley.

Langer, E. J. 1997. *The Power of Mindful Learning*. Reading, MA: Perseus.

Lapsley, D. K. 1990. Continuity and Discontinuity in Adolescent Social Cognitive Development. In R. Montemayor, G. Adams and T. Gulotta (Editors), *From Childhood to Adolescence: A Transitional Period?* Newbury Park, CA: Sage.

Lapsley, D. K. 1991. Egocentrism Theory and the "New Look" at the Imaginary Audience and Personal Fable in Adolescence. In R. M. Lerner, A. C. Petersen, and J. Brooks-Gunn (Editors), *Encyclopedia of Adolescence,* Volume 1. New York: Garland.

Larson, R. & Johnson, C. 1981. Anorexia Nervosa in Context of Daily Living. *Journal of Youth and Adolescence, 10:* 455–471.

Larson, R., Kubey, R. & Colletti, J. 1989. Changing Channels: Early Adolescent Media Choices and Shifting Investments. *Journal of Youth and Adolescence, 18:* 583–599.

Lasch, C. 1991. Beyond Sentimentalism, A Review of Feminism without Illusions: A Critique of Individualism by Elizabeth Fox-Genovese. *The New Republic,* February 18: 58.

LaVoie, J. 1976. Ego Identity Formation in Early Adolescence. *Journal of Youth and Adolescence, 5:* 371–385.

Lawrence-Lightfoot, S. 1999. *Respect.* Reading, MA: Perseus.

Layton, L. & and Schapiro, B. A. (Editors), 1986. *Narcissism and the Text: Studies in Literature and the Psychology of Self.* New York: New York University Press.

Leach, P. 1986. *Your Growing Child: From Babyhood Through Adolescence.* New York: Knopf.

Leonard, G. 1968. *Education and Ecstasy.* New York: Delacorte, 1968.

Leonard, G. 1972. *The Transformation: A Guide to the Inevitable Changes in Humankind.* New York: Delacorte.

Lepper, M. R. 1985. Microcomputers in Education: Motivational and Social Issues. *American Psychologist, 40:* 1–18.

Lepper, M. R. & and J. Gurtner, J. 1989. Children and Computers: Approaching the Twenty-First Century. *American Psychologist, 44:* 170–178.

Lerner, H. G. 1989. *The Dance of Intimacy: A Woman's Guide to Courageous Acts of Change in Key Relationships.* New York: Harper and Row.

Levinson, D. J. 1978. *The Seasons of a Man's Life.* New York: Knopf.

Levinson, D. J. 1996. *The Seasons of a Woman's Life* with Judy D. Levinson. New York: Knopf.

Lickona, T. 1991. *Educating for Character and Responsibility.* New York: Bantam.

Liebert, R. M. & Sprafkin, J. 1988. *The Early Window.* New York: Pergamon.

Loeffelholz, M. 2000. An Anthropological Hand on a New Kind of Genre. Review of *Full Circles, Overlapping Lives: Culture and Generation in Transition* by Mary Catherine Bateson. *The Boston Globe,* March 12: C2.

Lynn R. 1979. *Learning Disabilities: An Overview of Theories, Approaches, and Politics.* New York: Free Press.

Lyons, N. P. 1983. Two Perspectives: On Self Relationships and Morality. *Harvard Educational Review, 53*: 125–145.

Mack, J. 1970. *Nightmares and Human Conflict.* Boston: Little, Brown.

Marchant, H. & Smith, H. M. 1977. *Adolescent Girls at Risk.* New York: Pergamon.

Marcia, J. E. 1991. Identity and Self-Development. In R. M. Lerner, A. C. Peterson and J. Brooks-Gunn (Editors), *Encyclopedia of Adolescence.* New York: Garland.

Marcia, J. E. 1994. The Empirical Study of Ego Development. In H. A. Bosma, T. L. G. Graafsma, H. D. Grottevant and D. J. de Levita (Editors), *Identity and Development: An Interdisciplinary Approach.* London: Sage.

Marcia, J. E. 1999. Representational Thought in Ego Identity, Psychotherapy, and Psychosocial Developmental Theory. In I. E. Sigel (Editor), *Development of Mental Representation: Theories and Applications.* Mahwah, NJ: Erlbaum.

Marcuse, H. 1964. *One Dimensional Man: Studies in the Ideology of Advanced Industrial Society.* Boston: Beacon.

Markus, H. & Nurius, P. 1986. Possible Selves. *American Psychologist, 41*: 954–969.

Marris, P. 1991. "The Social Construction of Uncertainty." In C. M. Parkes, J. Stevenson-Hinde, and P. Marris, *Attachment Across the Life Cycle.* London: Tavistock/Routledge, Chapter 5.

Maslow, A. 1962. *Toward a Psychology of Being.* Princeton, NJ: Van Nostrand, 1962.

May, R. 1977. *The Meaning of Anxiety.* New York: Norton.

May, R. 1983. *The Discovery of Being.* New York: Norton.

May, R. 1986. *Politics and Innocence: A Humanistic Debate.* New York: Norton.

McLuhan, M. 1964. *Understanding Media: The Extensions of Man.* New York: McGraw-Hill.

McLuhan, M. & Fiori, Q. 1967. *The Medium Is the Message.* New York: Bantam.

McLuhan, M. & McLuhan, E. 1988. *The New Science.* Toronto: University of Toronto Press.

McQuire, W. J. 1986. The Myth of Massive Media Impact: Savagings and Salvagings. In G. Comstock (Editor), *Public Communication and Behavior.* Orlando: Academic.

Mead, G. H. 1934. *Mind, Self and Society from the Standpoint of a Social Behaviorist.* Chicago: University of Chicago Press.

Mead, G. H. 1938. *The Philosophy of the Act,* edited with an introduction by Charles W. Morris. Chicago: The University of Chicago Press.

Mercer, J. R. 1973. *Labeling the Mentally Retarded.* Berkeley: University of California Press.

Merton, T. 1974. *New Seeds of Contemplation.* NY: Norton (revised edition).

Mezirow, J. 1991. *Transformative Dimensions of Adult Learning.* San Francisco: Jossey-Bass.

Micucci, J. A. 2000. *The Adolescent in Family Therapy.* New York: Guilford.

Miller, A. 1981. *The Drama of the Gifted Child,* translated by Ruth Ward. New York: Basic Books.

Miller, J. B. & Stiver, I. 1997. *The Healing Connection: How Women Form Relationships in Therapy and in Life.* Boston: Beacon Press.

Miller, J. G. 1991. A Cultural Perspective on the Morality of Beneficence and Interpersonal Responsibility. In S. Ting-Toomey and F. Korzenny

(Editors), *International and Intercultural Communication Annual* Volume 15. Newbury Park, CA: Sage.

Mills, C. W. 1963. *Power, Politics and People.* New York: Oxford University Press.

Minuchin, S. 1974. *Families and Family Therapy.* Cambridge, MA: Harvard University Press.

Minuchin, S., Lee Wai-Yung, & Simon, G. M. 1996. *Mastering Family Therapy: Journeys of Growth and Transformation.* New York: Wiley.

Minuchin, S., Rosman, B. L. & Baker, L. 1978. *Psychosomatic Families: Anorexia Nervosa in Context.* Cambridge, MA: Harvard University Press.

Montemayor, R., Adams, G. & Gullotta, T. (Editors), 1990. *From Childhood to Adolescence: A Transitional Period?* Newbury Park, CA: Sage.

Murray, J. P. 1990. President's Message: Once upon a Time: Television, Children, and Social Policy—A New Fairy Tale. *The Child, Youth, and Family Services Quarterly,* American Psychological Association, Division 37, 3, *13,* Summer: 8–11ff.

Musa, K. E. & Roach M. E. 1973. Adolescent Appearance and Self Concept, *Adolescence,* Fall, *8*: 385–394.

Muuss, R. E. 1968. *Theories of Adolescence* (2nd edition). New York: Random House.

Neuman, P. A. & Halvorson, P. A. 1983. *Anorexia Nervosa and Bulimia: A Handbook for Counselors.* New York: Van Nostrand.

Nichols, M. P. & Schwartz, R. C. 1991. *Family Therapy: Concepts and Methods.* Needham Heights, MA: Allyn and Bacon.

Noblit, G. & Dempsey, V. 1996. *The Social Construction of Virtue: The Moral Life of Schools.* Albany: State University of New York Press.

Noller, P. &. Fitzpatrick, M. A. 1993. *Communication in Family Relationships.* Englewood Cliffs, NJ: Prentice-Hall.

Nosek, K. 1995. *The Dyslexic Scholar.* Dallas: Taylor.

Novick, J. 1984. Attempted Suicide in Adolescence: The Suicide Sequence. In Howard Sudak, Amasa B. Ford and Norman B. Rushfords (Editors), *Suicide in the Young.* Boston: Wright/PSG, pages 115–137.

Nozick, R. 1989. *The Examined Life: Philosophical Meditations.* New York: Simon and Schuster.

O'Connor, B. P. & Nikolic, J. 1990. Identity Development and Formal Operations as Sources of Adolescent Egocentrism. *Journal of Youth and Adolescence, 19*: 149–158.

Offer, D. 1969. *The Psychological World of the Teenager.* New York: Basic Books.

Ogden, J. 1995. Psychosocial Theory and the Creation of the Risky Self. *Social Science and Medicine.* February, 3, *40*: 409–415.

Okagaki, L. & Sternberg, R. J. 1991. (Editors), *Directors of Development: Influences on the Development of Children's Thinking.* Hillsdale, NJ: Erlbaum.

Okihiro, G. Y. 1994. *Margins and Mainstreams: Asians in American History and Culture.* Seattle: University of Washington Press.

Oreskes, M. 1999. Book review of *Monica's Story* by Andrew Morton, *The New York Times Book Review,* April 4: 6.

Paley, V. G. 1990. *The Boy Who Would Be a Helicopter.* Cambridge, MA: Harvard University Press.

Paley, V. G. 1999. *The Kindness of Children.* Cambridge, MA: Harvard University Press.

Palladino, D., Jr. 2000. Poets to Come: Walt Whitman, Self Psychology and the Readers of the Future. Unpublished manuscript.

Paul, E. L. & White, K. M. 1990. The Development of Intimate Relationships in Late Adolescence. *Adolescence, 25*: 375–400.

Paulos, J. A. 1999. *Once upon a Number: The Hidden Mathematical Logic of Stories.* New York: Basic Books.

Pavao, J. M. 1998. *The Family of Adoption.* Boston: Beacon.

Peck, F. S. 1978. *The Road Less Traveled: A New Psychology of Love, Traditional Values, and Spiritual Growth.* New York: Simon and Schuster.

Peradotto, N. 1997. Little Women: A New Generation of Girls Growing Up Before Their Time. *The Buffalo News*. January 26: F1.

Perkins, D. N., Jay, E. & Tishman, S. 1993. Beyond Abilities: A Dispositional Theory of Thinking. *Merrill-Palmer Quarterly, 39*: 1–21.

Perkins, D. P. & Gardner, H. (Editors). 1989. *Art, Mind, and Education*. Urbana: University of Illinois Press.

Petersen, A. C. 1993. Creating Adolescents: The Role of Context and Process in Developmental Trajectories. *Journal of Research on Adolescence, 3*: 1–18.

Phillips, D. P. 1983. The Impact of Mass Media Violence on US Homicides. *American Sociological Review, 48*, August: 560–568.

Phillips, Jr., J. J. 1975. *The Origins of Intellect: Piaget's Theory*. San Francisco: Freeman.

Piaget, J. 1958. *The Growth of Logical Thinking from Childhood to Adolescence*. New York: Basic Books.

Piaget, J. 1932. *The Language and Thought of the Child*. London: Routledge and Kegan Paul.

Piaget, J. 1967. *Six Psychological Studies*. New York: Random House.

Piatelli-Palmarini, M. 1980. *Language and Learning: The Debate Between Jean Piaget and Noam Chomsky*. Cambridge, MA: Harvard University Press.

Pinker, S. J. 1997. *How the Mind Works*. New York: Norton.

Pipher, M. 1994. *Reviving Ophelia: Saving the Selves of Adolescent Girls*. New York: Ballantine.

Pirke, K. M. & Ploog, D. (Editors). 1984. *The Psychobiology of Anorexia Nervosa*. New York: Springer.

Plato, 1928. *The Republic*. Introduction by Charles M. Bakewell. New York: Scribners.

Plato. *The Meno*. 1961. In E. Hamilton, and H. Cairns (Editors), *The Collected Dialogues of Plato*. Princeton: Princeton University Press.

Pollock, W. 1998. *Real Boys: Rescuing Our Sons from the Myths of Boyhood*. New York: Random House.

Postman N. 1982. *The Disappearance of Childhood*. New York: Vintage.

Postman, N. 1986. *Amusing Ourselves to Death: Public Discourse in the Age of Show Business*. New York: Penguin.

Ratey, J. & Johnson, C. 1998. *Shadow Syndromes: The Mild Forms of Major Mental Disorders That Sabotage Us*. New York: Bantam, 1998.

Rawlins, W. K. 1992. *Friendship Matters*. Hawthorne, NY: Aldine.

Resnick, L. B. 1987. *Education and Learning to Think*. Washington, DC: National Academy.

Revenson, T. & Singer, D. 1978. *A Piaget Primer: How a Child Thinks*. New York: Plume.

Rich, J. M. & DeVitis, J. 1985. *Theories of Moral Development*. Springfield, IL: Thomas.

Riesman, D. 1950. *The Lonely Crowd*. New Haven, CT: Yale University Press.

Roberts, D. F. 1993. Adolescents and the Mass Media: From "Leave it to Beaver" to "Beverly Hills 90210." In R. Takanishi (Editor), *Adolescence in the 1990s*. New York: Teachers College.

Rogers, C. 1942. *Counseling and Psychotherapy*. Cambridge, MA: Riverside Press.

Rorty, R. 1979. *Philosophy and the Mirror of Nature*. Princeton: Princeton University Press.

Rosenblatt, R. 1983. *Children of War*. Garden City, NY: Anchor.

Rosenfield, I. 1995. Memory and Identity. *New Literary History*. Winter.

Rumney, A. 1983. *Dying to Please: Anorexia Nervosa and Its Cure*. Jefferson, NC: McFarland.

Ryan, A. 1999. Review of *The Revival of Pragmatism: New Essays on Social Thought, Law, and Culture* edited by Morris Dickstein. *The New York Times Book Review*, April 4: 10.

Ryan, R. M. & Lynch, J. H. 1989. Emotional Autonomy Versus Detachment: Revisiting the Vicissitudes of Adolescence and Young Adulthood. *Child Development, 60*: 340–356.

Sabbath, J. C. 1969. The Suicidal Adolescent: The Expendable Child. *Journal of the American Academy of Child Psychiatry, 8*: 272–289.

Sage, D. D. & Burello, L. C. 1979. *Leadership and Change in Special Education.* Englewood Cliffs, NJ: Prentice-Hall.

Salinger, J. D. 1951. *The Catcher in the Rye.* New York: Bantam Books.

Salvaggio, J. L. & Bryant, J. (Editors). 1989. *Media Use in the Information Age: Emerging Patterns of Adoption and Consumer Use.* Hillsdale, NJ: Erlbaum.

Santrock, J. 1998. *Adolescence* (7th Edition). New York: McGraw-Hill.

Sapon-Shevin, M. 1994. *Playing Favorites: Gifted Education and the Disruption of Community.* Albany: State University of New York Press.

Savi-Williams, R. C. & Demo, D. H. 1983. Conceiving or Mis-Conceiving the Self: Issues in Adolescent Self-Esteem. *Journal of Early Adolescence, 3*: 121–140.

Scarr, S. & Kidd, K. K. 1983. Developmental Behavior Genetics. In P. H. Mussen (Editor), *Handbook of Child Psychology* (Volume 2, 4th Edition). New York: Wiley.

Scarr, S. & McCartney, K. 1983. How People Make Their Own Environments: A Theory of Genotype-Environment Effects. *Child Development, 54*: 424–435.

Schave, D. & Schave, B. 1989. *Early Adolescence and the Search for Self: A Developmental Perspective.* New York: Praeger.

Schön, D. A. 1983. *The Reflective Practitioner: How Professionals Think in Action.* New York: Basic Books.

Schön, D. A. 1987. *Educating the Reflective Practitioner: Toward a New Design for Teaching and Learning in the Professions.* San Francisco: Jossey-Bass.

Schorr, L. B. 1989. *Within Our Reach.* New York: Anchor.

Schwartz, G. 1987. *Beyond Conformity or Rebellion.* Chicago: University of Chicago Press.

Scott-Jones, D. 1993. Families as Educators in a Pluralistic Society. In N. F. Chavkin (Editor), *Families and Schools in a Pluralistic Society.* Albany: State University of New York Press.

Scribner, S. 1977. Modes of Thinking and Ways of Speaking: Culture and Logic Reconsidered. In P. N. Johnson-Laird and P. C. Wartson (Editors), *Thinking: Readings in Cognitive Science.* New York: Cambridge University Press.

Seager, H. R. 1951. "Economics at Berlin and Vienna. In Charles A. Gluck, Jr. (Editor), *Labor and Other Economic Essays.* New York: Harper and Row.

Seidman, J. M. 1960. *The Adolescent.* New York: Holt.

Selman, R. L. 1980. *The Growth of Interpersonal Understanding: Developmental and Clinical Analysis.* New York: Academic Press.

Serious Times, Trivial Politics. 1990. *The New York Times,* March 25: E18.

Shaffer, D. & Greenhill, L. L. 1979. A Critical Note on the Predictive Validity of the Hyperactive Syndrome. *Journal of Child Psychology and Psychiatry, 20*: 61–72.

Shafritz, J. M. 1988. *The Dorsey Dictionary of American Government and Politics.* Chicago: Dorsey.

Shannon, C. L. 1989. *The Politics of the Family.* New York: Lang.

Sheehy, G. 1976. *Passages: Predictable Crises of Adult Life.* New York: Dutton, 1976.

Sheehy, G. 1995. *New Passages: Mapping Your Life Across Time.* New York: Random House.

Shucksmith, J. 1998. *Health Issues and Adolescents: Growing Up, Speaking Out.* New York: Routledge.

Siegel, E. 1998. Life, Celebrity and the Pursuit of Happiness, *The Boston Globe,* December 13: C1.

Siegler, R. S. 1991. *Children's Thinking.* Englewood Cliffs, NJ: Prentice Hall.

Sigel, I. 1977. *Cognitive Development from Childhood to Adolescence.* New York: Holt.

Sigelman, C. K. & Shaffer, D. R. 1991. *Life-Span Human Development*. Pacific Grove, CA: Brooks/Cole.

Signorielli, N. 1993. Television and Adolescents' Perception of Work. *Youth and Society, 24*: 314–341.

Silver, L. B. 1989. *The Assessments of Learning Disabilities: Pre-School Through Adulthood*. Boston: Little, Brown.

Silver, L. B. 1992. *Attention Deficit Hyperactivity Disorder*. Washington, DC: American Psychiatric.

Silverman, P. R. 1999. *Never Too Young to Know: Death in Children's Lives*. New York: Oxford University Press.

Skal, D. J. 1993. *A Cultural History of Horror*. New York: Norton.

Slavin, R. 1989. Cooperative Learning and Student Achievement. In R. Slavin (Editor), *School and Classroom Organization*. Hillsdale, NJ: Erlbaum.

Smith, H. 1995. *Unhappy Children: Reasons and Remedies*. New York: Free Association.

Smith, P. (Editor). 1966. *Boys: Masculinities in Contemporary Culture*. Boulder: Westview.

Solden, S. 1995. *Women with ADD*. Grass Valley, California: Underwood.

Sommer, B. B. 1978. *Puberty and Adolescence*. New York: Oxford University Press.

Specter Person, E., Fonagy, P. and Figueira Augusto, S. (Editors). 1995. *On Freud's "Creative Writers and Day-Dreaming."* New Haven: Yale University Press.

Stack Sullivan, H. 1953. *The Interpersonal Theory of Psychiatry*, edited by Helen Swick and Mary Ladd Gawel. New York: Norton, 1953.

Stattin, H. & Magnusson, D. 1990. *Pubertal Maturation in Female Development: Paths Through Life*. Hillsdale, NJ: Erlbaum.

Stein, M. 1998. *Transformation: Emergence of the Self*. College Station, Texas: Texas A&M University Press.

Steiner, D. 2000. Retreat from Judgment. Unpublished manuscript, Boston University.

Stern, L. 1990. Conceptions of Separation and Connection in Female Adolescents. In C. Gilligan, N. Lyons and T. Hanmer (Editors), *Making Connections*. Cambridge, MA: Harvard University Press.

Sternberg, R. J. 1986. *Intelligence Applied*. San Diego: Harcourt.

Sternberg, R. J. & Barnes, M. L. (Editors). 1988. *Anatomy of Love*. New Haven, CT: Yale University Press.

Sternberg, R. J. & Berg, C. A. (Editors). 1992. *Intellectual Development*. Cambridge: Cambridge University Press.

Sternberg, R. J., Conway, B. E., Ketron, J. L. & Bernstein, M. 1981. People's Conception of Intelligence. *Journal of Personality and Social Psychology, 41*: 37–55.

Stierlin, H. & Weber, G. 1989. *Unlocking the Family Door: A Systemic Approach to the Understanding and Treatment of Anorexia Nervosa*. New York: Brunner/Mazel.

Stone, J. L. & Church, J. 1973. *Childhood and Adolescence: A Psychology of the Growing Person*. New York: Random House.

Stout, M. 1999. *The Feel Good Curriculum: The Dumbing Down of America's Kids in the Name of Self-Esteem*. Boston: Perseus.

Strachen, A. & Jones, D. 1982. Changes in Identification During Adolescence: A Personal Construct Theory Approach. *Journal of Personality Assessment, 46*: 139–148.

Strasburger, V. C. 1995. *Adolescents and the Media*. Newbury Park, CA: Sage Publications.

Straus, M. B. 1988. *Abuse and Victimization Across the Life Span*. Baltimore: Johns Hopkins University Press.

Straus, M. B. 1999. *No-Talk Therapy for Children and Adolescents*. New York: Norton.

Strauss, M. A. & Gelles, R. J. 1981. *Behind Closed Doors*. Garden City, NY: Anchor.

Stuart, S. & Cottle, T. J. 2000. Adolescents Still at Peril. Unpublished manuscript, Boston University.

Sugar, M. 1993. *Female Adolescent Development*. New York: Brunner/Mazel.

Sussman, H. 1991. Americans Hurry into Future Without a Plan. *Sunday Camera,* Boulder, Colorado, January 20: 3B.

Takanishi. R. 1993. Changing Views of Adolescence in Contemporary Society. In R. Takanishi (Editor), *Adolescence in the 1990s.* New York: Teachers College.

Tanner, J. M. 1955. *Growth and Adolescence.* Springfield, IL: Thomas.

Tanner, J. M. 1970. Physical Growth. In P. H. Mussen (Editor), *Carmichael's Manual of Child Psychology* (3rd Edition, Volume I). New York: Wiley.

Tanner, J. M. & Inhelder, B. 1971. *Discussions on Child Development: A Consideration of the Biological, Psychological, and Cultural Approaches to the Understanding of Human Development and Behavior.* New York: International Universities.

Tarter, R. E. 1990. Evaluation and Treatment of Adolescent Substance Abuse. *American Journal of Drug and Alcohol Abuse, 16:* 1–46.

Tatum, B. D. 1997. *Why Are All the Black Kids Sitting Together in the Cafeteria? And Other Conversations About Race.* New York: Basic.

Tavris, C. 1990. Review of *The Psychology of Optimal Experience* by Mihaly Csikszentmihalyi. *The New York Times Book Review,* March 18: 7.

Taylor, J., Gilligan, C. & Sullivan, A. 1995. *Between Voice and Silence.* Cambridge, MA: Harvard University Press.

Teens: Here Comes the Biggest Wave Yet. 1994. *Business Week,* April 11: 76–86.

Thomas, A. & Chess, S. 1977. *Temperament and Development.* New York: Brunner/Mazel.

Thomas, A. & Chess, S. 1987. Commentary. In H. H. Goldsmith, A. H. Buss, R. Plomin, M. K. Rothbart, A. Thomas, A. Chess, R. R. Hinde and R. B. McCall. Roundtable: What Is Temperament? Four Approaches. *Child Development, 58:* 505–529.

Thornhill, R. & and Palmer C. T. 2000. *A Natural History of Rape: Biological Bases of Sexual Coercion.* Cambridge, MA: MIT.

Tigner, S. 1993. Homer, Teacher of Teachers. *Journal of Education, 3, 175:* 43–64.

Tigner, S. 1994. A New Bond: Humanities and Teacher Education. *Liberal Education*, 1, *80*, Winter: 4–7.

Tigner, S. 1998, Plato's Meno. ED 700, Intellectual History of Education, Boston University.

Torrey, E. F. 1992. Oedipal Wrecks: Has a Century of Freud Bred a Country of Narcissists? *Washington Monthly*, January–February: 32–41.

Townsend, D. 1999. Distractions from Real. Unpublished manuscript, Boston University, December 20.

Traniello, D. A. 1999. Inclusion of Students with Disabilities in Three Elementary Schools: Values, Policies, and Practices. Doctoral Dissertation, School of Education, Boston University.

Tremmel, R. 1993. Zen and the Art of Reflective Practice in Teacher Education. *Harvard Educational Review*, 4, 63, Winter: 434–458.

Tsai, L. Y. & Ghaziuddin, M. 1997. Autistic Disorder. In Jerry M. Wiener (Editor), *Textbook of Child and Adolescent Psychiatry* (Second Edition), Washington, DC: American Psychiatric, pages 219–254.

Tucker, L. A. 1987. Television, Teenagers, and Health. *Journal of Youth and Adolescence*, *16*: 415–425.

Turner, S. L., Hamilton, H., Jacobs, M., Angood, L. M. & Hovde Dwyer, D. 1997. The Influence of Fashion Magazines on the Body Image Satisfaction of College Women: An Exploratory Analysis. *Adolescence*, *32*, Fall: 603–605.

Udall, D. 1991. The Power of Stories: Learning from the Lives of Young People. *The Journal of Experiential Education*. 14, *34*: 35–38.

van der Kolk, B. A. 1987. *Psychological Trauma*. Washington, DC: American Psychiatric.

van der Kolk, B. A., McFarlane, A. C. & Weisaeth, L. (Editors). 1996. *Traumatic Stress: Effects of Overwhelming Experience on Mind, Body and Society*. New York: Guilford.

Varenne, H. & McDermott, R. 1998. *Successful Failure: The School America Builds*. Boulder: Westview.

Vitiello, B., Stoff, D. & Atkins, M. 1990. Soft Neurological Signs and Impulsivity in Children. *Journal of Developmental and Behavioral Pediatrics*. *11*: 112–115.

Wadsworth, B. J. 1996. *Piaget's Theory of Cognitive and Affective Development*. New York: Longman.

Walker, L. 1982. The Sequentiality of Kohlberg's Stages of Moral Development. *Child Development, 53*: 1330–1336.

Wallerstein, J. S. & Kelly, J. B. 1980. *Surviving the Breakup: How Parents and Children Cope with Divorce*. New York: Basic.

Wallerstein, J. S. 1984. Children of Divorce: The Psychological Tasks of the Child. In *Annual Progress of Child Psychiatry and Child Development*, Stella Chess and Alexander Thomas (Editors). New York: Brunner/Mazel.

Walters, M., Carter, B., Papp, P. & Silverstein, O. 1988. Toward a Feminist Perspective in Family Therapy. In *The Invisible Web: Gender Patterns in Family Relationships*. New York: Guilford, pages 15–30.

Wartella, E., Heintz, K., Aidman, A. & Mazzarella, S. 1992. Television and Beyond: Children's Video Media in One Community. *Communications Research, 17*: 45–64.

Waterman, A. S. (Editor), 1985. *Identity in Adolescence: Processes and Contents*. San Francisco: Jossey-Bass.

Weber, M. 1968. *On Charisma and Institution Building,* S. N. Eisenstadt (Editor). Chicago: University of Chicago Press.

Webster's New World Dictionary of the American Language. 1960. New York: World.

Weinstein, F. Forthcoming. *Freud, Psychoanalysis, Social Theory: The Unredeemed Promise*. Albany: State University of New York Press.

Weinstein, F. and Platt, G. M. 1969. *The Wish to Be Free*. Berkeley: University of California Press.

Weiss, R. S. 1973. *Loneliness: The Experience of Emotional and Social Isolation*. Cambridge, MA: MIT.

Wellwood, J. 1990. Intimate Relationship as Path. *Journal of Transpersonal Psychology, 1, 22*: 51–58.

Werner, E. E. & Smith, R. S. 1982. Vulnerable But Invincible. New York: McGraw-Hill.

Whitman, W. 1926. *Song of Myself* from *Leaves of Grass*. Garden City, NY: Doubleday.

Wicks-Nelson, R. & Israel, A. C. 1997. *Behavior Disorders of Childhood* (3rd Edition). Upper Saddle River, NJ: Prentice-Hall.

Wilhelmsen, B. U., Laberg, S. and Aas, H. 1998. Alcohol Outcome Expectancies in Adolescence. *Psychology and Health*, November, 6, *13*: 1037–1044.

Williams, F., LaRose, R. & Frost, F. 1981. *Children, Television, and Sex-Role Stereotyping*. New York: Praeger.

Williams, M. 1991. *The Velveteen Rabbit: How Toys Become Real*. New York: Doubleday.

Winnicott, D. W. 1965. *The Family and Individual Development*. New York: Basic Books.

Winnicott, D. W. 1986. *Home Is Where We Start From*. Compiled by Clare Winnicott, Ray Shepard and Madeline Davis. New York: Norton.

Winter, G. D. & Nuss, E. M. 1969. *The Young Adult: Identity and Awareness*. Glenview: Scott, Foresman.

Wolf, E. 1988. *Treating the Self: Elements of Clinical Self Psychology*. New York: Guilford.

Wollons, R. 1993. *Children at Risk in America: History, Concepts, and Public Policy*. Albany: State University of New York Press.

Yeats, W. B. 1938. *A Vision*. New York: Macmillan.

Young, A. 1995. *The Harmony of Illusions: Inventing Post Traumatic Stress Disorder*. Princeton, NJ: Princeton University Press.

Young, A. 1996. Suffering and the Origins of Traumatic Memory. *Daedalus*. Winter, *125*, No. 1: 245–260.

Youniss, J. & Smollar, J. 1990. Self Through Relationship Development. In *Coping and Self-Concept in Adolescence,* Harke Bosma and Sandy Jackson (Editors). Berlin: Springer Verlag.

Zelan, K. 1991. *The Risks of Knowing: Developmental Impediments to School Learning*. New York: Plenum.

Zentall, S. 1993. Research on the Educational Implications of Attention Deficit Hyperactivity Disorder. *Exceptional Children, 2, 60*: 143–153.

Zilboorg, G. 1937. Considerations on Suicide, with Particular Reference to That of the Young. *American Journal of Orthopsychiatry, 7*: 125–31.

Zillman, D. & Bryant, J. (Editors). 1994. *Perspectives on Media Effects: Awareness in Theory and Practice*. Hillsdale, NJ: Erlbaum.

ABOUT THE AUTHOR

THOMAS J. COTTLE is Professor of Education at Boston University. A sociologist and practicing clinical psychologist, he received his B.A. from Harvard University and his M.A. and Ph.D in social psychology from the University of Chicago. In addition, he has earned a Doctor of Humane Letters from Lesley College. He has served on the faculties of Harvard University, Amherst College, MIT, and Columbia College in Chicago as well as served on the staff of The Children's Defense Fund. Many of his more than five hundred essays, articles and reviews have appeared in *The New York Times*, *The London Times*, *The Washington Post*, *The Boston Globe*, *Newsday*, *The Los Angeles Times*, *USA Today*, *The Philadelphia Inquirer*, *The St. Louis Post Dispatch*, *The Hartford Courant*, *The Baltimore Sun*, *The Atlantic*, *Harpers*, *The New Republic*, *The New Leader*, *Saturday Review*, *Life*, *McCalls*, *Parents Magazine*, *The Yale Review*, *Daedalus*, *Antioch Review*, *Massachusetts Review*, *Psychology Today*, and *Television Quarterly*. His more than twenty-five books include *Children's Secrets*; *Time's Children*; *Barred from School*; *A Family Album*; *Busing*; *Children in Jail*; *Like Fathers, Like Sons*; *Hardest Times*; and *At Peril*. Dr. Cottle has received numerous awards for his research, including a Guggenheim Fellowship, and has appeared on radio and television. He and his wife Kay Mikkelsen Cottle, a high school teacher, live in Brookline, Massachusetts. They are the parents of three children and the grandparents of three children.

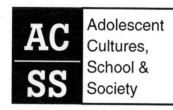

Adolescent
Cultures,
School &
Society

Joseph L. DeVitis & Linda Irwin-DeVitis
GENERAL EDITORS

As schools struggle to redefine and restructure themselves, they need to be cognizant of the new realities of adolescents. Thus, this series of monographs and textbooks is committed to depicting the variety of adolescent cultures that exist in today's post-industrial societies. It is intended to be a primarily qualitative research, practice, and policy series devoted to contextual interpretation and analysis that encompasses a broad range of interdisciplinary critique. In addition, this series will seek to provide a pragmatic, pro-active response to the current backlash of conservatism that continues to dominate political discourse, practice, and policy. This series seeks to address issues of curriculum theory and practice; multicultural education; aggression and violence; the media and arts; school dropouts; homeless and runaway youth; alienated youth; at-risk adolescent populations; family structures and parental involvement; and race, ethnicity, class, and gender studies.

Send proposals and manuscripts to the general editors at:
Joseph L. DeVitis & Linda Irwin-DeVitis
College of Education and Human Development
University of Louisville
Louisville, KY 40292-0001

To order other books in this series, please contact our Customer Service Department at:
(800) 770-LANG (within the U.S.)
(212) 647-7706 (outside the U.S.)
(212) 647-7707 FAX

or browse online by series at:
WWW.PETERLANGUSA.COM